ADENAUER AND THE NEW GERMANY

Adenauer AND

THE NEW GERMANY

The Chancellor of the Vanquished

BY Edgar Alexander

PREFACE BY Alvin Johnson

EPILOGUE BY
Chancellor Konrad Adenauer

FARRAR, STRAUS AND CUDAHY / NEW YORK

First Printing, 1957

Translated from the German by
Thomas E. Goldstein

Published simultaneously in Canada
by Ambassador Books, Ltd., Toronto.
Manufactured in the United States of America.
American Book–Stratford Press, Inc., New York

To
Dannie N. Heineman

ALVIN JOHNSON

Preface

Germany today stands balanced on a razor edge; West or East, America or Russia. What we offer is fellowship among the Free Nations, partnership in NATO, the powerful protection of the Associated Free Nations in case of a Russian movement toward the Rhine. What Russia offers is something very near to the hearts of all Germans, the restoration of the unity of Germany.

In the world of diplomacy nothing is given for nothing. Among the literate nations America alone is capable of fondly hoping for real concessions in return for a smile and a handshake. We were horribly disappointed at Geneva. That was all we got for all we offered.

Russia will give unification to Germany, but at what price? First, withdrawal from NATO, and neutralization: Germany to be disarmed, except for a militia capable of keeping domestic order but of nothing else. Second—and the Russians keep this in the background—an arrangement with East Germany that will safeguard the interests of the present Communist regime. Could that be settled by a plebiscite? No; the Russians will not hear of a plebiscite. A united Germany will have to be a further development of German federalism, if it is to have Russian consent.

And there is another condition to German union that the Russians do not mention at all. That is the acceptance by Germany of the Oder-Neisse line. This line gives to Poland much territory Germans have inhabited for a thousand years. The Poles expelled the German inhabitants, letting them carry away with them little but their blond complexions. At least 10 per cent of the present population of Federal Germany consists of such expellees.

The Germans aren't happy about that. But some of them murmur among themselves, "Russia does not love the Poles. If we play with Russia we may be able to revise the Oder-Neisse line."

There is no question about it: Germany could get a lot out of Russia, if she would but fall down and do obeisance to Russia. A certain kind of German may be willing to do that, believing that Little Red Riding Hood can outsmart a bear masquerading as a wolf masquerading as a grandmother. Whatever remains of the old Center Party under Bruening has a different but equally astonishing view of the practicability of outsmarting the bear-wolf-grandmother machine.

And we had best recognize, the appeal of this Russian solution is very powerful. No army; who in Germany wants to serve in the army? Unification; who in Germany is content with the division between East and West Germany? No monkeying with NATO. What German wants to be in NATO's first line of defense against Russia and her millions of soldiers advancing behind a "preparation" of atomic bombs?

What this all sums up to is, Germany a satellite of Russia. And with Germany in the Russian fold, NATO is a paper organization. It cannot check the advance of Russian influ-

ence to the Channel. For France is in no position to stand
against all Europe, thrusting forward from the East. Our own
policy would wisely retire into the "fortress America."

Against this powerful movement from the East stands one
mighty cliff, Adenauer.

We in America know little of Adenauer. We listen to the
Social Democrats, who seem to have a solution: we listen to
Bruening, whom we highly respect and who thinks Adenauer's
"dogmatism" keeps Germany from playing us against Russia
and Russia against us; but who are we to know anything
about the realities of German politics, except that they have
thrown the world twice into the agony of a world war in a
rather short generation?

What is it that made Germany, intellectually the most advanced of European peoples, a standing menace to civilization? West Germany drew from the French Revolution a
sense of the rights of man, of *Natural Law*, superior to governmental edicts and statutes. But Prussia would have nothing to do with the Rights of Man or the Natural Law. Prussia
saw all rights of man as derived from the State and its autocratic head. By nature the State could do no wrong. The individual could have no rights against the State.

This idolization of the State, supported by the German
philosophers from Hegel down, dominated German thinking. It spilled over into other countries. I know one of the
greatest of American jurists who pronounces in private pon-
tifically: "The rights of man are all bunk. Man has only the
rights the State grants him. The Declaration of Independence? A propaganda document."

The drift toward an Eastern solution in Germany is extremely strong. After two disastrous and devastating wars
within the space of one generation, the German masses do
not want any more war. The only war in the offing is a possible struggle between Russia, supported by China, against
America and her allies. If such a war should come, the Ger-

mans want to keep out of it. Therefore this traditionally militaristic nation doesn't want an army. They are afraid that an
army would again bring to the fore the nationalist, or indeed
the Nazi remnants in the population, to work on the surface
with the Western powers, but under the surface for the restoration of the evil Old Germany of blood and iron.

The granite cliff against which this drift dashes in vain is
Konrad Adenauer, Chancellor of the Federal German Republic, and his tried and true colleague Theodor Heuss, and
the Christian Democratic Union, a political party now com-
manding a majority in parliament, but much more than a
political party, a movement for restoration and maintenance
of democracy founded on the Christian conception of the
rights and the dignity of man.

We Americans are not completely at home in the international world of today. Most of us still feel it is enough of an
exercise to understand our own politics; how can we be expected to master the intricacies of the political situation of
another nation? Yet we realize that whether we may live in
peace or must go through the unimaginable horrors of another world war, an atomic war, depends not only on decisions reached in Washington, but often more importantly on
decisions reached in London, Paris and above all, in Bonn;
decisions in which we assert our right to a voice. It follows we
have to inform ourselves on the crucial problems of the other
nations with which we are indissolubly associated.

There has been no lack of newspaper and magazine studies
of Adenauer and his policies and party position; even a book
or two. But such treatment of a statesman who is still acting
is never satisfying. The contemporary writing on Lincoln
missed his meaning; the contemporary writing on Wilson
was hardly more adequate. A contemporary writer draws
heavily upon a statesman's acts; but before his article is in
print new acts emerge to refute the writer.

As a rule many years pass by before the real character of a

statesman, the real nature of the supporting political forces become intelligible to the historian. But in the crucial position of the world, we cannot wait for the historian to adjudge the merits and demerits of a statesman like Adenauer.

The author of this book, Edgar Alexander, is a highly accomplished historian. He has given many years to a painstaking study of Adenauer and his political environment. He has left it to others to present the annals of Adenauer and his party, devoting himself to their essential character and meaning.

To me, Edgar Alexander's achievement is astounding. The Adenauer of his book is precisely the Adenauer who has visited America, strong, modest, resolute, of penetrating and flexible intelligence. "Dogmatic" his critics call him. The "dogmas" he maintains are that all men are created equal, endowed by the Creator with certain unalienable rights, and that governments derive their just powers from the consent of the governed. Dogmas that we Americans carry in our minds and hearts and will carry until as a nation we die.

An American can't read this book without realizing: Adenauer is one of us, and in this moment of time, the greatest one.

One cannot escape the impulse to compare Adenauer with our two greatest statesmen of recent times, Woodrow Wilson and Franklin Roosevelt. The two Americans were, like Adenauer, dogmatic in their assertion of the rights of man, in their faith in democracy. Woodrow Wilson was master of words, and his words gave a thrill to millions. Franklin Roosevelt had an unprecedented confidence in chance and the future. He would take chances, believing that the mighty movement of the spirit of man would inevitably give us a world of freedom and democracy.

Adenauer is a man of few words, solid and pointed. The only thrill he gives you is the thrill of conviction. Like Wilson and Roosevelt his conceptions embrace the whole world.

But Adenauer has a special German problem, which is in essence a crucial world problem, the restoration of Germany to its old and rightful place in Christian civilization. To recover for Germany the Judaeo-Christian, Greco-Roman ethical values that a materialistic philosophy had thrust aside for an idolized State, absolute, whose only ethics was aggrandizement, whose only object was power. An imperial state, militaristic, under which the individual, shorn of rights, could yet preen himself on the national splendor in which as a molecule he was illuminated.

At one of the Hague Peace Conferences the representative of the Kaiser declared, "Universal peace is a mere dream, and not a lovely dream."

The Germans, from of old an honest and earnest people, no more adept philosophers than you and I, no less ready to follow after assertive superiority, were in the end dragged into the disastrous First World War, and later into the murderous Hitler regime, to achieve crimes unprecedented in history and to be utterly crushed in the Second World War.

To bring this disgraced and defeated people to its true German nature, to its rightful place in Christian civilization, to its place among the democratic nations in the new world order of peace, that has been the special object of Adenauer's statecraft.

He is succeeding.

May 28, 1957

Foreword

This book represents the first attempt to date of a socio-biographical profile of the German Chancellor, Konrad Adenauer, and his stature as a statesman. At the same time, it might serve as an introduction to the spiritual and political situation of present-day Germany—a situation profoundly stirred by the forces of regeneration, which have been released by the process of living German history since the catastrophe of 1945. Unmistakably, these forces stem from Germany's essential heritage, shaped in the historic community which links Germany, for life or death, to Europe and the Western World.

Such aims have resulted in a certain dual-level quality which characterizes this book—and which one might call the "historio-sociological" and the "socio-biographical" levels. On the first, I try to present the objective achievements on the road of social and political reconstruction and ethico-political regeneration in Germany. On the second, I show the

picture of the man and his personality, under whose statesmanship the new Germany has attained her present stature.

Scope and impact of Adenauer's personality can be gauged
from the widespread tendency, in Germany and abroad, to
identify the Federal Republic with the Chancellor's name
and personal prestige. The only meaning the often-heard
cliché about "Adenauer-Germany" can have is to epitomize
the outstanding role of Konrad Adenauer in the rehabilitation of the new Germany and the consolidation of her international status. This might be a sufficient reason for wanting
to know more about his statecraft and its achievements, both
as an individual expression and a sociological focus for the
spiritual and political forces on which the regeneration of
Germany depend. Because of this "focal" position, Adenauer's personality is uniquely suited to throw light on this
latest chapter in Germany history, its objective as well as its
personal components.

The present situation in Germany and Europe—especially
the German reunification problem and Germany's contribution to European security—has given rise to serious, even
apprehensive, efforts, so that the new energies, released since
1945, will be applied in Germany's best national and international interest. The present book attempts to highlight
the ideo-political facets of this situation, and to define the
present intellectual position of the forces and movements
upon which it is predicated. Yet such a survey of the objective forces will inevitably lead us back to Adenauer, the
statesman, and the movement of the "Christian Democratic
Union," which he heads. As a symbol and as an effective
sociological force—including the rallying of the opposition,
which may largely be credited to his impact—the German
Chancellor and his movement have appeared as a representative expression of the regeneration process in the Federal
Republic, the German contribution to reconstruction in

Europe and the German share in the great worldwide struggle of our time. The problem of tradition and the generations' problem in Germany today play their decisive role in
the historic framework in which these efforts are being realized. One must try to understand the problem of political
leadership in present-day Germany in its complex ethical
and political ramifications. Lastly, the German reunification
issue is extensively discussed. In view of the profound importance which a solution of this burning issue has for
freedom in Germany and peace in Europe, no elaborate explanation is needed why considerable space is given to its
discussion.

This book is the fruit of many years of intensive study of
German history; of close contact with the intellectual and
political movements and the leading personalities in the
German Federal Republic; and, also, of the more specific
studies which I made over the past few years in preparing a
comprehensive, two-volume socio-biography of Chancellor
Adenauer. To avoid interrupting the flow of the text, and in
particular to facilitate the understanding of these at times
intricate problems for the reader of the American edition,
I decided to forgo the inclusion of footnotes and source
references—especially since these are almost exclusively based
on German sources. The interested reader may easily consult
the comprehensive appendix of the original German edition:
Adenauer und das Neue Deutschland (Paulus Verlag, Recklinghausen, 1956). The sources and footnotes which will be
found there are equally valid for the American edition.

I consider it a most pleasant duty, in this foreword, to
express my sincere gratitude to the many eminent personalities and friends, foundations and organizations, both in the
United States and in the German Federal Republic, who
have given me their sympathetic support over these years for
my socio-biographical studies of Adenauer's development and
work. Above all, I am indebted for the gift of their ever-

present friendship to *Dr. George N. Shuster, Dr. William Roth* and *Dr. Toni Stolper.* My sincere thanks go further-more to the *Lucius Littauer Foundation* in New York, and the *Graduate Faculty of the New School for Social Research,* its distinguished President, *Dr. Hans Simons,* and its Dean, *Dr. Hans Staudinger,* for the help and support which they have given me. Finally, my thanks go to my German pub-lisher, *Dr. Georg Bitter,* Recklinghausen; and to *Dr. Thomas E. Goldstein,* New York, for the congenial understanding with which he has handled his masterly translation of my thoughts.

I wish to express my especially heartfelt gratitude to Presi-dent Emeritus, *Dr. Alvin Johnson,* whose paternal assistance and Socratic wisdom and energy have probably done most for the publication of this book. I feel a particular debt of gratitude to Chancellor *Dr. Konrad Adenauer* for his con-tribution of a personal Epilogue, with which he has dis-tinguished this edition.

The book is dedicated—as an expression of the collective gratitude of all the Chancellor's admirers and friends—to *Mr. Dannie N. Heineman* of Greenwich, Connecticut, for his magnanimous help and courageous assistance to Konrad Adenauer during his time of trial under the Nazi regime.

Bonn
——————   May, 1957   E. A.
New York

Contents

Part Two: **The Crucial Task: Reunification**

PART ONE

A New Germany

Introduction: Genesis of a Statesman

Konrad Adenauer's personality and influence, in their historical significance, have already left a lasting imprint on the history of Germany and Europe. It is above all founded on the new meaning which the German Chancellor's thought and action have given to the concept of "Christian," as an attribute of the intrinsically ethical achievements of his statesmanship.

The history of political movements shows how Christian ideas in the past have been misused as well as abused for political purposes. The deep-seated mistrust and the frequent misunderstandings of the application of Christian ideas to democratic politics and government—which one so often encounters, particularly in England and America—stem from this historical background.

It is precisely in this sense that Adenauer's personality, representing a new type of "Christian" statesman in a legitimate sense, has had a singularly persuasive impact. Ade-

3

nauer has been at all times a consistent foe of any political clericalism, in particular the misuse of certain Church doctrines and Papal teachings for partisan political purposes. More remarkable in view of his ideopolitical origins and sociological background, Adenauer has been able to outgrow all those denominational limitations, which many times have guided "Catholic" politicians of the old school.

Adenauer has restored those fundamental moral and spiritual principles in government and society which are at the root of Christian civilization and Western history and therefore are among the most powerful factors in the renewal of Europe and Western democracy. These principles are rooted in the dignity and freedom of man based on Natural Law, the intrinsic life principle of Western Christian culture and society. This specifically Occidental Jewish-Roman-Christian personalism has indeed left its imprint on the cultures and peoples of the Western world: understanding and respect for the human person, political freedom and social justice, which are as essentially native to the West as they are alien to the religious impersonalism of Eastern and Oriental Christianity, as well as to the spiritual and political collectivism of Russia and the Russianized East.

These Western "Christian" traditions and concepts of personal freedom need to be stressed by any political movement which seeks a truly fundamental renewal and strengthening of democracy in the Western world. They are equally necessary for a fruitful effort to lead the peoples of Central and Eastern Europe back into the Western community, and to integrate them with its spiritual, cultural, social, and political life.

In this sense, the term "Christian" is justly applicable to political ideas and actions as represented by Adenauer and his party, the Christian Democratic Union (CDU) of Germany. In this sense—and only in this sense—the term Christian may even be essential in the efforts to revive the truly Christian traditions and values in democratic government and society, as well as for all those movements of today which consider themselves obliged and authorized to represent the authentic traditions and vital interests of the peoples of Central and Eastern Europe in the struggle of ideas in the now all-encompassing political and social sphere.

Since the idea of "Christian" politics, as it was practiced by certain political parties and so-called "Catholic" politicians and statesmen in the old Europe, down to the close of the prewar era, requires a fundamental revision and restructuring for the job of building a "new order" in Germany and Europe—particularly along genuine democratic lines— the new "Christian" meaning in politics and social reform, as embodied in Adenauer, his personality and work, are indeed of a pioneering significance. Without a Christian democratic renewal of Germany, the idea of establishing true and lasting democracy in Europe, perhaps even in the Central and Eastern European countries, would, if it were not totally hopeless, face a highly uncertain future.

There is no need to create a legend around Adenauer to account for his prominence as an international statesman. An inborn political instinct and a strong desire to live a life of action led him most naturally into politics. In addition to his innate aptitude for the tools of politics, he possesses a Christian world view, which is firmly anchored in a political ethos.

These qualities have enabled him to fulfill himself politically in the high calling of statesmanship in a way which is unparalleled in the tragic history of German politics, and specifically in the history of German Catholicism.

Politically and socially, Adenauer represents the best heritage of his native Rhineland. The traditions he follows, which bear the specific imprint of the *Civitas Coloniensis* and the orbit of Cologne (*Koelnischer Raum*), offer the most truly European expression of *Deutschtum* and at the same time the best German expression of Occidental culture and

of the European spirit. These traditions, with their strong
emphasis on the idea of the Christian democratic state and
social doctrine grew from the same historic and cultural soil
of the Rhineland, with its innate European heritage. Adenauer's ethicopolitical *Weltanschauung* and democratic realism have been formed and nourished by these traditions.
It is, in fact, the unique feature of Adenauer's political development that he has always been consistently sustained by
these traditions. Here is the core of a real understanding of
Adenauer's sincere European orientation and genuine Western policy.

Almost all the prevalent misconceptions about Adenauer's
position and policy, in Germany and abroad, are essentially
due to an inability to comprehend these ideopolitical roots.
For the first time in German history, these traditions have
produced a statesman called upon to guide the political
destiny of Germany in a truly democratic and European
sense.

These are the same intellectual and political traditions
which enabled Carl Schurz—perhaps the only genuine democratic statesman whom the environment of Cologne produced during the nineteenth century—to bring his particular
concept of democratic realism to bear upon American politics. Reflection on the ideohistorical kinship between Carl
Schurz and Adenauer and the resulting similarities in their
respective political mentalities might deepen American understanding of the kind of political realism that sustains
Adenauer's Western policy.

Konrad Adenauer has remained true to these traditions.
Their democratic and social-reformist heritage became the
foundation of the political and social movement of the CDU.

Adenauer's political career was as difficult as it has been
successful. He began by accumulating a valuable stock of experiences with the elite of the German civil service officialdom who were responsible for the exemplary administration

of German cities and communes. At the age of thirty, Adenauer, then a lawyer, was elected a member of the city council of Cologne, the third largest city in Germany. Seven years later he was elected deputy *Buergermeister* and five years later, in 1917, he became mayor (*Oberbuergermeister*). In this office, until 1933, he initiated the spectacular organization and cultural development of the great Rhineland metropolis, gaining for the city an international reputation as one of Europe's most important modern cultural and commercial centers. During this period, from 1920 to 1933, Adenauer, as permanent President of the Prussian State Council, exerted a decisive influence in the efforts to establish a firm democratic structure for the Prussian state, and in the development of a conscious democratic policy for the Center Party in the Prussian Parliament.

Adenauer, despite or perhaps because of his authentic conservative position, was equally hostile to reactionary political movements and social radicalism. He firmly rejected both a narrow confessionalism and clericalism. Twice, in 1920 and in 1926, he thus refused a call to seek office at the Chancellory of the Reich. This would have obliged him either to enter a one-sided alliance with the radicals of the Left; or he would have been forced to compromise with the reactionary politics of the Right.

He was consistently dedicated to a defense of the Weimar Republic, in the spirit of genuine Christian and democratic responsibility. Two acts of his were especially significant in this connection. In 1922, as President of the German Catholic Convention in Munich, Adenauer sharply rebuked the conservative Monarchist Cardinal Faulhaber for his attacks on the legitimacy and democratic foundations of the Weimar Republic, reminding him of the constitutional basis and the democratic spirit of the republic. On February 6, 1933, as President of the Prussian State Council, he once more showed his extraordinary courage, when he categorically refused to dissolve the Prussian Parliament on the basis of an anticonstitutional emergency decree issued by Hindenburg. He thus openly defied the Chancellor of the Reich, Hitler, declaring that this decree represented a "crude violation of the Constitution, creating a double standard in law, of justice and injustice!"

At this time, Prelate Kaas and Bruening, the leaders of the Center Party, were already negotiating with Hitler. The tragic results of these dealings are well-known. They led to the moral and political suicide of the Center Party, through its endorsement of the "Empowering Act" which all but deprived the German people of their rights.

When the catastrophe broke, Adenauer remained in Germany, because his political conscience would not permit him to leave, even though the hatred of Hitler and Goering was especially directed against him. During the Nazi rule, he was subjected to serious pressures and repeated arrests. Those years of stern privation and suffering were fruitful years; the convictions were then taking shape within him which were later to fit him for his call to statesmanship. His hour came after 1945, when Adenauer became the "Chancellor of the Vanquished" to set his people on the road to a better future.

The most impressive achievements of the new forces at work in the German Federal Republic are the masterful reconstruction of the administrative machinery, the reorganization of society and of the political parties, and the astounding resurgence of the economic and cultural life. But the visible manifestations of these imposing achievements of German efficiency and the German sense of duty conceal the invisible spiritual transformation, as represented particularly in the political thoughts of Konrad Adenauer and Federal President, Theodor Heuss. We have in mind here the revival of those ethicopolitical traditions of Natural Law, linked to both the liberal and the conservative traditions in Western democracy, whose influence had been opposed in Germany since the days of the reactionary Romanticists, until they were utterly submerged by the Nazi state with its innate hatred of Europe and its contempt for the people.

Both the constitution and the state laws of the new German Federal Republic reflect the best traditions of the Western-oriented order of Law. They are admirably in accord with the personalist concept of freedom, rooted in the Natural Law of democracy and the material concept of justice of the welfare state.

On this foundation, a new type of public and social thought has emerged under the leadership of Adenauer and his supporting movement of the CDU, in which the best traditions of German life merge with the ideopolitical core of European civilization and the Christian cultural community of the Occident. These efforts to achieve a new direction and order of Germany's moral and political life one may indeed view as a truly "new" element in German political thought. Adenauer has constantly exercised the full power of his statesmanship, drawing upon his many years of experience in German politics and administration in order to carry forward this reorientation.

The justification for the basic ethicopolitical principle of Adenauer's entire Western policy lies in this interdependence between the spiritual option of the German people for the cultural community of the Occident and their practical decision for a political community with a renewed Europe. For this reason the Federal Chancellor has consistently opposed the tendencies toward a one-sided Eastern orientation or an isolationist neutralism, expressing his emphatic belief that "Because of our view of life, Germany cannot and should not seek an alignment with the East. For ideological and cultural reasons, we Germans belong to the West in our total concept of life, and only by aligning ourselves with the West can our isolation and defenselessness come to an end."

As a result of World War II, the old European balance of

power has been eliminated once and for all. As a result, Eastern and Central Europe have fallen under Russian influence, and all Western Europe has been subjected to the intercontinental tension between the new world powers, America and Russia. From these hard facts there arose the need for a remaking of Europe, by securing its freedom in a new economic and defensive community with America—the only power capable of stemming the Russian advance in Europe. Germany had but two alternatives. She could decide to secure her freedom and the freedom of the West against the Soviet danger in an alliance with the European community and the United States of America. Or she could betray her power and freedom to the Russian neo-imperialism, thereby sealing the fate of Europe, which, without Germany, is unable to survive either politically or economically.

In signing the Paris treaties and the NATO pact, Adenauer chose the first of these alternatives. At the same time, he regained the full sovereignty of the Federal Republic and, as "Chancellor of the Vanquished," led his nation back to the community of the free nations. The existence of this new European community strengthens the hope that Germany will one day be reunited and all Germans will be in a position to enjoy the benefits of freedom. The steadfast character and political dependability of Adenauer, particularly illustrated in his meeting with the Russians in the Moscow Conference, is also a guarantee that he will unceasingly search for a solution of the problem of Germany's reunification. For this solution Adenauer will above all have to take into account Germany's responsibility toward Europe, as it was expressed by Frederic Gentz in 1806:

"Europe has fallen through Germany,
Through Germany it must rise again!"

I

The Legend: Adenauer-Germany

"The kind of plunge into the abyss which we Germans have experienced compels us to recognize that we must break with the past. Lost illusions cannot give us a fruitful life. I do not happen to believe in fairy tales!"

With these words, the German Chancellor gave a clue to an understanding of the miracle of the "new Germany" which has aroused so much astonishment. The great sobriety of the political thinking which is at the root of Adenauer's realism was to be the guiding light for any attempt to fit the political forces and ideological currents underlying the rehabilitation of Germany into their proper place in the historic pattern of our age. To appreciate the forces involved will make serious demands upon our knowledge of German history and our familiarity with the German political scene.

There is considerable confusion abroad, and even among large sectors inside Germany, as to the motives and premises as well as the actual results of the German resurgence, and

11

the most serious confusion centers in Adenauer's policy, the composite elements of his personality and its foundations in the objective conditions. The ultimate reason for all this confusion may be seen in the inadequate familiarity with, or the insufficient understanding of, the tragic course which German history and German political thought have taken since the days of the great French Revolution in 1789. On the whole, the sentiments of the world with regard to things German tend to oscillate between an irrational, metapolitical fear, sober respect, and enthusiastic admiration for the achievements of German efficiency and the self-effacing sense of duty —the forces which have made the German come-back possible. And yet, any of these attitudes suffers from profound ignorance of the innate emotional and political dualism of German history. This dualism has indeed resulted in the actual duality of Germany's destiny, with its dual faces of the official and the nonofficial Germany.

These considerations justify an attempt to aid in the understanding of recent German history and politics, by tracing the growth and achievements of Konrad Adenauer, the new Germany's leading statesman.

No one familiar with the present German scene would deny that such an effort must commence with the political soul-searching and the self-education of the German people. The sympathetic interest in the new Germany which the world is increasingly showing indicates that the results of such a study will meet with a friendly reception also outside of Germany, especially in the Western European countries and in the United States. In so far as this interest in the neo-German "miracle" seems increasingly centered in the person of the Chancellor—for reasons which we shall present in detail—it appears to be an increasingly important task to promote the understanding of the internal as well as the international aspects of the German problem through a social-biographical study of the statesman and his development.

The extraordinary impact of Adenauer's personality and work upon the political developments in Germany and Europe ever since the disaster of 1945 has caused an increasing number of people in and outside of Germany, especially in the United States, to identify the new Germany almost exclusively with the person of the Chancellor. The resulting catch phrase of an "Adenauer-Germany" has all the defects of ideological oversimplification of complex historic facts. It shares the fate of all those generalizations and slogans which have always blocked the understanding of the complex as well as tragic evolution of German history and political life.

This oversimplified approach seems particularly deplorable for the most recent phase of German history, because it tends to further another distortion of the true image of Adenauer-Germany in its essential features, its intellectual and political reality. The current and, even more, the future chief problem of the German Federal Republic on the domestic front—i.e., the problem of political leadership—has been particularly obscured by such misconceptions. This is shown not only by the confusion now reigning among the coalition parties of the Adenauer government—where open crisis has meanwhile broken out—but in particular by the ambiguous way in which this crisis has been evaluated abroad, especially in America. If one analyzes the origins and effects of the Adenauer-Germany legend, one is at once confronted with a development which, despite its grave political implications, has found much too little attention both in Germany and abroad. What we have in mind is the fact that virtually any problem of the German political scene, however unimportant, is hardly ever discussed except in connection with Adenauer's name. Moreover, it begins to be assumed that no conceivable solution of any of these problems can ever be worked out except in direct connection with Adenauer. And finally, the new Germany's entire moral and political credit, and therewith the confidence in her national and international future, are assumed to be indissolubly linked with the moral eminence and political prominence of this great statesman.

Such an over-all identification, however fruitful it may be in its concrete significance for the present-day Germany, may in fact turn out to be fatal for the problem of Germany's future political leadership. As a matter of fact, this wholesale identification of Germany's present policy with Adenauer's name is unhealthy even from the inside German point of view. It is just as undesirable abroad, especially in the United States, where practically all the confidence and all the hopes for the German Federal Republic are inevitably tied in with the person of its Chancellor. It is no doubt true that the actual course of German resurgence would seem to justify the unique confidence in Adenauer's moral and political integrity and effective statecraft; and certainly no one can say whether Germany after 1945 would have gone the same way, and would have enjoyed the same confidence and the same degree of assistance from abroad, without Adenauer's presence. His achievements are indisputable in this respect. The figure of this statesman represents the real core of the neo-German development between 1945 and 1956—that period which has already been recorded in the annals of history as the "Adenauer era." And yet, this dubious type of metapolitical legend of the *Life* magazine picture-story type is an inadequate tool for the perilous craft of high policy, as well as for the responsible task of the political sociologist and the historian of his own time. Beyond the arousing and satisfaction of political sensations and sentiments, there is also the indispensable job of political education, the striving for a genuine understanding and constructively critical penetration of this outstanding figure, and thus a comprehension of the deeper historic and political forces of the new Germany.

As a rule, a legend tends to form around a living statesman only where there is something basically wrong either with the statesman or the political reality which he represents.

This is why political legends are apt to spring up especially during great political crises, when politicians of mediocre talents, or outright political demagogues, prefer to assume the disguise of the "statesman," acting as the tools of political power groups or mass movements. Thus, the Bruening legend is a typical product of the political life-and-death crisis during the last years of the Weimar Republic. In those days, Hitler's enemies sought to forge an effective weapon against the rising Nazi mass movement by borrowing Bruening's Catholic traditions and personal prestige. His historic failure in the final struggle for the Weimar Republic is evidence enough that the Bruening legend was essentially misleading.

According to the Bruening legend, he was Germany's instrument; Bruening in fact becomes one with Germany. According to the Adenauer-Germany legend, on the other hand, Adenauer is identified with Germany's image, Germany is being identified with Adenauer, Germany becomes one with Adenauer. In the first case, the propaganda created a defensive front acting under Bruening's leadership; but two years later, the course of events refuted the notion that this front represented Germany and would be able to save it from the abyss. In the latter case, Adenauer's statesmanship created and strengthened the positive front of the forces of reconstruction, and the course of events during the past ten years confirmed its achievements, with the universal recognition that through these Germany was once again led away from the abyss.

The legend of the "defeated Chancellor" and, on the other hand, the legend of the "Chancellor of the Vanquished" express the fundamental difference between that which "had been" in the policy of the Weimar days and that which has developed anew in the policy of Bonn: Bruening as the symbol and exponent of the political failure of large segments of the German bourgeoisie during the Weimar history, ending in the disaster of 1945; and Adenauer as the symbol of accomplishment under the challenge of a new era of German ascent.

To understand the current situation in the new Germany and the resulting problems for the development of Germany's domestic and foreign policy, one simply must reduce the legend of Adenauer-Germany to its factual historic aspects and its real political substance. It is imperative to distinguish the facts which are relevant for Adenauer, the statesman's personality from those objective historic forces and political realities which are behind the actual shape and growth of the so-called Adenauer-Germany. We shall term the *personal* facts—i.e., those relating to Adenauer's personal talents and achievements—the *sociobiographical* aspects; while those objective facts which are related to the historic and political reality will be viewed as the *ideopolitical* and *sociological* conditions.

Such a distinction offers perhaps the only way to clarify the confusing aspects of the Adenauer-Germany legend, while at the same time doing justice to Adenauer's personal achievements and furthering the understanding of the political developments in Germany since 1945.

Thus a special new kind of biography is called for, different from the run-of-the-mill character of the political biography, in order to grasp the growth of the Christian statesman Adenauer out of the social and political traditions of the Rhineland and of German Catholicism, within the framework of ideopolitical developments and the evolution of government in Germany during the past fifty years. Adenauer's personality epitomizes the specific complexity of recent German history—its implicit dichotomy of ideas and politics— the kind of interrelation which the historian and the sociologist tend to view as the characteristic German problem of the interrelationship of religion and State, and hence of Church and Society. Only the sociobiographical presentation, combining the methods of ideohistorical analysis with the historicosociological interpretation, can lead to a deeper under-standing of these problems.

Such a method of presentation is particularly indebted to the sociobiographical principle of the historical method, which was founded by the famous German philosopher Wilhelm Dilthey (1833–1911):

"One must understand that peculiar kind of interaction," Dilthey wrote, "in which the individual is determined by his environment, and is reacting to it. All history is concerned with such interaction. The historian penetrates more deeply into the historic world, by sorting out the various contexts and studying the life within them. The most basic among all these contexts is represented by the way the life of the individual evolves within the environment, by which it is affected and influenced, and upon which it exerts its own influences in return. The life of the historic personality represents a type of interaction in which the individual receives influences from the historic sphere and is molded by these particular influences, while he in turn exerts his influence upon the historic level. And in the same way, biographical achievement does not make the individual a prey to the unbounded forces of the historic world. The sphere in which the individual lives is the state, religion, science—in short, a unique system of life, or a context of similar systems. It is the inherent structure of such contexts which attracts the individual, molds him, and determines the direction of his activity. From the potential contained in this inner structure for a historic figure emanate his historic achievements as well."

This ideohistorical principle is particularly fruitful for a sociobiographical interpretation of Adenauer's figure as a statesman, when it is closely linked with the method of ideopolitical interpretation of the historic process—the method which the great German historian Friedrich Meinecke (1861–1952) and, similarly, Gerhard Ritter, handled in such masterly fashion. These methods are especially applicable in Adenauer's case, for the life of the Chancellor, in its now more than eighty years, appears ideally suited to be viewed as a phenomenon making as well as interpreting history, singularly apt to express the creative forces of history in their role of historic realities, in their impact upon the present time.

"History," Gerhard Ritter wrote in his biography of Luther, "if correctly interpreted, involves the recognition of the fact that we must remain incomprehensible for ourselves without an understanding of what has gone before. Why is that so? Because our lives, born from the womb of the past, continue their growth more consistently than we are aware of in any single moment. To the extent that historical consciousness calls these facts to our minds, we enrich the substance of our thinking, and the striving of our will gains in clarity of purpose. It is certainly true that the impulse of living in the present, the more powerful it is, tends to interpret the past after its own fashion; and yet it cannot do without such an interpretation, for only with its aid can it gain any clarity about itself. A truly objective, historically faithful interpretation of the past may perhaps succeed only at a distance from the great decisive battles of the mind with their heated passions: but the clarity and the inner meaning of these intellectual decisions will become more evident, the more deeply we are able to penetrate into the core of the historic forces, the more clearly we are able to grasp the past in its unique nature, the more objectively and widely we are able to interpret its meaning." (Gerhard Ritter: *Luther,* Munich, 1925.)

These insights into the nature of a historic and political comprehension of reality, which proceeds along sociobiographical as well as ideohistorical lines, may afford the only fruitful approach toward replacing the Adenauer-Germany legend with an objective comprehension of present-day German political realities. Any facts and interpretations which will be presented in this book are therefore primarily offered to serve this purpose. To anticipate the result of our study, we shall see the unique inner relationship and interaction which exist between the personal achievements of the statesman Adenauer as the architect of the new German Federal Republic on the one hand, and the historic background and political realities of the neo-German development since 1945 on the other.

In his achievements as a statesman since 1945 Adenauer has been as much indebted to historic traditions as to the specific domestic situation in Germany during the last ten years. Or, putting it differently: Adenauer has given at least as much to the new Germany—in terms of personal talent and political achievements—as he has benefited from Germany in terms of traditional values, political forces, institutional entities, and actual support. Germany has always included a greater historic and political potential and sum total of objective achievements than even her greatest statesmen have ever been able to represent or realize.

Therefore the political legend of Adenauer's Germany is only relatively valid, and it is limited by the historic and political realities of the German Federal Republic. Its relativity is obvious to anyone familiar with the German domestic and international situation—unless he prefers to close his eyes to a realization that the so-called Adenauer era of this latest phase of German history is coming to an end. The fact is that even the personal aspects and potentialities of the Adenauer era are approaching their conclusion, in view of the advanced age of the Chancellor himself. No matter how highly we appreciate the personality and work of the octogenarian Chancellor, we cannot shy away from the question: after Adenauer —what? Who shall be his successor? Can there be any succession at all, in keeping with Adenauer's characteristic individuality?

At this point, only an indirect answer is possible to the first question, because on the one hand it will depend upon international factors which will be decisive for the German and European future—especially upon the peaceful solution of the international tensions between America and Russia. On the other hand, the answer depends essentially on the problem whether it will be at all possible to continue the fundamental achievement of the Adenauer era—the job of reconstruction in the Federal Republic—which has been accomplished under Adenauer's leadership in an organic way. There are above all two forces which will be decisive for a healthy transition from the Adenauer era to a reunited Germany in the near future.

From the international point of view, it is the question of reunification and the position which a unified Germany would occupy in the future framework of European politics, especially a modified NATO, and especially vis-à-vis Russia and her Eastern European satellites.

Domestically, however, the problem would be to find an answer which would satisfy both the European responsibilities and the Western-oriented conscience of the Federal Republic. At the core of this problem is the grave issue of political leadership, which in its connection with Adenauer's towering figure and achievements includes the problem of his succession as well.

II

The Problem: Political Leadership

It is a safe assumption that Konrad Adenauer harbors few illusions about the fundamental difficulties inherent in the question of the successorship. For he knows perhaps better than anyone else what problems the transition from the "Adenauer era" will raise for the future domestic evolution of Germany. Quite regardless of the fact that the personal conditions for his succession are fundamentally different from those which made it possible for Adenauer to grow into his role, even the objective sociological and political premises of the coming era will be materially different from those conditions which the "Chancellor of the Vanquished" found when he took office. And it was those conditions of the earlier period which determined the way in which he tackled the job of rehabilitation in the Federal Republic.

Adenauer's mentality and government system have often been described by the term "autocratic." This book is designed to show how little such a characterization accords with

21

the true state of affairs. Even the often used term "patriarchal" does not really fit the personal attitude and style of
government of the Chancellor. It is, however, quite fit and
proper to apply the term "paternal" to designate the awareness of an especial responsibility toward the kind of community which, due to its social structure, is in need of a stern
leadership, in order to fulfill its purpose in accordance with
the given social and political conditions. Any such activity is,
in a functional sense, at the same time conscious "leadership,"
i.e., the direction of the individual members of the community toward the better fulfillment of the common purpose.

Autocratic rule subjects all the rights and privileges of the
individual members of the community, as well as of the community as a whole, unqualifiedly to the sole will of the leader.
The exercise of both personal and community rights is exclusively tied to the will of the apex of the social edifice, its
head and ruler. Thus, the right of other social elements and
historic forces in regard to the decisions of the individual and
the sociological unit has been excluded from the start. The
German people had its drastic lesson in the nature of this
type of "leadership" in the guise of the Nazi dictatorship,
reason enough at least for the Germans to recognize the
absurdity of the term "autocratic" as applied to Adenauer's
kind of government.

As far as *patriarchal* rule is concerned, according to its historic meaning and sociological function, it represents a certain definite type of autocratic family rule. Moreover, especially in the age of Enlightened Absolutism and in the former
Papal territory, it used to represent a type of social and political association in which the rights of the community were
determined, as well as exercised, by its head. The personal
rights, on the other hand, of the individual members are as
a rule absorbed by the patriarchal authority only in so far as
they are in a direct sociological relationship with the patriarchal leadership. This is, for example, the case with the

Catholic patriarchal system, where this relationship has a distinct religious or ecclesiastical character. This type of patriarchal form of government and society exists in the Western world today only as a historic memory. This is true, even if one must recognize that patriarchalism as a system of family rule still survives, especially in certain Catholic countries.

The nature of true *paternalism* is founded on the fact that it arises out of certain sociological situations and patterns of community life—and will always arise from these again—where the basic conditions of life of a natural community, of family and State, require a stern personal type of leadership. In this context, the natural family pattern is at the same time the natural pattern for other, more comprehensive forms of the community, such as State and nation, or, rather, a nation supporting the State, and a State protecting the nation. In this case, any essential disturbances of the equilibrium and any threats to the natural stability call for a visible gathering of all energies in the person of a political leader and statesman. In such situations as appeared especially after the German catastrophe of 1945, the individual instinct of self-preservation begins by mobilizing the next higher instinct of preservation in human nature, the instinct of family preservation. Hence, the natural position of the father in a special and elevated role, the natural center of the family and sociological core of all family life. In this regard, true paternalism is as much of a *natural* phenomenon on every level of life—originating in the family and naturally integrated into the *family* organization, as patriarchalism must be considered a *sociological* phenomenon, produced by the need for a social organization of family life and the family community.

Patriarchalism is based on the authority of a RULER; paternalism is only concerned with the authority of a LEADER. This difference between patriarchal ruling and paternal leading is fundamental for its application in a democratic system, in which only the function of leading, but not of ruling, is possible. Also important is the fact that only a genuine *moral authority* can justify and sustain paternal leadership; without moral authority it must degenerate into autocratic rule of the type of patriarchalism or autocracy. Those facts bear decisively on the problem of the possibility or even necessity of paternal leadership in a democratic system in times of emergency. If there is no genuine moral authority for the task of a paternal leader, his job—i.e., his leadership—degenerates into autocratic rule: the so-called "authoritarian democracy" which is no democracy at all. (Hindenburg's and Bruening's system of governing with emergency decrees. Also typical was Dolfuss' and Schuschnigg's authoritarianism in Austria.)

Even those who did not share the experience of the life-and-death crisis of the German people in 1945 can understand that these disastrous upheavals tended to revitalize both the individual and the family instinct of self-preservation. Herein lie the elementary causes of the origin and success of Adenauer's paternal system of government. The immediate postwar years, with their implicit revitalization of the family instinct, roused at the same time the wish for a kind of paternal leadership—as the sociological analysis with the privilege of hindsight may note today. It is obvious that Adenauer's origin in the strong paternal traditions of Cologne family life, as well as his own exemplary life as a family man, were particularly apt in meeting this urge. Perhaps this explains the profound human impact which the personality of the "Chancellor of the Vanquished" has exercised upon the German people, from the days of the collapse down to the immediate present.

But two other essential factors of a sociological and political nature, aside from the human and personal elements, have been responsible for Adenauer's paternalism and the success of his type of government. Its effects and implications have been decisive for the political individuality of his system, and they make it inevitable that this system will be replaced by a new form of government under Adenauer's successors.

Let us consider first the sociological premises of Adenauer's paternal style of government. They are founded, on the one hand, on the impact of the Nazi system upon the political mentality of the people and, on the other hand, on those catastrophic results of the sudden collapse of Hitler's totalitarian order in 1945, which cut across all sectors of political and social life. In this situation, it would have been futile to expect an abrupt change of the political mentality of the people away from the Hitler system to a type of political thought and feeling in line with the democratic governments of the Western nations—especially France, England, and America. The only possibility in 1945 of guiding the German people toward a gradual understanding of genuine democracy, and a step-by-step progress in the use of their political values and institutions, consisted in replacing Hitler's autocratic system with the type of government that has evolved under Adenauer's paternalism.

I do not wish to be misunderstood on this point. What I am dealing with is by no means the overcoming of the Nazi dictatorship and the Hitler autocracy by the device of an authoritarian regime in the Federal Republic under Adenauer's patriarchal leadership—the type of system some of the Chancellor's opponents claim actually exists now. What we are concerned with here, and what was indeed in line with the sociological and ideopolitical necessities of 1945, is the replacement of the Hitler dictatorship and the liquidation of its sociological and political heritage by a system and technique of government which, while scrupulously respecting democratic freedoms, seeks to overcome the prevailing chaos through stern order and with a firm hand, thus providing the right kind of leadership for the new start in political life and for the reconstruction of the State, together with an impressive show of personal responsibility. Adenauer's type of government has fully demonstrated its validity. It was in this framework that the young German Federal Republic, so often termed "Adenauer-Germany," was born. In the following chapters we shall examine the essential stages and contents of this development.

A true understanding of the Adenauer type of system also requires a greater familiarity with those unique political conditions which have molded the specific individual character of Adenauer's policy—the policy that has been called the "policy of fulfillment" on the Chancellor's part, in relation to the Allied victors—and the emphatic "pro-Western orientation" of this policy. We shall study these developments in the following chapters as well. For the moment, it is enough to state that, in the circumstances, Adenauer's extraordinary personal vigor and determination, and the largely personal responsibility of the Chancellor, have made it possible for these developments to succeed. It may be that this fact, and the moral and political credit which the Chancellor has been able to gain abroad due to these developments, is the most precious foundation upon which a visible successor to the Adenauer system may be able to build.

All these reflections result at least in one important conclusion, especially significant for the confidence of the outside world in Germany's future development: the present system of government in the Federal Republic is rooted in Adenauer's personality. In this manner, Adenauer's paternal government style has fulfilled itself both in personal and objective ways, sociologically as well as historically. Any attempt by his successors to continue this type of paternalism, or to perpetuate it as a system of government in the Federal Republic, would be utterly doomed to failure. What is more, such an attempt would probably set up serious obstacles for a healthy development of German political life, and might conceivably lead to an actual life-and-death crisis.

On the other hand, it seems vital that Adenauer's basic ethical and political attitude should be preserved, together with his basic political conception, the substance of which has been termed his "European orientation" and his loyalty toward the West; and these basic attitudes should in time be developed further and indeed be consolidated and deepened. Hence it is not Adenauer's paternal style of government—distinctly linked with his own personality and the peculiar conditions of his era—which could and ought to be continued, but his unique approach to the tasks of statesmanship. Thus the widespread concern one encounters, both inside Germany and abroad, that the possibility of an organic transition from the Adenauer era into the next phase of German history shall find a constructive solution, if this distinction is observed.

But this concern tends to lessen perceptibly as soon as one takes a closer look at Adenauer's actual achievements in the growth of the German Federal Republic. In studying the record of these achievements, we shall at once become aware of certain unexpected aspects of German development during the past decade, which were largely concealed by the unfortunate legend of "Adenauer's Germany." They are essentially related to the *problem of generations* and their impact upon the neo-German political scene, and the *problem of traditions* and their creative influence in the rise of the German Federal Republic.

In 1945, Adenauer observed that it was necessary to break with the past—referring, of course, only to the negative aspects of the German tradition. One must certainly guard against a misinterpretation of this postulate, as if the Chancellor had meant to reject all that belongs to the past in Germany's political tradition or history. His profoundly conservative philosophy safeguards Adenauer from the perils of such a position. The outspoken realism of his political philosophy quite naturally involves a full recognition of all the genuine traditions and values in Germany's political and social history, including her heritage of political freedom and her democratic philosophy of the State.

In this attitude, it must be noted, Adenauer is completely in accord with the intellectual and political outlook of Theodor Heuss, the President of the West German Federal Republic. Heuss's contribution, inspired by a genuine political humanism, has probably been the single most important factor, next to Adenauer's achievement, in the rise of the new Germany. One may even state that some of Adenauer's own contributions in the field of political institutions would have been unthinkable without the support and consolidation of Heuss's outstanding activities in the cultural and ideopolitical field—or at least would have lacked much of their actual impact.

It is impossible to evaluate either the achievements of the Chancellor's statesmanship or the history of the Federal Republic in general without due attention to the President's contributions on the cultural, and especially on the constitutional, level. Even a correct analysis of the problem of political leadership in Germany depends to a large extent upon an assessment of Theodor Heuss's specific contribution and ideopolitical share within this entire complex. Any sociobiographical history of the German Federal Republic, its origins, and evolution to date must largely be focused upon Adenauer's and Heuss's personalities. And only through such an approach can we do justice to the historic achievements of these two men and to the full constitutional meaning of their respective offices of Chancellor and President, within an objective historical framework.

The fact that, in all the discussions and analyses of this subject thus far, the emphasis has chiefly been on Adenauer's personality, is for two main reasons. The office of the Federal Chancellor, for one thing, carries a particular degree of executive power and responsibility. Adenauer, moreover, has up to now attended to the duties of this office with an energy and a degree of success indicative of extraordinary gifts of statesmanship and a creative passion dedicated to political aims.

Compared to the prominence of the chancellorship and the personality of the Chancellor himself, it was natural that the office of the Federal President, and the manner in which Theodor Heuss has conducted it, have received relatively little attention, especially in world public opinion. According to the Bonn Basic Law, the constitutional position of the Federal President is largely limited to the formal representative duties of a head of state, including certain rights of proposal and nomination, the signing of international treaties, and similar functions. Consequently the office of the German Federal President involves chiefly three things: absolute passivity in international affairs, an essential passivity regarding the executive branch of government, and complete neutrality in all issues of party politics. In other words, the official role of the Federal President requires absolute self-restraint in all institutional and executive functions of the government. Thus any active application of statesmanship, any creative use of passionate political convictions, are definitely barred to the President.

In his role as Federal President, Theodor Heuss has so far scrupulously observed the inherent limitations of his office. He has been able to pursue this course, because even during the years of his greatest political activity he practiced that "sacred sobriety" in the political sphere which consistently places the human above the purely institutional factor. Heuss once said, "One must keep a realistic view of things; thus one will see human beings rather than mere institutions and paragraphs. . . ."

As a result, Heuss has consistently viewed political institutions primarily as opportunities for the creative adjustment of the life of the community and the citizen. Along with the other institutions of society—above all, the inherent educational powers of church and school, literature and art—the political institutions are there to serve as "tools for the formation of human beings," in order to safeguard the "natural life" of the individual citizen, and therewith the "worth of the individual person and his liberty." This humanistic concept of the cultural and civilizing role of politics was pointedly expressed by Heuss when he said: "One may not be able to create cultural values by political means, but perhaps it is possible to make the right kind of politics through a cultured and civilized approach." What Heuss meant was that any genuine political activity must be predicated on certain definite cultural premises, if it is to evolve in the service of civilization; for while a political action based on materialistic, mechanistic attitudes can never promote cultural progress, a civilized human approach may indeed lead to a humane, humanistic type of political activity.

This position reflects the best traditions for the spiritual foundation of political life, transmitted to Heuss through the heritage of Swabian liberalism and South German democracy. These forces have animated and inspired Heuss's extraordinary activity in his nonpolitical role since 1949, and in his contribution to the social and cultural rehabilitation of Germany. But his constantly growing influence upon the development of the new German educational and cultural life is also indicative of the enormous authority which Heuss has been able to gain as a genuine political leader, especially through his fundamental contribution to the shape and substance of the constitutional foundations of the new Germany, the Bonn Basic Law.

In this regard, Adenauer aptly characterized Heuss's achievements when he said: "The indirect election of a head of state has been proposed by Heuss. This concept, together with the abandoning of the institution of the plebiscite, echoes the experience that in a vast democracy demagogues may all too often succeed in exploiting the political inexperience of the broad masses through their cheap methods. One may view as Heuss's particular achievement, as the fruit of his role as a mediator, his contribution to the school provisions of the Basic Law. His experience from Weimar days enabled him to contribute toward the relaxing of the rigid and inflexible rules particularly in this field, and to the projection of a middle line, which ultimately helped to avoid disintegration."

Adenauer similarly recognized Heuss's over-all contribution to the growth and development of the new Germany in his words of appreciation for a successful partnership, dedicated to the Federal President on the occasion of his seventieth birthday: "What was important and effective above all was the uniting force of common objectives, as in the approach to social tensions, to the Jewish problem, to the treatment of the real and emotional plight of the expellees. If an atmosphere of confidence has sprung up abroad, and has materially contributed to restoring German prestige in the world, this represents only one, and hardly the least, among the achievements of the Federal President, who incidentally nourishes no illusions as to the difficulties still before us, despite all that has been achieved and which no one would have believed possible only four years ago."

Recently, Heuss published a comprehensive selection of his speeches, writings and letters of the years 1949–1955, in a volume entitled *Wuerdigungen (Recognitions)* (Tuebingen, 1955). This collection reveals the intellectual vitality and political scope of the educational and political activities of the German Federal President. In fact, these documents represent ideopolitical achievements of the best kind. They are a testimony to the creative power of a humanistic approach to politics, an approach in the best traditions of conservative liberalism; a political activity in the cause of the German present and a fruitful European future, oriented to a responsible and living sense of history.

We have important reasons for trying to determine the personal relationship and the interaction of the respective achievements of Adenauer and Heuss; they are of considerable significance for the deeper sociobiographical understanding of the Chancellor. We may shed some light upon the problem of the generations inside the present political leadership in Germany. Here we find significant clues to the historic currents and developments which have shaped the particular sociological and political structure of the new Germany, as well as to the specific differences between the new German Federal Republic and such earlier entities as the Weimar Republic. And from the relationship of these two outstanding figures we may gain an understanding of the unique ideopolitical traditions and values of the German past which have influenced and guided the new patterns of government and political life, including the leading institutions of the new Germany. Above all, this perspective permits us a glimpse into the problems of specific ideopolitical traditions and political experiences that have determined the growth and actual work of Adenauer, or that, in a dialectic process of interaction between personality and historical environment, have been shaped by Adenauer himself.

III

The Dilemma: The Generations' Problem

The gravity of the political leadership problem in the German Federal Republic is underscored by the fact that its two highest offices are filled by men who have passed the seventy mark. One does not have to feel particularly strongly about the generations problem in order to worry about the health of these "veterans," if only because of the physical strain attendant upon these offices; and, even more serious, because of the future of the issues which confront them every day.

It was an impressive demonstration of popular confidence when, in September, 1953, the German people confirmed the then seventy-eight-year-old Chancellor by a conspicuous majority for another four-year term in office, and in July, 1954, reelected the then seventy-one-year-old Federal President for another five-year term. Anyone familiar with German conditions knows that the outstanding statesmanship and political

33

experience represented by these two men can indeed not easily be replaced. Next to them, all other potential candidates, some of whom will ultimately have to succeed them, seem lacking in political experience—aside from a few politicians of the Weimar era, who have been so severely compromised by the course of events that the fate of the young Federal Republic could not possibly be entrusted to their hands. Even among the representative leaders of the various German states, political parties, and labor unions, all of whom belong to a younger generation, there is hardly a name that seems qualified, on the basis of the record, to become Adenauer's or Heuss's successor. In stating this, we mean in no way to imply any value judgment as to the individual abilities and qualifications of these men. We are merely registering the dearth of political talent and experience inside the new Germany—a fact which some circles, for understandable reasons, prefer to ignore.

This lamentable condition is likely to cause grave future complications, domestically as well as on the international scene. This is especially true for the problem of Adenauer's succession, unless the Chancellor should even now apply the whole weight of his experience and genius to the problem of insuring a smooth succession. The training and systematic encouragement of a leadership elite for government and social institutions might best be approached once the causes underlying the current dearth have been analyzed. We are here touching upon a problem which, in its various historical, ideopolitical, and specific sociological implications has found little consideration so far.

The generations problem is, in fact, at the very core of the political leadership problem in the Federal Republic. By analyzing its deeper ideopolitical and sociological implications, we may thus be able to contribute much toward the clarification of all those basic questions linked with the rehabilitation of the new Germany. With almost perfect clarity this entire complex of problems is focused in Adenauer's personality and achievements. Indeed, the way in which the personal and social elements cross-fertilize each other in the sociobiographical pattern of the octogenarian Chancellor's life—the interaction of biographical and sociological forces—throws light on the political biography of the past three generations of the German people. Adenauer's figure represents an ideopolitical continuity in the sequence of generations which is simply nonexistent for the younger generations, due above all to the gap torn in the sociological continuity of German history by the Nazi regime. Or, to put it differently, Adenauer's political personality reflects the historic forces of the more recent German past in a way that the younger generation cannot claim for itself, because the National-Socialist break in the continuity of the generations also involved a sharp ideopolitical break in the German traditions. What in Adenauer's personality manifests itself as vigorous continuity, as an implicit unity of generations and traditions, appears as a mere flaw, a weakness, in the younger generation's striving to capture the leadership.

One must grasp this fundamental fact in order to understand the deeper implications of the leadership problem in Germany today. How little the old shopworn methods of the political biography and the one-sided political historiography are suited to illuminate these problems, becomes evident almost at first glance. The total inadequacy of these old methods is, incidentally, revealed in their importance in dealing with a truly timely interpretation of the German problem as a whole. Perhaps this is the principal reason for the absence, to this day, of a systematic history of the Weimar Republic and of the German developments since 1945, as well as for the absence of a comprehensive discussion of Adenauer's growth and record—not forgetting also the crucial problem of the generations and traditions and their interrelationship.

By contrast, the purely biographical aspects of the Nazi

period have been treated with an almost dizzying copiousness. Viewed for their value in political education, all these treatments are of a particularly dangerous type because, on the one hand, they work with the old positivist methods of the pure biography, and on the other with the allegedly purely "factual" method of relating political processes and developments. Thus the whole ideological background remains in a complete haze, and the significance of the "negative" traditions of German nationalism and the German expansion of power is altogether overlooked. We shall have occasion to come back to these problems which Adenauer had in mind when he spoke of the "past," and to the "lost illusions" with which the new Germany must break.

Any discussion of the purely private biographical material suffers from the defect of obscuring the role of the human element in the political sphere, i.e., the scope and impact of the political leader. The positivist, pragmatic method, on the other hand, tends to present history exclusively as a pattern, or sequence, of political and economic events. Thus both these old methods neglect the sociological problem of the generations, and its impact upon the individual, in favor of the purely objective political and economic sequence of events, while the ideopolitical and spiritual problem of traditions appears reduced to the mechanistic views of political pragmatism and economic utilitarianism. In any of these concepts there is always the danger that the generations problem will resolve itself into the mere triviality that the "older" and the "younger" generations, respectively, are out for power—or, more simply, that the first tend to cling to their positions of leadership, while the latter exert considerable pressure in order to succeed to these positions. The issue of traditions appears in this light as a mere ideological dead weight in the struggle for power, conjuring up immediate suspicions of conservative ideologies or reactionary power politics behind it. Most views of German and non-German observers of German development since 1945, and in particular of Adenauer's policy, suffer more or less from their inadequate appreciation of the twin problems of generations and traditions and their fundamental significance for the issue of political leadership.

Any valid historicosociological evaluation of the German present must start from the understanding that the German revival was predicated upon the utilization of the most mature store of experiences within the older generation of German politicians, together with the best traditions in German history, for their combined impact upon the German present. The accomplishments of men like Adenauer and Heuss represent the historic heritage inherent in the German traditions combined with the sociological heritage represented by their respective generations, working for the rehabilitation of Germany. True, there are those who maintain that the job of reconstruction begun in 1945 represents a direct continuation of the pre-1933 "past," a mere revival of the "old" forces enshrined in the political order of the Weimar Republic. But such an interpretation overlooks the incisive impact of the Nazi era upon the sociological structure of German political life and upon the over-all ideopolitical fabric of German traditions.

National Socialism, with its implicit political dynamism and the revolutionary *élan* of its nihilist ideology, had a far deeper impact upon the course of German history than the mere temporal measure of its rule, 1933–1945, would indicate. Its influence dominates the life span of at least an entire generation. For, after all, the disintegration of the political structure under the Weimar Republic commenced long before 1933, and the effects of the Nazi nihilism, on the other hand, are felt in German life far beyond the end of its actual rule. Essentially three main consequences of the Nazi era may be distinguished in their effect upon the life of the German nation, and, therefore, three historic and political results

for the German present and future. We may classify them as
the sociological impact upon the generations problem; the
political impact in the sphere of the political institutions and
movements; and, lastly, the ideological impact in the sphere
of the German traditions.

National Socialism has on its conscience the elimination of
an entire generation from sharing in the creative evolution
of political life in Germany. There can be no doubt that the
chief reason for the present dearth of qualified political prac-
titioners and general leadership material is the result of the
suppression of all political education and practice of a non-
Nazi type during the Hitler period. But no less perceptible
are the results of the fact that, many years prior to the actual
Nazi ascent to power, the Nazi doctrine had poisoned the
political thinking and the emotional life of millions of young
people, some highly gifted, who were definitely interested in
political affairs. It was inevitable that this group, which until
1945 had known nothing but the Nazi brand of politics, after
the collapse became prey to a state of political despair or total
indolence; and that this mental void could at best be replaced
by political cynicism or a chronic state of indifference, not
by an active political interest in the "new" forces and problems confronting the present German nation. Besides this
group, however, we should remember the tragically lost potential of political talent which was extinguished by the Nazi
terror, or else by the disastrous effects of the Second World
War. We should mention in this context, above all, the victims of the Hitler terror of July, 1944, and its murderous
aftermath, the destruction of the substantial remainder of the
liberal as well as conservative political talent of pre-Nazi days.
And finally we should recall those men and women in the
spheres of the political sciences, sociology and law, who went
abroad after 1933 and who—those who were still alive in 1945
—for a variety of reasons refused to return to their native

country, thus contributing to the "generations gap" in German political life.

This brief survey should suffice to show how the generations gap caused by the Nazi regime, amounting to the loss of almost an entire generation for the political life of the nation, could not fail to add its burden to the leadership problem. All the more reason to recognize the efforts of that small group of political leaders of the older generation who, under the leadership of the "old man" have laid the foundations of the Federal Republic, both on the Bonn level and in the individual states. They had to proceed with little help from the intermediary generation—poor in political experience—but with definitely vigorous support from the ranks of the young Germany.

Our view of the generations problem should help to explain why Adenauer has been popularly nicknamed *der Alte,* which expresses infinitely more than mere civil respect for the "old man" in the Anglo-Saxon sense: the younger and youngest generations of the German people consider the "old man" of Bonn as the living embodiment of all the genuine political experiences and traditions of recent German history. Their confidence in his leadership, therefore, is far more sincere and deep-rooted than was that of the generation of the Bismarck admirers in the "old man of the Sachsenwald." Adenauer's personality and work, therefore, seem to represent, at least for the present, the successful bridging of the generations gap. The only remaining question is whether the busy "old man" will find the time and the strength, in order effectively to initiate the more talented among the younger generation in the intricacies of professional statesmanship. For only in this way would the generations problem, in its effect upon the political leadership of Germany, find a lasting solution.

But there is, of course, one great obstacle in the path of a constructive solution of this problem, the paternalistic nature of Adenauer's style of government. Notwithstanding the admiration we owe to the person of the octogenarian Chancellor; notwithstanding the recognition due his record as a statesman up to now; and even despite the unqualified support every good German, European, and American owe to Adenauer's policy in and outside of Germany in the interest of German freedom and Western security, one thing must be stated with perfect clarity:

Much in contrast to his astonishing statesmanship, and the acumen and farsightedness which have so far distinguished his judgment in all important issues, he appears to have relatively little understanding of the political and psychological implications of the generations problem. The aging Chancellor does not seem to see that a gradual change has taken place even within the problem of the generations, with the result that at least the more vigorous intellects and personalities among the intermediary generation are increasingly conscious of their right to make their opinions heard and to display a greater freedom and more independent initiative in their political actions. Thus the latent personal tension that exists between Adenauer and the former Minister President of Rhineland-Westphalia, Karl Arnold—a man a quarter of a century his junior—must primarily be explained by their different outlook on life based on the difference in generations. Despite the identity of ideas and political objectives, this difference points to different methods and ways in which to realize their common aims.

In a similar way, a perceptible change has taken place in the concept of the highest leadership echelon in the Christian Democratic Union. It is highly indicative that the middle generation among the leaders of that movement are striving, with growing purposefulness, for a modification of the paternalistic leadership methods of their "old chief" Adenauer. The Stuttgart party convention of the CDU, in April, 1956, brought these tendencies into the open, while manifesting at

the same time Adenauer's ability and readiness to recognize
and accept any genuine manifestation of an independent political activism arising from the middle generation. Adenauer's ungrudging acceptance, at the Stuttgart conference,
of the enlarged vice-chairmanship of the party from two to
four members (Arnold and Gerstenmaier, in addition to the
original members, Kaiser and von Hassel)—although this decision went counter to his own proposal as well as to prevailing custom—and his consent to Karl Arnold's election as the
Chancellor's new deputy in the CDU leadership, gave clear
evidence of two things:

For one, that Adenauer the realist, despite his paternalistic
mentality and his great age, is both willing and able to recognize the inner dialectics of the generations problem, and their
inherent pressure for a change in the paternalistic system of
government both on the level of the Federal Republic and
within the leadership of the CDU movement.

Secondly, with the frankness and clarity which characterize his statements Adenauer, during the same party convention, took the opportunity to head off any possible speculation
concerning his impending retirement, by countering one of
Khrushchev's remarks—that he is holding his German plans
in abeyance until Adenauer retires—by saying: "Well, gentlemen, that about retirement is a problem, you know. As long
as God gives me the vigor and strength [to carry on], it is up
to you whether Mr. Khrushchev shall succeed, or not!"

It may be worth noting, in this context, that next to God
and the "gentlemen" of the CDU to whom he referred, it will
depend very largely upon the results of the 1957 elections for
the Federal parliament whether Adenauer will actually be
permitted to officiate as Chancellor of the Federal Republic
for a third time. In fact, this contingency may depend on yet
another factor, the solution of the crisis caused by the defection of the Free Democratic Party (FDP), under Thomas
Dehler, from the government coalition. Let it be noted also

that the conflict between Adenauer and Dehler has some significant roots in the generations problem, which is now gaining such increasing acuteness. The bold and independent
action of the Rhineland-Westphalia FDP, led by the younger
Free Democratic forces, has been a clear enough indication
of this trend.

What has been said here on this subject should make it
plain that the solution of the generations problem appears
not only as the factual basis for any future solution of the
political leadership problem in the Federal Republic, but at
the same time involves a fundamental challenge for the new
generation, which sooner or later will be called upon to assume the leadership in the new Germany, to show whether it
shall be willing and able to recognize, appreciate, and successfully continue the decisive achievements of the Adenauer
era.

IV

The Past: Tabula Rasa

Besides interrupting the continuity of the generations, the Nazi system produced two other incisive effects upon political life in Germany, both of tremendous significance for its entire sociological and ideopolitical fabric. The Nazi claim to totalitarian power made a clean sweep, indeed a *tabula rasa*, of government institutions and all other forms of political life in the Weimar Republic.

Already during the early thirties, the profound crisis which had gripped these institutions revealed their lessening cohesion and inner strength, their inadequacy in coping with the necessary adjustments. Outstanding among these institutions requiring either a complete overhauling or obliteration were the political parties of the Wilhelmian and Weimar eras, both multiple-party states. Next, there were the more extreme forms of the Weimar parliamentary system, the essentially unrealistic and doctrinaire formalism of the Weimar constitution; and finally, the fatal dualism between Prussia and

43

the Reich, with all its perilous implications. Among these implications, the overwhelming influence of the military (the Reichswehr) and of the Prussian Junkers were probably the most dangerous.

Secondly, the Nazis were so completely thorough in their mobilization of all the open and latent resentments which were the by-product of the profound crisis through which the German nation had for a long time been passing, that all those intellectual heresies and political ideologies—nationalistic, pan-Germanic, or plain imperialist—which had burdened German history since the days of the French Revolution, were suddenly laid bare in their utter absurdity. In point of fact, this Nazi *tabula rasa* among the doomed and decadent sociological and ideological manifestations of the Weimar Republic was one of the most vital premises for rebuilding government and political life after the war. The fact that this was, at first glance at any rate, a purely negative development can hardly diminish its decisive historic significance. We are here faced with one of the Nazi accomplishments by which the evil intent produced a lasting good. Indeed, the impact of this clean sweep with everything "past" and all those "lost illusions" with which, in Adenauer's words, the present-day German must break, was so profound, that any effort at resurrecting the past in order to build political life in Germany today has long been proved futile. Adenauer's example shows above all that the effective reorientation of German domestic and foreign policy must proceed from the candid recognition of this fact. The same holds true for the correct sociological assessment of these efforts and their results up to now.

Of all these phenomena of the past, only the fate of the political parties and social institutions or movements of the Weimar days concerns us here, in connection with our problem of political leadership. At a later point in our study, when we shall discuss the administrative structure of the Federal Republic, we shall have occasion to deal more specifically with the other developments. Nor is this the place to discuss the totalitarian party formations of Nazism and Communism. Later, when we consider the problem of how the new Germany may be secured against the threatening irruption of a neo-German nationalist or bolshevist collectivism, we shall give our attention to the dangerous antidemocratic influences emanating from them.

The crisis of the political parties and philosophies of the Weimar Republic found its most manifest expression in the permanent crisis of the German National and Democratic parties. By the time the Hitler regime sounded the death knell both to reactionary conservatism and political liberalism —the latter weakened by its intrinsic rationalistic-positivistic philosophy—the history of these two parties of the bourgeois Right and Left had shown how far the implicit perversion of these two ideologies had already progressed.

The inner insecurity and administrative confusion which pervade their respective successor parties in the Federal Republic reveal how pitifully little of the past of these parties survived the Nazi *tabula rasa*. The *complexio oppositorum*, the meeting of opposites, represented in the present Free Democratic Party (FDP), is in reality an uneasy marriage between the heirs of the true liberals and democrats and the successors to the heavy-industry and nationalist wing of the former German People's Party. This is an apparent indication that these groups have not as yet managed to find a valid political expression in exchange for the lost structures of the Weimar days. Incidentally, the political confusion reigning among many of their so-called "leaders" shows how little these groups have as yet understood the ideological changes in the new Germany. The great mass of the electorate, in particular the younger generation, seems to realize the extent of past dead weight and the exceedingly small share of "new" forces present in this party—as indicated by the rather modest following which the FDP has been able to attract on both federal and state levels.

But the fullest impact of the Nazi *tabula rasa* was felt by the two largest among the constitutional parties of the Weimar Republic, the Center and the Social Democratic parties. The effects on the one party were completely different from the effects on the other—a fact which has left its decisive mark on the face of the present successor parties. The ideology and the platform of the Social Democratic Party, products of crisis and depression, were made entirely obsolete in the Nazi period. On the other hand, the external forms of party structure of the SPD, especially the party bureaucracy and the well-organized hierarchy of party functionaries, survived in their essentials and are preserved in the new Germany. In decided contrast, the sociological structure and outward forms of the Weimar Center Party were totally destroyed by the Nazi *tabula rasa*, while the democratic core of its political and social philosophy has been substantially preserved. It has in fact become one of the essential ideopolitical ingredients of the new party of the Christian Democratic Union (CDU). We shall observe the concrete political and ideological contribution which these two parties are making to the new era out of their heritage. A detailed discussion of the platforms and performance to date of the present-day Social Democratic Party and Christian Democratic Union will provide us with the opportunity for such an analysis. What interests us particularly here is the way in which the breakdown of the old Center Party's social structure as well as the ideological disintegration of the Weimar Social Democratic Party affects the problem of political leadership in the Federal Republic.

We may begin with a general observation: The handful of undaunted followers of the resurrected Center Party may not be contented with it. There can be no doubt that the demise as organizational entities of these two largest among the parties loyal to the Weimar constitution involved certain moral problems over and beyond the entirely new social conditions with which they were faced after 1945. It is this fact which has militated against resurrecting the old Center Party, but in favor of the Social Democratic revival. Despite the undeniable failure of the SPD in concrete matters of party politics and tactics, the Socialist leadership summoned the moral courage, during the last decisive fights, for a courageous stand against Nazi temptations and threats—especially on the issue of the Enabling Act. Much in contrast, the Center leadership failed, particularly in ideopolitical and moral respects.

The psychological and moral implications of these reactions and attitudes affected the leadership problem in Germany in a much more decisive way than is usually conceded or assumed. The Social Democratic Party, due to its attitude during those decisive months, managed to save the moral prestige of the party leadership of the time, and even preserved a measure of moral sanction for the Social Democratic émigrés. As a result, in 1945 the exiled Socialists, together with the SPD functionaries who had stayed at home and borne the brunt of Nazi persecution, were able to undertake successfully to restore the party, under the leadership of that tragic and heroic figure, Kurt Schumacher. The newly founded SPD came out of every single election since 1946 as the second largest, in some states even as the strongest party, with almost 30 per cent of the total vote. The attempt to restore the old Center Party, on the other hand, ended miserably with less than 1 per cent of the total vote. There were, no doubt, other factors—some of them very important—behind this result, above all the powerful appeal of the interdenominational idea. Still, the way in which its leadership had discredited the Center Party was without a doubt the primary reason for the rejection by the mass of the Catholic electorate of attempts to restore the party. Painful experience had taught them that the old Central Party and the majority of its surviving leaders inexorably belong to that past with which the new Germany must break.

The fact that this break also involves the loss of a valuable store of experience in political and social organization and practice has of course contributed materially to the current leadership crisis in German political Catholicism. We shall see how Adenauer's personality and impact take on an added significance against this background, for Adenauer belongs to the circle of significant Catholic politicians of the Weimar period which was not in the least compromised by the course of events. This fact alone would entitle him to the role of continuing the best of the social and political traditions of German Catholicism and, hence, of preserving for the new order after 1945 whatever is left of positive social and political forces in the heritage of the Center Party. This heritage which fell legitimately to Adenauer became one of the major assets in the Christian reorientation of political life, in the pattern of the Christian Democratic Union.

Today's Social Democratic movement, however, plainly suffers from a lack of such spiritual continuity, precisely because it is too definitely bound to its own past. For the new SPD not only salvaged its old party apparatus and the sum total of the experience of its party bureaucracy and hierarchy, all through the *tabula rasa* of the Nazis. But it staggers under the burden of the crisis in Marxist theory which the present-day SPD has inherited, plus the ideopolitical crisis of the Weimar days—which proved a grave additional complication for the problem of political leadership.

As we shall see, this is indeed one of the chief causes for the current ideological crisis of the SPD, and a serious drawback for the ideopolitical regeneration of German life in general. The SPD experiences its own leadership crisis primarily as the problem of a "party without a program," a "movement without ideas." The SPD now confronts a situation which is the exact reverse of that in which the CDU finds itself, where the type of traditions and experiences personified by Adenauer amounts to a basic program and a repertory of forward-looking ideas, although on the other hand the CDU lacks the underpinning of solid organizational patterns and experience. To this very day, the young party of the Christian Democratic Union represents, despite its successes, more of a program and a promise than a political reality or a set of tested experiences. The leadership problem, chiefly an ideopolitical issue for the SPD, is for the CDU mainly a problem of inadequate personal experience and day-by-day practice in the political field.

This is not the place for an exhaustive discussion of the ideological crisis of the SPD. For the present purpose it may suffice to state that the present crisis in the German Social Democratic Party stems essentially from three facts, whose ideological premises and political interrelations should be clearly recognized: one, the ideological crisis of Marxist philosophy in general; two, the international crisis of the Socialist movements and parties as a phenomenon of the contemporary political scene; and, three, the crisis of the German Social Democratic movement as a specific German problem.

The best survey of the ideological crisis of the Marxist philosophy, as an ideohistorical problem of our time, is presented by *Studies in Marxism (Marxismus-Studien)* published by the Study Group of the Protestant Academies, Tuebingen, 1954, by Edwin Metzke and numerous collaborators. The religio-sociological and sociophilosophical aspects of the problem are impressively summarized in the collective volume, *Christian Faith and Social Action*, New York, 1953, edited by John A. Hutchison. This joint effort by a number of former "religious Socialists"—including Paul Tillich and Eduard Heimann—is especially significant because, with perfect intellectual integrity and a particular open-mindedness toward the problems of religion and socialism, it deals with the decisive change which the effort toward a synthesis of Marxism and

Christianity underwent during the last twenty years—the type of effort expressed in Tillich's and Heimann's ideology of religious socialism during the 1930's. The present clear-cut rejection of Marxist socialism on the part of this group is not only expressed in the change of name from "Socialist Christians" to "Christian Action," but also in the change of their concept of socialism. As early as 1946 they reflected this change in the statement: "Our concept of Socialism has undergone a progressive modification, which is predicated upon a deepening of our theological insight; a progressive assimilation of European experiences, as communicated by our members who have immigrated to this country [Tillich and Heimann]; and, furthermore, a close scrutiny of the Soviet Russian developments and the activities of the Communist Party in the United States."

British socialism, too, has gone through substantial changes, leading in particular to a distinctly positive emphasis on the interrelation of socialism and Christianity. A characteristic expression is the changed attitude of Sir Stafford Cripps in his book, *Towards Christian Socialism* (London, 1944), as well as the position of Ernest Bevin, who, in his study, *The Job to Be Done* (London, 1947), has stated:

"The chief source of the British Labour movement is a *spiritual* one. For after all, whence did we take our ideals? About a hundred years ago, our movement was born in the villages, the small parishes and adult schools. From these primitive beginnings there arose men and women with a desire to throw off all shackles which were tying them down, and to found the great community of freedom."

German Social Democracy never possessed such a religious-Christian tradition. Thus the party now finds it particularly difficult, if not impossible, to tap the source of religious tradition for new energies with which to master its spiritual crisis. The new edition of Kurt Schumacher's writings and speeches is all too clear in this respect. The same holds for the memoirs of the well-known Socialist Julius Braunthal, *In the Search for the Millennium (Auf der Suche nach dem Millenium,* 2 volumes, Nuremberg, 1948). Braunthal's experience of the "rediscovery of the meaning of freedom and democracy within the concept of Socialism," in contrast to the inhumanity of the Fascist and Communist dictatorships, leaves him essentially baffled.

The universal crisis of the Socialist movement has become especially evident in England after the war. This has been a fatal contributing element to the ambiguous attitude of the Labour Party toward the new Germany. Thus the influence of the Leftist Bevan wing of the Labour Party has done much to stiffen the neutralist attitude of the German Social Democrats. The German Social Democrats, however, have remained altogether unaffected by the serious soul-searching of the moderate majority of the British Labour Party in regard to the contemporary crisis of socialism. With an intellectual honesty and courage rare in Socialist quarters, the British Socialists, to throw off outdated Marxist ideologies, demonstrated in the *New Fabian Essays* (London, 1952), that true Socialist convictions are quite compatible with a conscientious and realistic appraisal of the requirements of actual political life. They confessed:

"Following the election of the Labour Government in 1945, and the rapid realization of the Fabian program, in theory as well as in practice, one was faced with a *dangerous vacuum*. What was needed were not just new ways and means or a set of new party principles for an election platform, but, rather, an analysis of the political, economic and social situation as the basis for a *new formulation of Socialist principles"* —(R. H. S. Crossman). The German Social Democrats, however, clinging to their old and obsolete concepts, seemed to prove that their leaders had little inclination to follow the example of the British Socialists.

Later, we shall deal more extensively with the specific problems of the German Social Democratic crisis. However, it should be pointed out here that the problem of the synthesis of nationalism and socialism—which plays such an important role in this crisis—has been thoroughly discussed in the excellent book by Erich Matthias, *Socialdemokratie und Nation* (Stuttgart, 1952). On the basis of a wealth of documentary material from the publications of the Social Democratic émigrés, this study presents a brilliant analysis of the many facets of the psychological and ideopolitical elements leading to the nationalistic neutralism and neutralist nationalism of the present German Social Democrats.

For a deeper understanding of the causes of the present ideopolitical crisis in the SPD, a thorough study of Kurt Schumacher's collected writings and speeches seems indispensable. It will make clear the isolationist and nationalist implications of the party's current neutralism, in opposition to Adenauer's European policy.

But one should also emphasize the achievements and efforts of that minority within the SPD which aims at a constructive Social Democratic contribution to the new Germany, as well as an ideopolitical regeneration of their own program. In this context, one should above all mention Ernst Reuter—who met with an untimely death—and the Bavarian Minister President Wilhelm Hoegner, as deserving credit for being the only figures among the politicians returned from exile after 1945 who were able to utilize the experiences of their emigration years for a constructive and outstanding contribution to the new Germany. Credit should also be given to the Hamburg SPD leader Max Brauer. Even those who hold different political convictions must recognize the unique merit of these men, and of a number of other Social Democratic politicians and labor leaders, in stemming the radicalization of the German labor movement and almost completely eliminating the Communist influence in the Federal Republic and West Berlin. In this these men have made a fundamental con-

tribution to the rehabilitation of Germany and the basic
stabilization of political and economic conditions in the Federal Republic. This recognition is especially due for the
achievements of the Social Democratic labor leaders within
the German Trade Union Federation. Without the moderate
attitude of the labor leaders in questions of social and economic policy, the recovery and substantial stabilization of the
German economy would certainly have been inconceivable.
In acknowledging these contributions, the leaders of the
Christian labor movement inside the CDU retain and emphasize their just claim to credit for their own remarkable
achievements in this field of political action. Similar acknowledgment is due, in the political sphere, for the outstanding
cooperation shown by the Bavarian Social Democratic movement under Hoegner and Vollmar's disciple, Waldemar von
Knoerringen, in effecting a remarkable body of social reforms
inside Bavaria. In cooperation with the Christian Socialist
Union the particular achievements of the Berlin Social Democrats, under the leadership of Ernst Reuter, in the crushing
defeat of the Communists in West Berlin, deserves the fullest
recognition.

In these facts we may see some of the practical and political
premises of a reasonable cooperation between the two mass
movements of the Social Democrats and the Christian Democratic Union (CDU-CSU): without it, there would not be
any significant future either for the internal consolidation of
the new Germany or the ultimate reunification with the
alienated areas. Nor would there be any future for the European idea.

In any account of the debate inside the SPD, which has
picked up considerable momentum since Schumacher's death,
one should especially stress the efforts of the Berlin group of
Otto Suhr and Otto Stammer; and the Bavarian group around
the Vollmar school at Kochel, as well as of a younger group
in Westphalia. The group around Carlo Schmid, and the

religious-Socialist circle of Willi Eichler, deserve equal attention, although the highly centralized official party propaganda
of the SPD is making every conceivable attempt to restrict
publicity for these efforts.

For all these issues the best introduction is the book by the
well-known Social Democratic writer Klaus-Peter Schulz,
Sorge um die deutsche Linke (Concern for the German Left),
a critical analysis of SPD policy since 1945 (Cologne, 1954).
The book should be listed among the most significant publications of the German postwar period; in fact, it may do for
the current SPD situation what Eduard Bernstein accomplished, by way of ideological revision and courageous criticism, in his *Premises* and his *Revisionism*.

But the havoc wrought by the Nazi regime created a far
more devastating impact in the field of the social movements
and sociopolitical institutions than in the field of the political
parties. Hitler was well aware that—next to the large parties
loyal to the Constitution, the Social Democrat and Center
Parties—the strongest pillar of the social and democratic edifice of the Weimar Republic was the impressive structure of
the German labor unions.

The growth of the trade unions was, after all, closely linked
with the history of these two parties. And due to this condition, the German labor movement developed along lines which
substantially differed from those of other countries, especially
the labor movements in Britain and the United States. Quite
in accord with the unique character of the German political
parties—which, unlike the political parties anywhere else, had
primarily been ideological, or *Weltanschauungs,* parties—the
German trade-union movement bore a distinct ideopolitical
stamp. This was evident in the different attitudes of the various "tendencies" inside the trade unions on the issue of capitalism and on the economic order in general. The German
trade unions were thus, above everything else, the organized
exponents of economic or sociopolitical ideologies; proudly

they called themselves *Richtungs-Gewerkschaften,* i.e., "tendency" trade unions. But inasmuch as these ideologies could only express themselves politically within the framework of the political parties, these "tendency" trade unions in turn became a determining factor in the political shape of the parties.

The unique pattern of the German trade-union movement was based on the dialectic interaction of social ideology and party politics. What this meant in practice was the close collaboration of the social movements of the Social Democratic, Christian, and Liberal trade-union movements with the SPD, Center, and Liberal parties, as they existed until 1933. In no other country had the labor movement and the political parties developed a similar social and ideological interdependence and political interaction as existed between the German trade unions and the political parties. This explains why the trade-union leaders were always among the leading personalities of the political party, and why every labor union quite naturally assisted "its" party during an election campaign.

Political life during the Weimar Republic was affected far more than was apparent by this close relationship between the trade unions and the political parties. The two largest government parties of the Weimar Republic, SPD and Center, doubled in the role of political agents for the two largest trade-union associations, the Socialist Free Trade Unions of the General German Trade Union Association (ADGB) with an approximate 4,570,000 members, and the Christian Trade Unions of the German Trade Union Conference (DGB) with roughly 1,284,000 members. Besides, the liberal splinter parties shared among themselves the representation of the so-called Free-National and the "Yellow" trade unions and employee associations of the German Trade Union "Ring," with about one million members.

These data may highlight the tremendous potential of political power which was vested in the German trade unions.

It is one of the most tragic chapters in the annals of the Weimar Republic that its downfall must partly be ascribed to the belated formal agreement providing for a combined trade-union movement to oppose the Nazi threat; it was not before the period from February to April, 1933, that such an agreement was drawn up by the union leaders, and by that time it was plainly too late.

Understandably, the power-lusting Nazi politicians along with their associates in the heavy-industry and military groups were anxious to break this impressive aggregate of power. After the Enabling Law had provided Hitler with the necessary means for dissolving the political parties, the "abolition" of the labor unions no longer presented much of a problem. The Nazis so thoroughly wrecked the German trade-union movement with its great social and educational institutions by confiscating their large money reserves and cooperative enterprises, and by ruthlessly persecuting a large number of the trade-union leaders and functionaries, that there was practically nothing left to be salvaged for the new era.

The involvement of the trade unions in the Nazi *tabula rasa* intensified the leadership problem in the new Germany in a way which it is still difficult to estimate. In this field especially, the need for giving up a past which was in fact already dead, made the creation of new institutional patterns an absolute necessity. For years to come, the consolidation of Germany's domestic policy and the development of truly democratic social and economic policies may depend upon the proper solution of this grave problem.

In view of experience to date, it is difficult to consider the present solution, i.e., the joint organization of all workers and employees within the Federal Republic in the German Trade Union (DAG), as more than an experiment. Its consolidation will largely depend upon two premises, which we shall presently discuss. Meanwhile, the schism in the new united labor movement, with the formation of "Christian Trade Unions" beginning in 1956, makes it very clear that this is not as yet a final solution, even though the new opposition movement has so far preferred to stay inside the DGB.

The new joint German trade-union movement was organized in 1949 under considerable pressure from the occupation powers, and modeled after the American example, as a purely professional association. In contrast to the old pattern, the new movement seeks to act as spokesman for the professional interests completely independent of the political parties or any other organized social or ideological special-interest groups. In our analysis of the "new" forces we shall inquire to what extent this has been a successful attempt so far. For the moment, we are merely concerned with noting a dual problem: First, that the age-old devotion of the political and social movements in Germany to ideologies and *Weltanschauungen* is still a strong factor in current political thinking in Germany, even after the Nazi regime destroyed the external manifestations of this factor. The serious tensions inside the DGB, which produced some highly explosive conflicts during the last Federal elections, were an indication of the dead weight of the past and its ideopolitical heritage that are pressing down upon the growth of the "new" forces and patterns. To eliminate these tensions would call for considerable organizing experience and leadership talent in the social and labor fields. Unfortunately, this talent is simply not available, in consequence of the break in the continuity of the generations and the murderous persecution of many former trade-union functionaries and leaders by the Nazi regime. Even such outstanding personalities as Tarnow, Kaiser, and Karl Arnold are unable to replace the accumulated experience and leadership qualities of men like Leipert and Stegerwald. The premature death of these two labor leaders deprived the German trade-union movement of a wealth of organizing and political experience in the social sphere, the type of experience that has been so abundantly available in the political and cultural areas, as personified in Konrad Adenauer and Theodor Heuss.

But another highly significant fact bears upon the German labor movement today. The Catholic social movement had been especially hard hit by the holocaust of the Nazis. The destruction of the world-famous *Volksverein* of Munchen-Gladbach spelled the end of an organization that had given training to the best elements of the school of social and political realism within the German Catholic fold; these had supplied a core of democratically minded leaders for the Center Party and the Christian trade unions. It was due largely to the *Volksverein* that, in the unhappy conflict of methods and tendencies within the Catholic movement of Weimar days, the realism of the Catholic social philosophy, founded on Natural Law precepts, finally won the upper hand. The strong influence which the social and political ideas of the *Volksverein* exerted upon Adenauer's philosophy was vividly evident in the stand which he, together with Stegerwald and Mausbach, took at the Munich Catholic Conference of 1922. Adenauer's personal development reflects among other historic factors the tragic gradual weakening of the ideopolitical and structural cohesion of German Catholicism—an outgrowth of the inherent traditional dualism of the Catholic doctrine of the State and society.

Even the German episcopate and its influence upon the course of German Catholicism under the Weimar Republic felt the unfortunate impact of this dualism. This is the only explanation for the almost incredible absence of even a word of protest against the destruction of the *Volksverein,* from either the German episcopate or the Vatican in 1933. Rome, in its Reich Concordat with Hitler, finally sanctioned this destructive act. The same inner conflicts may explain why the German episcopate to this day has failed to assist, or take the lead, in a revival of the *Volksverein* movement after 1945.

The gap in ideopolitical education left by the absence of the *Volksverein* has undoubtedly contributed to the scarcity of political and social leadership material in German Catholic ranks. That break in the continuity of the generations, wrought by the Nazi system, has taken its heavy toll also among the middle generation of the Catholic leadership; and no one is more painfully aware of this fact than Adenauer. It is hardly a secret how deeply the Chancellor's policy suffered from the dearth of qualified leadership material among the middle and younger Catholic generations. Adenauer's tireless efforts to strengthen both the ideological and organizational foundations of his Christian Democratic Union are severely impeded by this same lack.

This brief survey of the bearing of past factors upon the current leadership problem cannot be concluded without at least mentioning three important sectors of German life which escaped the National Socialist scourge, which in fact were even considerably strengthened and expanded under the Nazis. These are the fields of German government administration, German technology, and the German economy. The rise of the new Germany after 1945 is primarily due to the combined effort of these three sectors. Administrative patterns, technology, and the economic life are by definition indifferent to ideological matters. They are philosophically neutral. Hence these sectors were wide open to unlimited utilization and expansion by the Nazi system, as well as to the influences of its successor, the new Germany. Of course, the Nazi abuse of these institutions in ideological and political respects had been as disastrous as their proper utilization in the framework of the Federal Republic has been wholly salutary. But as neither of these systems needed the actual and functional political participation of the men who were active in these fields, even Hitler sensed that he could not ask for their total devotion to the National Socialist ideas, as long as he needed the effective cooperation of the German

administrative official, engineer, industrialist, or business-
man. This, then, was one area where the Nazi regime practiced an almost inconceivable tolerance, contenting itself
with a formal rather than genuine show of loyalty. It is true,
on the other hand, that in 1933 the German officials, engi-
neers and technicians, businessmen and industrialists, most
of whom had kept aloof from politics until then, accepted
the formal "coordination" (*Gleichschaltung*) with as little
resistance as they had put up against the new order in 1918,
and as they did again in 1945. But any different attitude
would have meant that vital contributions by the administrative, technological, and economic sectors would have been
lost to the regime of Hitler as to the new order after 1945.

It has been recognized even outside of Germany that there
is no sound reason for holding the average German official,
technician, or industrialist responsible for his enforced sub-
mission to Hitler. This should have been a reason for the
majority to silence the small minority of genuine Nazi fanatics in this group, and to demand an accounting of all those
bureaucrats, technicians, and militarists who had placed their
specialized professional skills at the service of the organized
bestiality of Nazi mass murder and concentration camps.
The sad chapter of the "denazification trials" has shown
that all these differentiations pose an extremely difficult task.
And yet, despite the heavy burden of these experiences, the
objective traditions and capabilities of the administrative,
technological, and economic sectors perhaps suffered least
from the changing tides inside Germany.

German officialdom and the spheres of military and technical activity were thus spared the break in the continuity
of the generations, which cut so deeply into almost every
other sector of German life. Hence, after 1945, it became
extremely urgent to integrate the talents and experience of
those elements, which for the most part had not been compromised, with the process of over-all rehabilitation. The

startling results in the reconstruction of the German communities, cities, and states in administration and organization, and the successes of technology, industry, and business in the Federal Republic today testify to Adenauer's ability in drawing on the best experience and traditions of the past for the building of a new order.

This process, however, involves certain dangers more serious than the occasional errors in personnel policy would indicate. When the administrative, technological, and economic sectors were freed from the grip of the Nazi dictatorship there was the danger that the very opposite tendencies might be released, in unbridled liberty and license. When freedom is misunderstood or used for the wrong purposes, there is always the danger that officialdom and administration become "bureaucracy"; that a misused technology may degenerate into "technocracy." Only when these fundamentally neutral functions are sustained and guided by spiritual values and true statesmanship is it possible to protect their basic nature as servants of the community against an unhealthy arrogance, and to prevent the economic life from degenerating into ruthless profiteering. Hence we are faced with some decisive questions: How far has the Federal Republic been able to cope with these problems in its reconstruction and rehabilitation work? To what extent has the latent danger of bureaucratization and technocracy been checked in the new Germany? We are thus touching upon the question of the ideopolitical traditions, which in Adenauer's and Heuss's work have taken up the guardianship of the spiritual values of German policy.

V

The Traditions: Conservatism and Liberalism

It is surprising, in view of the many critical treatments and analyses of the new Germany, how little attention has been given to the origins of the spiritual values and ideological forces behind the job of reconstruction in the German Federal Republic. These issues are almost completely misunderstood outside of Germany. The paradoxical course of recent German history eludes the political pragmatist, as well as the positivistic sociological view. Only the objective accomplishments of German organization and technology can look impressive from such a perspective. On the other hand, Konrad Adenauer's personality and achievements as the prime architect of the neo-German "miracle," and the ideopolitical forces in which they are rooted, remain undefinable. For want of a more intelligible description, they were often labeled as "Catholic conservatism" or even "clerical authoritarianism." Even inside Germany, the crisis in the sociological discipline—particularly acute due to the problem of the break in the generations—has prevented a deeper historical and sociological understanding of these problems. Moreover, the opposition of Adenauer's political adversaries, extremely primitive in ideopolitical respects, has tended to discredit the Chancellor as a "Chancellor of the Allies," the agent of a "fifth occupation power" in Western Germany— an obvious allusion to the Catholic Church. Even those who have at least a vague notion that significant forces arising from Germany's tradition are now at work, often are barred from a deeper understanding by such misleading labels as the "return to the early Victorian era," or the "conservative Restoration period."

For anyone trying to pierce this smoke screen of misconceptions, it soon becomes obvious that the Nazi system cannot possibly have extended its *tabula rasa* into the orbit of the genuine conservative and liberal traditions of German history. National Socialism, it is true, with its innate tendency to pervert the essence of any and all traditions within reach, engulfed indeed the more negative aspects of German conservatism and liberalism, exposing their inner absurdity. One should not forget that, after all, the whole *complexio oppositorum* of the Nazi ideology and philosophy of power was concocted very largely from the heresies of German conservatism and liberalism. Ever since the first quarter of the nineteenth century, the genuine conservative principle has been systematically perverted into political reaction, and the genuine liberal view into the liberalistic rejection of the innate laws of State and society; and both these false doctrines have increasingly jeopardized life in Germany. Historically we are here face to face with the ideological starting point of German nationalism and the German defection from the Christian legal and international order of the West. In the guise of Prussian militarism—the so-called "Borussianism"—

the national-liberal ideology of the Pan-Germanic power
state, German anti-Semitism, the false religious doctrine of
a "German" Christianity, and the religiopolitical movement
of neo-paganism from the days of romanticism and the Restoration to the reign of neo-Romantic nihilism of the Nazi
regime, these ideologies had kept Germany and the whole
world in a turmoil.

To anyone familiar with the contemporary German scene,
it is obvious that all these destructive traditions have been
so heavily compromised by the Nazi system that they now
quite definitely belong to the part of the past with which
the new Federal Republic must break. This is true, even
if there are still small groups in the Federal Republic today
which continue to cling to obsolete conservatism and liberalism along with their musty dreams of power.

We have entered upon this ideohistorical digression in
order to straighten out at least some of the confusion, prevailing inside as well as outside of Germany, concerning the
nature of German conservatism and liberalism. One has only
to talk with some German Catholics to see what a tremendous amount of ideopolitical confusion exists in these circles
on the subject of genuine liberalism. And exactly the same
confusion exists in German liberal quarters on the subject
of conservatism. It goes almost without saying that the confusion in the Social Democratic camp extends to both concepts, naturally, in view of the anticonservative and antiliberal background of that movement. And all this fuzziness
leads to the strange result that the Social Democratic Party
today is more susceptible than ever before to the ill effects
of certain negative traditions of German conservatism and
liberalism, in particular the ideology of the Prussian bureaucracy and the type of nationalism of national-liberal
origin.

This situation makes it all the more important that the
present German generation should be alerted to the true

positive values and traditions of German conservatism and liberalism. After all, the most important accomplishments in the political and cultural rehabilitation of Germany have been achieved thanks precisely to those traditions and values. They are alive in the leading personalities in this development, especially Chancellor Adenauer and President Heuss.

We may now proceed to a deliberate historicosociological attempt to determine the ideopolitical positions of Adenauer and Heuss—without doing violence to a deeper ideohistorical understanding of the most recent chapter in German history. Putting it summarily, one might say that Adenauer's personality and development symbolize the best traditions of German conservatism, while Heuss represents the best in the German liberal tradition. And since both conservatism and liberalism, in their unadulterated forms, have grown on the common soil of the rational interpretation of Natural Law, the two currents have achieved a point of interpenetration and interaction which might be termed a genuine "liberal" version of the conservative tradition, or on the other hand a genuine "conservative" variant of the liberal school. Through the medium of concrete political action and present-day experience "liberal Conservatism" and "conservative Liberalism" have come to complement and cross-fertilize each other. It thus seems fair to call Adenauer, as the exponent of the former position a "liberal conservative," and Heuss, as the representative of the latter position, a "conservative liberal."

Until 1945, both these currents were largely excluded from active participation in German politics, because the dominating influences in recent German history were the antiliberal, authoritarian and reactionary version of conservatism and, at times, an anticonservative, individualistic type of liberalism. Even under the Weimar Republic such a mutual impact and interaction were, for a number of reasons, possible only on a very limited scale. Men like

Adenauer and Heuss hence were exceedingly limited in their
scope. But the utter collapse of the old order in 1945 tore
down also these obstacles and limitations.

*Thus probably for the first time in German history there
now exists an opportunity for a constructive unfolding both
of a genuine liberal conservatism and a conservative liberalism. We have here the most significant feature among the
"new" developments in the German Federal Republic.*

One would be ignoring a crucial issue in the new Germany if, out of narrow ideological prejudice, one chose to
push these fundamental facts aside. Many a German Catholic
of conservative stamp will never fully grasp the liberal heritage of tangible political liberties, because of his unfounded
fears of the specter of "liberalism." And yet he, too, is indebted to these freedoms for the liberal postulate of a "free
Church in a free state," as well as for the entire framework
of free political institutions under a constitution founded
on the sovereignty of the people and on the concept of parliamentary democracy. The more extreme German liberals,
on the other hand, are similarly hard put to it to realize that
certain genuine conservative principles should be preserved.
Primarily these are the conservative principles according to
which the only lasting guarantee of intellectual and political
freedom for the contemporary citizen lies in the personal
freedom and individual dignity founded upon the concept
of Natural Law and the organic traditions of cultural life.
Despite its theoretical rejection of these traditions, even the
Social Democratic Party has always benefited from the conservative and liberal patrimony of freedom. The present
futile opposition of this party and its inner ideological crisis
are very largely due to its political blindness in ignoring that
genuine conservative and liberal heritage.

When, after the war, these traditions became fully fruitful
in the reconstruction of Germany, the SPD in effect blocked
its own path to active participation in the job of reconstruc-

tion. One may see a sign of the intrinsic logic of history, as well as the instinct of political self-preservation of the German people, in the fact that the leadership of the new Germany was not entrusted to the spokesmen of the traditional opposition to these principles—men of Kurt Schumacher's type—but to the representatives of the genuine conservative and liberal traditions, Konrad Adenauer and Theodor Heuss. This is not the proper place to elaborate our description of Adenauer as a liberal conservative or of Heuss as a conservative liberal. Let us merely refer here to the ideopolitical concept, which will help us to differentiate between the perverted forms of the liberal and conservative philosophies and their genuine expressions, while at the same time exhibiting their close kinship and interdependence in the political sphere.

This is the principle of the natural freedom and morality of the human person, as expressed in the doctrines of the rational Natural Law, and valid on all social and political levels in the life of the individual and the community. It takes no supernatural revelation to recognize it, nor does it call for any theological sanction in order to be valid. The principle of the rational Natural Law is indeed "written into every man's heart" as a natural moral law, a *lex naturalis,* as the Apostle Paul knew. A man may recognize the binding force of this principle in his own life in the form of a natural right, a *jus naturale;* it also demands recognition as a natural obligation for all action. This doctrine of the rational Natural Law received its specific theological motivation in the theonomous Natural Law of Christianity. In this, the *lex naturalis* appears as the natural expression of the *lex aeterna* of the Divine Creation; accordingly, the *jus naturale* appears as an expression of the *jus divinum,* the Divine Law, whose universally binding order is recognizable without any particular difficulty to the natural human reason, the *ratio.*

This means that, while the rational Natural Law in general may be ethically deepened and morally reenforced with the help of the specific theonomous Natural Law, the rational Natural Law nevertheless maintains its independent character as a universally binding norm of all human action, both for the individual and the community, even without the theological sanction, as Suarez and, above all, Grotius have emphasized. This is why it may be recognized also by those who, for philosophical reasons, reject the theonomous Natural Law of the Christian faith, in particular the strict Thomistic version of Catholicism.

The centuries-old "strife over Natural Law" was always concerned with finding a correct solution of the problem of the theonomous versus the autonomous character of Natural Law. The various solutions that have been offered have influenced, through their sociological implications, the development of both conservatism and liberalism. One might say that the ideopolitical development and the actual fate of the conservative and liberal movements in the various civilized countries clearly reflect the influence of this debate on the interpretation of the Natural Law philosophy. These relations have received far too little attention in the past. This is why we are here concerned with a closer examination of them.

The creative solution of the leadership problem, and the consolidation of the "new" order in Germany in general, will very largely depend upon the extent to which the tradition of rational Natural Law may become effective in the future ideopolitical evolution of Germany; and above all, on the tradition of British and American democracy and the conservative and liberal philosophies behind them, which reflect an important current in the Western tradition of Natural Law.

Here we may present a general observation regarding the functional concept of conservatism and liberalism, as clearly defined expressions of certain individual and political attitudes. The conservative mind is indebted to tradition. It acts in a constant awareness of the fundamental unity of the spiritual and political forces which are at the root of its own existence. For the true conservative mind, the past is always equivalent to a tangible historic reality extending into the present, so that any "new" development appears to this kind of thinking as an implicit obligation to continue and further develop this historic reality. This true conservative, acting from such an awareness of tradition, does not indulge in a mere "reminiscing" and meditating about history, nor does he resort to the past in order to secure a polemic argument for his own time. Instead, he is guided by an acute awareness that the present—that which is *now,* bears a political responsibility for the *future*—for that which ought to be. Yet this readiness and open-mindedness toward the inevitable transformation of the past into the future involves a liberal attitude: liberal in this sense to be understood as the attitude of true *liberalitas,* which strives for the ever-increasing realization of liberty and ethical values in the course of history.

Wherever such a genuine liberal attitude is lacking and the conservative principle acts solely as a tendency to cling to the past, obstructing the rise of new forces which announce themselves in the present as pressures toward historic progress, conservatism degenerates into regression and reaction. The awareness of historic traditions, in this *reactionary conservative view,* is narrowed down to a mere traditionalist attitude basically hostile to the present, *the true enemy of all intellectual and political progress.* The whole movement of modern conservatism has been determined by this dialectic conflict between the historic realism of a progressive, liberal, and hence genuine conservatism, at all times open to any opportunity for realizing a greater measure of freedom; and, on the other hand, the pseudohistoric, formalistic attitude of a traditionalism which is focused upon the past, and hence has its back turned to life. If one wishes to trace the origins of this dialectic process, one should turn to the life and writings of the great English statesman Edmund Burke (1729–1797), the true founder of liberal conservatism, or else to the life and writings of the French conservatives De Bonald (1754–1840) and De Maistre (1754–1821), the real founding fathers of reactionary traditionalism.

Any attempt to evaluate the liberal mind should start from a proper understanding of the functional role of the liberal concept. On principle, the attitude of *liberalitas* expresses a genuine open-mindedness toward any real or potential opportunity for the progressive realization of freedom. Different from the conservative mind, the liberal mind is not primarily interested in the significance of the past, the traditional implications and aspects of freedom and their historic patterns. The liberal mind, especially in the social and political sphere, is entirely focused upon the present, and is therefore particularly sensitive to any not yet fully exploited opportunity for a greater degree of tangible freedom. The liberal sense of history incessantly presses for social reforms, striving for the substitution of new values for obsolete patterns of political and social life.

From the days of the Renaissance, this genuine liberal principle has been the dominant motif of historic progress, present especially in the intellectual and political reform movements. It has been historically effective in extending the area of social and political freedom, especially where the efforts for the improvement of contemporary conditions and the drive for greater freedom in the future have been coupled with respect for the spiritual values and intellectual traditions of the past. For without the preservation and living action of these traditions in the unfolding of contemporary history there is no lasting stabilization nor development of any expressions of freedom directed to the future.

The basic conservative attitude of any genuine liberalism is founded precisely in the realistic sense of responsibility toward history in the critical, as well as tradition-minded, culturally conservative sense of history. Perhaps the most vigorous expression which the ideopolitical and historic realization of this conservative liberalism has found has been in the life and works of Thomas Jefferson (1743–1826), Alexis de Tocqueville (1805–1859), and the great Englishman Lord John Acton (1834–1902).

Since the idea of freedom can materialize only in the concrete human being and in its relations to a concrete society, all genuine expressions of both liberal conservatism and conservative liberalism are founded on the sociological principle of the full and frank recognition of the historical and political reality. Liberalism, therefore, degenerates when the rational, that is, the reasonable reality of the relations between the individual and the community begins to evaporate into rationalistic schemes and utopias, with the disintegration of the natural and historic patterns of society due to the infiltration of radical and revolutionary ideologies. Whenever liberal concepts of freedom have been twisted into liberalistic misuse, these revolutionary tendencies have always been active. From this point of view, a misconceived liberalism has indeed been the starting point and breeding ground for revolutionary movements. *The whole Marxist and communist philosophy stems from the liberalistic misuse of the liberal idea.* It is equally responsible for all those movements and trends ever since the days of the French Revolution which have threatened the natural foundations, based on Natural Law, of the idea of personal freedom and the life of society; such as the atheist secularism, the revolutionary libertinism, the liberalistic school of nationalism as well as of capitalism.

We may well say that the core of both genuine conservatism and liberalism is the principle of a rationally conceived

Natural Law. It is quite compatible with the Christian teachings of this rational Natural Law—although over the everlasting protest of the theological Integralists and Absolutists—to detach the sociological categories from the formal relation to the theological categories of the principle of absolute Natural Law. Thus it is entirely possible for the Catholic followers of Natural Law to work together with all the forces outside the Catholic fold, and even outside of Christianity, striving for a tangible expansion and stabilization of freedom, while observing the universal orders of the Natural Law for the individual and the community. At any rate, in the interest of historic and social progress, especially in the sphere of politics and affairs of state, there is ample room for such cooperation.

The ideopolitical cooperation of Adenauer and Heuss, which for the first time introduces this element into recent German history, represents a renewed historic justification for the late Scholastic doctrine of the realist concept of Natural Law, including the basis for the democratic tenet of the sovereignty of the people which that concept entails. Both the genuine liberal principles present in basically conservative social teachings of Catholicism, and the traditions of the German brand of liberalism founded in Natural Law —as represented by Theodor Heuss—have been brought to bear upon the job of German rehabilitation.

And therewith a basis has been found for the renewal of German life and its full reintegration with the Natural Law and the political traditions of the Western cultural community. In 1922, the great German sociologist Ernst Troeltsch had already predicted that a reintegration of the Natural Law would be prerequisite to any renaissance of German values, as a historic necessity. As far as the task of renewal and rehabilitation is concerned, this probably settles the old sociophilosophical and methodological dispute among the German Catholics; the losers are the exponents of those antidemocratic tendencies within the German Catholic fold, which, from the days of Adam Müller's romanticism to the dubious "political theology" of Carl Schmitt and the even more highly questionable "universalism" of Othmar Spann, have so unhappily influenced the work of social and political education in the German Catholic camp. In the reintegration of Natural Law and sound political traditions we see the ultimate justification of Konrad Adenauer's position during his dramatic dispute with Cardinal Faulhaber at the Munich Catholic Conference of 1922.

Later, we shall explore the fundamental significance of the late Scholastic doctrine of rational Natural Law for the Chancellor's political world outlook. Suffice it to state here that in this position Konrad Adenauer is proving himself the legitimate disciple of the greatest and most sincere liberal-conservative figure in German Catholicism during the nineteenth century, the great political leader and bishop Emanuel von Ketteler.

Concerning Theodor Heuss and the true liberal tradition he represents, it is important to trace the background of Württemberg democracy from which he stems. The best traditions of Swabian humanism are responsible for his intellectual growth. What he once said about the influence of the old Swabian democracy upon the formative years of his political teacher, Konrad Haussmann, may well be applied to himself, namely, that its political thought has been guided "by a thoroughly rational idealistic trait, aiming at a Constitutional order in accordance with certain postulates of Natural Law, and a political life guided by pure principles."

Heuss's political and social philosophy differs substantially from the run-of-the-mill variety of political liberalism in Germany. To grasp its uniqueness, one must understand the firm roots of the liberalism of Heuss in the "rational-idealistic and Natural Law" traditions of Swabian democracy. This definitely places his ideopolitical position within the liberal tradition as a whole. The position of Theodor Heuss is very aptly characterized by what he once said of the liberalism of Hugo Preuss, that he "was never an unquestioning follower of the Manchester school, nor did he ever content himself with singing the praises of individualism." It is a characteristic of Swabian humanism that it defends the unique value and intellectual freedom of the human person, in its commitment to the community against both intellectual collectivism and anarchic individualism. The political Natural Law of Swabian democracy consistently defends the social and political freedom of the individual citizen, within the framework of the community, against any collectivist tendencies in the social and political sphere.

In these respects Heuss's political and social ethical philosophy, in its inherent orientation toward the idea of Natural Law, definitely approaches the specific Christian social doctrine, in so far as the theories and movements of the latter are close to the realistic philosophy of social and political democracy, founded on the concepts of Natural Law. It is here that Heuss's social and political ideas have a certain common basis with the movement of social and political realism, oriented on Natural Law, within German Catholicism—as represented by von Ketteler and Hitze, up to Stegerwald and Adenauer.

Theodor Heuss's intellectual and political world view offers an approach to an essential understanding of the historic fate of the rational Natural Law tradition in Germany. Only the Swabian brand of liberalism has preserved the rational concept of Natural Law of the German Enlightenment from degenerating into rationalistic tendencies, thanks to its links with the implicit Christian ethics of Swabian humanism. Only in the Swabian brand of democracy has its ideopolitical tradition been preserved, while all the other variants of German liberalism have led to rationalistic disintegration, toward a liberalistic positivism in the concept of law. Hence, one of the best German traditions has once more been revived for the benefit of all of Germany, in Theodor Heuss's ideopolitical world view, through the medium of its characteristically Swabian manifestation. Like all his great compatriots, this stubborn Swabian has always known that the best Swabian heritage also involves the best forces in the German tradition. The same is true for Konrad Adenauer's origins in the Catholic Rhineland, whose liberal and conservative wide-openness toward the world has always served the best traditions of German civilization and politics.

Such attitudes and such traditions have shaped the genuine German, truly national precept which, through the leadership of men like Adenauer and Heuss, guides the establishment of the "new" order in Germany—the precept that any personality linked to a cultural heritage of a specific region, any religious individuality tied to a certain philosophical attitude, any social concept motivated by a natural regional outlook, and in general any specific political manifestation or movement which has a firm ideological basis, will always tend toward the unity of German civilization and the nation as a whole.

The New Order: Democracy and
European Unity

To understand the new Germany one must grasp the fundamental changes which the Second World War wrought both in Germany and Europe. Even before trying to assess whatever "new" elements these changes have brought to the surface, one needs to realize the full extent to which the familiar order of the "old" Germany and the "old" Europe have been implicated in the disaster of 1945. The "old" historic order, and the new political manifestations in the resurgence of Germany and Europe, are closely linked.

More than in any previous historic change the well-laid plans of the victors were thwarted by the actual developments in postwar Europe. The democratic Allies against Germany had proceeded on the assumption that the results of the Nazi defeat in Europe would present no particular complexities—other than those which could well be mastered with such palliatives as the Atlantic Charter, such absurdities as the "unconditional surrender" formula, the Morgenthau Plan, or the Teheran and Yalta treaties. Nor can it be said that the reconstruction and rehabilitation blueprints which were drawn up by Hitler's opponents, either inside the German Reich or in exile, were inspired by a keener wisdom and foresight, in particular the schemes of the exiled German Social Democrats in London, or the German Communists with their headquarters in Moscow.

The obvious failure of all these blueprints had essentially three causes, easily recognizable today. First, there was that fatal mixture of genuine enthusiasm over the triumph of the democratic idea, on the one hand, with the resentment against everything German, on the other, understandable during the phase of the fight against the Hitler tyranny. Clearly, this unfortunate mixture had the effect of cramping the thinking of these masterminds of the German and European future to a point where they felt they could safely ignore the inner laws and dynamics of German and even more so of Russian history. Secondly, the masterminds suffered from an almost criminal ignorance of this particular chapter of European history, and in their ignorance they underestimated the importance of the negative, as well as the positive, forces in the German and Russian ideopolitical tradition. And finally, there was that dubious optimism inherent in the pragmatist political philosophy with an added shot of unadulterated historical materialism, climaxing in the belief that the military power and the political skill of the victorious "democracies" would suffice to ensure the realization of these plans. Confident in this view, they saw no need to bother about the intellectual traditions and the less tangible political elements in the historic realities of the nations concerned, in particular of Germany.

It is this same threefold misconception of the implicit potentialities and the actual political impact of the past which explains the astonishment of non-Germans in the face of the "new" German phenomenon, the "miracle" of Adenauer's Germany. Even the difficulties many Germans have in appreciating the new things that are rising before their eyes stem from this very same misconception. This holds true in particular of the opposition of the Social Democrats, who apparently still fail to see that the mere recognition that something fundamentally new has come about is by no means tantamount to an endorsement of Adenauer's policy. Even those critics who, because of their political convictions, are unable to put a stamp of ideological approval upon Adenauer's policies must admit that it is impossible to understand the new Germany without knowing something about the Chancellor's personality and work. The close and inescapable ties linking German rehabilitation since 1945 with the international situation have forever identified the German problem in its European implications with Adenauer's personality. His work symbolizes the creative potentialities of the best traditions of the old Germany and Europe in their vigorous impact upon the new time.

The chief task of this book, then, is to demonstrate that in Adenauer's person an altogether new type of German politician has stepped before the curtain of history, precisely the type that was called for by the fundamental changes which have taken place in Germany and Europe.

Since 1945 the German problem has been broadened into an eminently European problem. Similarly, the European problem has been inextricably linked with the problem of Germany. In this way the personal growth and work of the Christian statesman Adenauer are integrated with the vital unity of the best in both the German and the European traditions. Only from such a perspective may one try to grasp the intrinsic German implications, as well as the European relations of the new "Adenauer-Germany," its origins, and increasing consolidation.

It has almost been forgotten, in the amazement of the outside world and the complacency inside Germany over the
German achievements to date, that in 1945 Germany was
utterly defeated in the greatest and most terrible of all wars.
When Adenauer cautioned against "lost illusions" which
would have to be discarded for good, he probably had this
fact in mind, as did Theodor Heuss when he cautioned the
Germans against the danger of turning the "blessing of being
able to forget into a rapid method of forced forgetfulness."
Those who have opposed Adenauer's policies have been
blinded by this type of forgetfulness of the stark necessities,
domestic and international, under which the first "Chancellor
of the Vanquished" had to operate. Even Kurt Schumacher,
that talented leader of the opposition, became a victim of
this amnesia as early as 1949, when he flung the unsavory
question at the Chancellor before the West German parliament—a question affecting Adenauer's basic patriotism: "Are
you speaking as the Chancellor of Germany"—adding the in-
vective thrust, "Chancellor of the Allies?"

To his tragic end, Schumacher held to the delusion that
the best German interests were fundamentally incompatible
with the realistic policy of the "Chancellor of the Vanquished" in its courageous shouldering of the consequences
of the defeat. Writing in his foreword to the "Action Program of the Social Democratic Party," on July 26, 1952,
Schumacher was still able to say: "Since 1945 the Social
Democratic Party has proceeded in the belief that we must
strive for cooperation with all the freedom-loving elements
throughout the world, while not permitting the German people to sink to the level of a subject nation." Adenauer's vision
has been more honest also on this point, because it was less
obstructed, when he spoke of the "plunge into the abyss" of
the German people in 1945—a plunge so profound that it
was simply not possible for the Germany Schumacher was

talking about to sink any lower "to the level of a subject nation."

Heinrich Bruening feeds on rather similar illusions. From the safe haven of America's Harvard University, he calmly looked on while the German people were working their way out of the abyss of 1945 until at last, in 1954, Germany could afford the luxury of offering Bruening, who meanwhile had returned to his native country, a suitable platform for his attacks upon the "pure dogmatism" of Adenauer's foreign policy. "The opportunities for a happy German foreign policy," he now proclaimed in his Düsseldorf speech, "lie in the utilization of Germany's geopolitical position in the interest of the political balance in Europe, and thereby of peace. Thanks to her geographical position, Germany might once more have fulfilled this task after the Second World War. Whether that possibility still exists, I cannot say. Again, for years after the Second World War, we have conducted our foreign policy along purely dogmatic lines, as has consistently been the case from the day Bismarck retired till 1926."

It would be difficult to give a more telling illustration of a complete misunderstanding of Germany's changed position in the European and international interplay of forces since 1945 than this censorious condemnation of the foreign policy of the defeated German nation.

Critics like Bruening conveniently forget all the unfavorable aspects in the changes which have taken place in Germany and Europe, while pursuing their own special interests on the strength of Germany's growing stabilization and returning vigor.

Bruening, then, cherishes the illusion that Germany in 1945 could have taken up where she left off in 1933, at least as far as her foreign policy was concerned. To begin with, this view overlooks the fundamental fact that Germany—in the sense Bruening uses the term—simply ceased to exist in

1945. He moreover ignores the fact that the old Europe as well went down in 1945, a fact of hardly less crucial importance. And this illumines a third fact, namely, that 1945 saw the crumbling, for the foreseeable future, of any tangible bases for what Bruening calls the "political balance of Europe."

Russia's undisputed supremacy in Eastern Europe and the Balkans today has spelled the end of all possibilities of a European balance of the type that existed from the Congress of Vienna until 1938. Russia's imperialistic designs on Europe, which were halted in Vienna, attained their full realization only after the Second World War. The intelligent policies of a Metternich, a Talleyrand, a Castlereigh at the Congress of Vienna, and their fruits in terms of European security—including the security of Germany against Russia— were definitely lost, due to the pathetic failure of Western diplomacy at the Yalta, Potsdam, and San Francisco conferences. Later on we shall see that the weakening and the partitioning of Germany, which were part and parcel of these colossal diplomatic errors, cannot be explained by these developments alone. For the moment it suffices to state that the surrender of European interests to Eastern Europe, including the breakup of Germany's territorial integrity, established some highly tangible facts for any concrete European policy after 1945—this surrender which was inaugurated at Yalta, executed at Potsdam, and at last received its moral sanction at the San Francisco conference. It is these facts which have determined the fundamentally changed position of a defeated Germany toward a changed Europe.

Any statesman who had to face the tough job of realizing the relationship of a defeated, divided Germany toward a changed Europe, whether Schumacher or Bruening, would have had no choice except to shape his policy in accordance with these facts. What Bruening seems to forget is that even prior to this failure of the Western powers—and quite inde-

pendently of it—the Russian advance to the Oder-Neisse line
had been made possible by the Nazi German betrayal of
Europe. Adenauer, in his responsible insight, is well aware
of this. Karl Marx had foreseen the dangers which would
arise from a nonfulfillment of Germany's European mission
in relation to Russia. His foresight had been infinitely clearer
than the Russophile critics of Adenauer's foreign policy will
ever be able to see. As early as 1853 Karl Marx the "historian," not the revolutionary ideologist, with reference to
his critique of Russia, in an article in the New York *Tribune*
had warned of Russia's imperialist policy in Europe; the
same policy which Stalin so successfully realized at Yalta and
Potsdam. "Once Russia has progressed this far on her road
toward a mighty empire," he wrote, "will it be at all possible
that this huge and far-flung power will be content with what
she has attained? Once Russia flanks the Austrian protector-
ates to the north, east and south, it is unavoidable that
Austria herself must become a Russian satellite. Then, Russia's interrupted and undulating western borders will require
to be supplemented and safeguarded, in the sense that Russia's 'natural frontier' will then run perhaps from Danzig,
or even Stettin, to Trieste. And just as victory follows victory
and annexation follows annexation, the Russian annexation
of the Turkish possessions in the Balkans would be no more
than a preparation for the ensuing annexation of Hungary,
Galicia and Prussia. And thus, the mighty Slavic empire of
the Russians, which the fanatical Pan-Slavists are now dreaming about, would become a reality."

It does not take much imagination to see how Karl Marx's
prophecy has been fulfilled since the Second World War,
precisely up to the Oder-Neisse line. Even more amazing is
the way in which Marx seven years later, in 1860, writing
from London, warned the Germans of the concrete political
and territorial consequences if Germany should betray Europe's true interests to the imperialism of Russia—exactly

the betrayal which Hitler did commit later. "What we Germans will lose through this operation will be no more than East and West Prussia, Silesia, parts of Brandenburg and Saxony, all of Bohemia, Moravia and the remainder of Austria, plus our national existence. Russia will thus receive parts of German Federal territory, pushing her western borders a full 65 miles to the west. This would seal the partition of Germany. The direct road from Vienna to Berlin would then run across Russia and the same would even be true for the direct road from Munich to Berlin."

The purpose of this historical digression is to bring out a fact which is not usually recognized in its full significance: that Germany's defection from Europe is essentially responsible for the present weakness of both, as well as for the surrender of parts of Germany to Russian imperialism. For the foreign policy of the new Germany this plainly means that German security depends upon her return to Europe; just as the recovery of the new Europe depends upon the substantial cooperation of the new Germany. Friedrich Genz' insight of 1806—which he gained by witnessing the results of Germany's defection from Europe at that time—is still valid today: "Europe has fallen because of Germany, Germany must make it rise again!"

Since 1945 no one has had a clearer perception of these German obligations toward Europe, and no one has tried more sincerely to meet them than Konrad Adenauer. In his political realism, firmly rooted in the tradition of the Rhineland and the *civitas coloniensis* and its European heritage, Adenauer saw that this historic obligation is a mutual concern. He saw that there is something like an equally valid European obligation toward Germany. This vision seemed ever more compelling as the neo-Russian imperialism became an increasing handicap and an actual threat to the rehabilitation of the new Germany. Adenauer's entire European policy, as we shall see more clearly later, has consistently been guided by the vision of this dual and mutual obligation.

Adenauer is well aware that the Germany of the Federal Republic, the part that has been spared the fate of Russian tyranny, can avail herself of her opportunity only in close, open, and direct cooperation with the West—that opportunity which was given Germany by the Allies of gradually working out both her external and inner freedom. There is no place for "neutrality" in Adenauer's statecraft, neither for "political" neutrality in relation to the security and defense requirements of Europe, nor for an "ideological" neutrality toward the intellectual and ethical traditions of the Western community.

It is precisely this view with which Adenauer introduced an entirely new element into the conventional pattern of Germany's policy in Europe which prevailed the last 150 years. Adenauer's emphatically Christian statesmanship is animated by a strong feeling that the new Germany will be able to live in a fruitful community with the new Europe only if she is able to reweave those vitalities with the intellectual and ethical traditions of the West—over and beyond the mere community of political and economic interests— which were increasingly weakened during the nineteenth century, and at last abruptly broken under the Nazis. In this sense, Adenauer's European policy is at all times essentially based on the traditions of Western civilization—a policy, that is, aiming at the realization of ethical principles, intellectual potentialities, and cultural values.

To Adenauer's thinking even that highly controversial issue, the European defense community, NATO, possesses these same fundamental implications. He is aware that the unavoidable establishment of German armed forces at once raises the question of their responsibility toward Europe, or, in other words, their moral dependability. After the bitter experience the world has had with previous versions of German militarism it is easy to understand why Adenauer saw only one solution: to tie the German forces closely to the armed forces of the other European nations, and in this way to achieve a close integration of the spirit and leadership of the new German army with the moral order and the traditions of Europe. True, even this solution would not necessarily have banished all the old familiar risks and dangers. Yet Adenauer's solution seemed all the worthier of support, as it presented the smallest possible risk as compared with more formidable dangers. The discussion of the integration of the German Federal Republic into the European defense system brought to light great diversity of opinions on the European problem as a whole.

The one thing always overlooked by the neutralists is the factor of Russia as a world power, which is inextricably linked with this problem. To an almost disastrous extent this holds true of the illusion that the new Germany could play the role of an independent and self-supporting "European" mediator, in the dubious sense of the Rapallo and Locarno strategy, that illusion for which Bruening has become the representative spokesman. The neutralists try to convince themselves that the present-day world power, Russia, is actually serious about its Platonic assurances of peaceful coexistence between the democratic Europe and Communist-imperialist Russia, as if Russia were gratefully ready to respect a "neutralized" Germany wedged in between herself and the West. Men like Heinrich Bruening either ignore or minimize Russia's actual and potential threat to all of Europe. They look back to a state of affairs, now long past, when a weak Russia was only too willing to try out the Rapallo strategy against the West, together with an equally strong if not actually stronger Germany. Bruening was still wrapped up in these illusions when, speaking before his Düsseldorf audience, he made the statement: "Thanks to her geographical position, Germany might once more have fulfilled this task after the Second World War. Whether that possibility still exists, I cannot say."

A simple reference to Russia's real attitude should suffice to meet these misconceptions on the part of Bruening and those who feel like him. It is understandable that the Russians and Russophiles reject any scheme which aims at the consolidation of Europe. Their rejection will undoubtedly harden to the extent that the integration of Germany in the European community becomes part and parcel of such schemes. Russian diplomacy most keenly understands Germany's changed position in the international play of forces. More keenly than the neutralists will ever understand, Russia realizes that *Germany's once independent role in the European balance-of-power structure based on the equation, Western Europe–Germany–Russia, went down forever in 1945.* Russia understands, too, that the new European pattern will never permit Germany again to play its unique geopolitical role between East and West with any measure of independence, whether in the weakened form of the Federal Republic, or as a future reunited Germany. And Russia knows equally well that this Germany will never again be in a position to play "both ends against the middle," through mutual-assistance pacts, based on her economic and military potential, of the Rapallo and Locarno type, facing the West in an alliance with the East, or turning against the East in a Western coalition.

Above all, Russia knows that there are only two alternatives left to Germany in her new situation: to decide whether to help secure Western freedom and thereby her own against the threat from the East by voluntarily joining the European community; or else, whether to turn to the East, thereby surrendering her own energies and freedom with equal finality to the neo-Russian imperialism, sealing the end of freedom in Europe without which Germany cannot live.

Today, these inescapable alternatives cannot be stressed heavily enough.

From 1945 on, Adenauer's entire effort in the international sphere has been committed to the one goal: to secure German freedom in conjunction with the West; and to help secure Europe against the threat from the East.

By his actions as well as by his countless pronouncements, Adenauer has given overwhelming proof that he has understood Germany's new role in Europe, with all its geopolitical and military implications, quite as keenly as the Russians. Actually, these insights of a penetrating political realism should have been enough to make this great statesman into a good European for his country's sake. Yet his convictions, born out of tradition and the inherent bent of his mind, had already made him a good European as early as 1919. As a trustee of the University of Cologne, which he had founded, he declared during the inauguration ceremonies: "Whatever shape the peace treaty will take [following the First World War] here on the Rhine German civilization and the civilizations of the Western democracies will meet during the coming decades. Unless they can be reconciled, unless the European nations learn, over and above their concern for the protection of their national individualities, to realize and cultivate that which is common to all European civilizations; unless these nations can once more be united in a cultural community; unless another war among the nations of Europe can be prevented in this way, Europe's leadership in the world will be forever lost."

Again and again, Adenauer has been criticized for subordinating the reunification of a divided Germany—the question which has such an overpowering importance for the Germans themselves—to his concern for European unity. No doubt, from a purely formal point of view this criticism is natural. The problem of reunification is now at the very core not only of Germany's European but also of her domestic policy. And, no doubt, Adenauer's adversaries and foes have gained significant psychological momentum and propaganda fuel from this unhappy state of affairs. It is a dangerous sort of propaganda, which knows how to make clever capital out of the natural reactions of the German people and their understandable indignation over the outrageous mutilation of the national unity and energies. And yet any objective examination of the issue proves that Russia's present terms for the reunification of East and West Germany cannot possibly be met. Russia's policy since Yalta has consistently aimed at eliminating from the European pattern of forces the geopolitical positions and economic and military potentialities of the German area between the French border and the Vistula, by weakening and splitting up the German territory.

Meanwhile, Russia's policy in Europe up to the Geneva and Moscow conferences of 1955, and the Soviet visit to London in the spring of 1956, has given definite proof that Moscow has no intentions of limiting or abandoning these objectives. On the contrary, Russia's proposals at Geneva and London for the reunification of Germany called for "neutralization." This proposal was predicated upon Germany's elimination from all European security pacts and its consequent helplessness before the Eastern power sphere of Russian imperialism. If Germany is ready to pay this price, she may indeed have reunification with the alienated area, with Russia's fullest "sympathy." But the price, obviously, involves two things: *Germany's betrayal of Europe, and the surrender of German freedom to the despotism of the East.*

It is axiomatic that no European in his right mind, much less a patriotic German, would ever consent to such a price. Germany's neutralization along these lines would mean opening the rest of Europe to Russian influence, since the American security guarantees—the only bulwark against the Sovietization of Europe—would become a mere illusion without the German potential. What is more, neutralization would amount to the surrender of the Federal Republic to a Russian-sponsored "reunited" Germany. The formal return of 18 million Germans in the East would be bought with the actual loss of liberty for 50 million West Germans. An objective analysis of the German problem in its present shape shows clearly that Adenauer, as a responsible statesman, could never consent to such a solution.

"It is perfectly clear," Adenauer said on October 18, 1952, at the Berlin party congress of the Christian Democrats, "that at this juncture the Soviet Union does not want to see reunification in freedom. Recent events present overwhelming proof that Soviet Russia is not willing at this point to permit Germany's reunification in peace and freedom."

When and how the 18 million East Germans shall recover their freedom, without a betrayal of European security or of the actual freedom of the 50 million West Germans, nobody can say today. That is, of course, precluding the horrible contingency of a new war. But there is the prospect that the growing economic strength and political consolidation of West Germany—and, along with it, the growing vigor of Europe—may ultimately create a situation which could compel the Russians to revise their attitude. In such a situation, German reunification would be conceivable without the implicit surrender of the freedoms which have to date been achieved in the Federal Republic, along with their safeguards. Adenauer is increasingly able to envisage such a contingency to the degree that European integration and the resulting economic and political alliances of the West are progressing.

"It is now up to us," the Chancellor said on the same occasion, "and above all up to Germany to advance the integration of Europe. In so doing we shall prove the latest Russian hope of disintegration of the Western alliance, opening the path for further successes in the cold war, to be unfounded and vain. Then the day for negotiating with the Soviet Union

with some prospect for success will be in sight. Once the
Soviet Union realizes that it can achieve nothing by means of
the cold war, it will also dawn upon its leaders that the heavy
priority they are giving to the production of war materials at
the expense of consumer-goods production is no longer worth
while. Then the Soviet Union will be ready, in its own best
interest, for a change in policy. Our task—that is to say, the
task of the Western world, including the Federal Republic—
consists in hastening such a realization on Soviet Russia's
part. Reasonable and promising negotiations will then be
held, and the reunification of Germany will come in peace
and freedom. Despite all my efforts I can see no other way
than this."

What has been said so far should leave no doubt that, once
the old European balance of power had collapsed, the only
basis for Germany's continued political existence was her
orientation toward the West. Yet one would ignore the deeper
problems inherent in the building of a "new" German system, if one were to isolate the international and the closely
related economic and military necessities from the ideopolitical aspects of the German problem and its European solution.

*Security, in foreign or defense policy terms, can never be
pursued as an isolated objective. Security must always serve
the safeguarding of all the specific liberties, which are at the
basis of the new pattern of political, intellectual, as well as
social and economic life for the German people. This new
pattern must be created out of the spirit of Western democracy and the tradition of Western civilization. This is the
only way for the German nation to draw a truly fundamental
lesson from the disaster of 1945. Only along these lines can
the effort in rehabilitating Germany have a deep and lasting
meaning. European orientation in political terms, therefore,
is no more than a premise for the vitally needed intellectual
Western orientation for the new Germany. In this, there is
as little room for a "neutralism" of any kind, still less for a*

dubious "Eastern orientation." Adenauer has never tired of stressing over and over that the political orientation toward the West can only have a meaning and—especially in view of the Russian threats—can only be justified if it is paralleled by an ideopolitical return to the cultural and intellectual values of Europe, above all the Natural Law concept of man and society.

Again in the same speech, Adenauer said: "As a matter of life and death, Germany must get out of her current isolation and defenselessness. That Germany, according to our entire philosophy, can and must never look for an Eastern alliance is clear beyond a doubt. For reasons of philosophy and cultural tradition, we Germans belong to the West, and only when we join the West can our isolation and defenselessness be overcome."

Such a realization, however, calls for the strength and intellectual honesty to face the tragic facts of German political history and the evolution of legal thought in Germany during the last hundred and fifty years. Such an examination will show that the tendency to isolate the European factor in German policy is just as old as the old "European balance of power" concept, which went down once and for all in 1945. History shows that the Germans have made the worst possible use of their measure of independence which they enjoyed above all in the sphere of foreign affairs; their "independent choice," as far as it was that, between East and West; their intermediary and mediator's position. The reason why they played that part so poorly is that Germany's independence of the old European order, that was buried with the great French Revolution of 1789, provided the Germans not only with a relative freedom of political and diplomatic action, but at the same time with the fatal freedom to reject the intellectual and cultural traditions of the West.

The man who perhaps most clearly grasped the tragic implications of this progressive defection from Western civilization, to which Germany's growing independence was contributing so much, was Ernst Troeltsch, as early as 1922. Under the impact of the disastrous results of the First World War this highly gifted German theologian and sociologist undertook what may have been the most thorough act of soul-searching by a German at that time. Unhappily, his profound insight that Germany needed a spiritual and cultural orientation toward the West remained totally without effect. After the 1945 disaster the validity of his view suddenly dawned upon many a serious German. Troeltsch's "Program for a Self-scrutiny of Historical, Political and Ethical Thought in Germany" might prove highly illuminating reading for all neutralists—who like to think that their ethical and political concepts are quite as fully European as those of Chancellor Adenauer. Troeltsch offered a clear distinction between the Bruening-type concept of the European problem and that allegedly "all-too-dogmatic" concept of the true European statesman, Adenauer. It is the "gulf separating German political, historical and ethical thinking from the thinking of Western Europe and America" which, according to Troeltsch, is the most pressing problem for the intellectual and political leaders of Germany to solve. Implicit in this tenet is the only possible criterion for judging the new elements in Germany which have so far come to the fore. The question must therefore be asked: *Is this new Germany, under Adenauer's leadership, moving toward the realization of freedom and democracy in the sense of European tradition and Western civilization in general?*

Once the question has been thus posed, it becomes apparent that the "new" German problems must be viewed on an ethical rather than a purely political level, on the ideohistorical rather than the sociological plane. Similarly, those concrete political and sociological aspects of the German evolution since 1945 which have so far been discussed in these observations call for a further discussion of the intellectual and cultural situation of the new Germany. In fact, what first looked like a predominantly political problem—Germany's efforts to build a stable democracy—and the manner in which these efforts relate to the European idea, in its purely economic and political aspects, reduces itself to the problem of *the German return into the moral and legal order of the Western community*.

Such is indeed the focus from which the "intellectual situation" of the new Germany should be viewed, both for its present shape and with regard to its decisive significance for the German future. Such a focus will at the same time highlight the unique features of Adenauer's intellectual make-up, steeped in tradition, and his political ethics—the unique mentality of this emphatically European and emphatically Christian statesman.

If we reduce the problem to its most basic form of a general political order, it boils down to the fundamental issue which has aroused such passionate and, in part, successful struggle in Germany ever since 1945, in which Adenauer and Theodor Heuss have taken a significant lead. The issue is: What kind of freedom and democracy may be most suited to the German character, and how can these be realized and insured permanence in political as well as cultural terms?

It is enough to raise this question to make clear the eminently ideopolitical or ideological character of the problem. An intellectual and cultural consolidation of democracy presupposes the existence of intellectual values and categories to which they may be related; just as any political consolidation must relate itself to the existing social and civic forces.

In sociological terms an intellectual and cultural consolidation requires a concrete ethical frame of reference, and an equally concrete legal and constitutional frame of reference for the political consolidation. If such frames of reference do not exist, they must be created. Thus the cultural problem of building a German democracy reduces itself to the problem of creating a new legal order, resting on ethical foundations; and a new order of the State, especially its constitutional bases, in line with the new concept of law.

In reducing the problem to these terms, many other issues, some of them highly significant, are left aside (such as the religious and philosophical implications). These issues would go far beyond the scope of the present study. Nor are they particularly relevant for a sociological understanding of the political interaction of "law and ethics" and "law and government," the issues which alone concern us here.

In point of fact, the relationship between ethics and law involves the more fundamental relationship between ethics and society, in the sense that any law-abiding order must be ruled by a universal ethical law. The legal norm is, in other words, determined by some ethical principle. Ethical legitimacy serves to sanction the natural legality of a social order based on law. Concrete man is subject as well as object of his freedom. And therewith he is subject as well as object of any social organization regulated by law. Man's natural birthright determines both the extent of his freedom and his obligation to society, as reflected in the State. Indeed, throughout the history of Western freedom this concept has never tolerated an independent "law of the State" to hold sway at the expense of the "natural and inalienable rights" of man, as the guiding principle of government.

It would take no less than a recapitulation of the entire history of Natural Law and its transcending significance for the concepts of human dignity and freedom in the evolution of Western man fully to substantiate this statement. From Cicero and St. Augustine to the Paris "Declaration of Human Rights" of the United Nations, and President Eisenhower's inaugural address of January, 1953, this has been the great underlying principle.

All the efforts to realize this principle have been signposts in the progressive triumph of a concept of freedom and law, the Natural Law tradition of Western democracy. It is this tradition which has managed to avoid or, rather, to bridge the gulf between ethical validity and formal legality in the theory and practice of law. Failure to resolve this conflict has characterized the purely positivist philosophy of the state in Germany during the last hundred and fifty years. In fact, Germany's fatal revolt against Europe is most strikingly illustrated by the ascendancy of the idea of the authoritarian state. From Hegel and the days of the romanticists, down to Hitler's crown jurist Carl Schmitt's excesses in legal theory and the legal anarchy of the Nazis, the German concept of law has progressively moved away from the Natural Rights traditions of the West.

Even the constitution of the Weimar Republic was never able to overcome the cleavage between the ethical validity of the democratic order of law, common to the Western world, and the purely formalistic legality of a positivist concept of law, based on the state. Gerhard Anschuetz, leading commentator on the Weimar constitution, gave a classic expression to its inherent positivist formalism when he declared that it was entirely immaterial for the legal validity of a law whether it, actually, or in the opinion of some, "contradicts all ethical and moral rules; whether it flies in the face of all decency and good faith; whether it constitutes a complete denial of all the tenets of Natural Law; and whether or not it will stand up to such values as justice, fairness and logic," so long as the law has come about by constitutional means. Small wonder, against the background of such a concept of law, that Hitler was able to evolve the terrible Enabling Act of 1933 out of the formal legalistic ground of the Weimar Republic. The Act proved to be a "formal" instrument for depriving the German people in perfectly legal fashion of their basic rights.

By that time, it is true, Bruening's system of an "authoritarian democracy," based on his famous emergency decrees, had already become hopelessly entangled in this formalistic type of legal thought. In the end, even Bruening knew of no better solution than to give his blessings to this same Enabling Act.

The new constitutional law (*Grundgesetz*) of the Federal Republic and the contributions of the individual German states represent a definite break with this anti-Natural Law position—and was therefore a conscious endorsement of the great Natural Law tradition of the West.

Konrad Adenauer stated clearly why this break was needed. "Respect foi the rights of the individual and nations must once more become the foundation for the life of the community both within the nation and in the international sphere—respect for rights which were not created arbitrarily but have their roots deep in the Natural Law. Unless we deprive the state of its all-inclusive power; unless we free ourselves from the idea that the state is the fountainhead of law, and may at will rescind the law; unless we come to recognize laws, for the individual and for entire nations, which are not subject to change or rescission, because they are firmly anchored in Natural Law, there will be no more peace, order or security on earth. Our Christian convictions compel us to strengthen and revive such a concept of law."

An attitude like this is quite obviously conducive to an intensified sense of democracy, in the best Western tradition. It is equally obvious that it will help to overcome the narrow positivism of a purely formalistic democracy, as represented by the Weimar Republic. Adenauer gave exemplary leadership also when he proclaimed the concept of individual freedom rooted in the Natural Law philosophy, as the basic law of the new democratic order: "I consider democracy the only possible form of government for a great and civilized nation, such as the German, in ruling its own affairs." . . . "Personal freedom is and will remain man's greatest good. This is why we must carry the fight against the excessive authority of the State, of the local authorities, or wherever else it may manifest itself, and assert the freedom of the individual, to the last corner of the last office of the Government." . . . "He who concedes any rights to the State which would interfere with the fundamentally private sphere of a human being, is committing a sin against the supreme law of democracy."

Adenauer, it may be pointed out here, had already expounded these ideas under the Weimar Republic. He did this at a time when Heinrich Bruening was engaged in a passionate effort to realize the highly dubious idea of an "authoritarian democracy," of an antidemocratic government under Hindenburg's presidential aegis.

One who wishes to understand the intellectual climate of Germany today must consider the changed concept of freedom and democracy, its ideopolitical substance, and legal implications as indeed crucial. It is here that the change from the old Germany to the new post-1945 nation has been most significant. In her new concept of democracy and freedom the new Germany proves that she now endorses the philosophy of the individual and of democracy which is ingrained in the Natural Rights tradition of the West.

Here is a deliberate break with the gradual narrowing down of the idea of freedom, so characteristic of the old Germany; a break even with the liberalistic formalism of the Weimar Republic. Here in fact is one area where the German nation, between 1945 and 1950, has used its God-given, inalienable right to intellectual freedom by deciding for the Western tradition and spirit. It was a decision, at the same time, determining the spiritual direction of Germany's political alliance with the West, even though this alliance itself could only come about gradually, as Germany regained her freedom of action after 1950.

Viewed against such a background the so-called "neutralism" is an untenable position in the Federal Republic today. That particular concept of freedom which underlies the various West German constitutions clearly expresses the Western concept of the individual. Democracy which is growing up on this basis must be a genuine Western-type democracy, complete with the sovereignty of the people and the full-fledged parliamentarian system. Neutralism has been as good as excluded on ideopolitical grounds by the constitutional development in Germany between 1945 and 1951. Here, then, is the ideological foundation for Germany's political orientation toward the West. Here is the same drive for political community between the Federal Republic and the Western world as is evidenced in Adenauer's European policy.

There has been a considerable amount of confusion emanating from the neutralist camp. This is all the more reason why responsible Germans, who are sincerely striving and struggling for freedom and democracy and their genuine realization in Germany, must face these fundamental facts and their inescapable political implications. There is an inner, extremely practical logic in these facts which should be clear even to the most elementary political understanding.

Between 1945 and 1951 Germany made an effective decision in favor of the tradition of the West, by the particular way in which she developed her new constitutional and social legislation. And this, intrinsically and inescapably, involved another decision: for German alliance with the West, that is to say with Western Europe and America.

There is a close interdependence between the German decision for the cultural community of the West and the practical decision for the political community of interests between the new Germany and Europe. It is in this interdependence that we find the objective core, the spiritual and political principle of Adenauer's Western orientation and his European policy. Adenauer never tired in stressing "that Germany can and must never seek an alliance with the East, because her entire outlook on life refers her to the West, and because only the alliance with the West will bring an end to her isolation and defenselessness!"

Unfortunately, very little attention has been given so far to the ideohistorical aspects of the evolution of constitutional law in postwar Germany.

There exists indeed a considerable list of text collections and commentaries on the new state constitutions and the Bonn Basic Law, containing some excellent discussions of the facts from the point of view of constitutional and administrative law. There even exist some valuable discussions of these matters by non-German, especially American, authors—in particular, some analyses of constitutional law and the sociopolitical aspects of the Bonn Basic Law. Lastly, one should refer to a number of studies by lawyers and legal sociologists concerning various special problems of the new German constitutional law, and the Bonn Basic Law in particular. But all these are scattered throughout the professional literature and buried, and hence difficult for the general reader to find. In fact, all these studies make it seem even more imperative to attempt an ideohistorical synthesis of the new German evolution in the field of constitutional law. Only a historical and sociological synthesis can bring out the ideopolitical significance of these German achievements in the sphere of constitutional law between 1946 and 1951.

These achievements are spectacular. The outside world in particular should know more about them, if only for the reason that this work was done in an atmosphere of inner freedom and ethical as well as political soul-searching—an atmosphere which the German people knew how to preserve even in the years of their lowest political decline, as an expression of their inalienable right of spiritual self-determination, under the formal political authority of the occupation powers. This is of course particularly true for the states of the West German occupation zones which in 1950 were combined into the Federal Republic. At an early juncture, Konrad Adenauer insisted that this area should have the right of spiritual, constitutional, and political self-determination. As

early as 1947, during the constitutional debate in the North
Rhineland Westphalia Diet, he declared, with respect to certain interferences on the part of the British occupation authorities: "In the Inter-Zonal Council, spokesmen of all political
parties have fortunately insisted that such an interpretation
of the rights of the Allies, or, in this case, the British Military
Government, would create an intolerable situation. If it
should really be true that our rights depend solely and exclusively upon the will and whim of the respective Supreme
Commanders, then I must say that all our work is in vain,
and without purpose or meaning. But in that case, they should
not keep telling us that we should learn to understand the
meaning of democracy!" Especially in his much discussed—
and much misunderstood—great speech before the Inter-
Parliamentary Union, meeting in Berne on March 23, 1949,
Adenauer stated this contention vigorously, before an international forum. He said then that the German people, by the
unconditional surrender of the *Wehrmacht* in 1945, had not
surrendered their right to moral and political self-determination; and this involved the inalienable natural right to carry
through the fundamental reorganization of the government,
the social and cultural life, with freedom and responsibility.

Happily, with unimportant exceptions, the Western occupation powers—much in contrast to the Russians—have never
seriously intruded into the ethical and spiritual sphere of the
evolution of constitutional law in the new Germany. And
wherever the occupation powers were in fact able to exert a
lasting influence in the reestablishment of the German states
and their federal integration, as for instance in the abolition
of the old Prussia, it turned out to be a very wholesome influence indeed. This is true, although some future corrections
in the structure and boundaries of the states may be unavoidable.

There is one essential fact that interests us particularly in
this connection. That is the astonishing freedom of spiritual

self-orientation and ideopolitical self-determination which the German people manifested wherever they were given the chance, in the rehabilitation of state constitutions and the integration of the states in the Federal Republic. Even more astonishing is the extent to which this process has been guided by principles of legal philosophy and social ethics that are on a par with the best Western traditions of freedom and democracy. This process also exhibited the creative manifestation of the values and traditions which are rooted in a genuine German conservatism and liberalism, and ultimately hark back to the Natural Law traditions, traditions which are best exemplified in the persons of Konrad Adenauer and Theodor Heuss. A truly comprehensive historicosociological discussion of that spiritual turning point in German history will one day have to go back to those constitutional debates in the records of the West German parliaments and the Parliamentary Council in Bonn from 1946 to 1951.

These records represent important ideohistorical source material for the turning point in the German tragedy and the story of Germany's ethical and political reorientation. They constitute the basic commentary on the results of those debates: the individual state constitutions and the Bonn Basic Law. The stenographic record of these debates presents an objective documentation of the share which the individual states and all the political parties may one day claim before the forum of history as their contribution to the moral and political change in Germany and her return to the West.

At the same time they offer objective evidence of the contribution of the specific ideopolitical traditions of the individual German states to the rehabilitation of Germany. With an incomparable objectivity and the authority of the historic source, these records reveal in particular the share of the two largest political parties, the Christian Democratic Union (CDU-CSU) and the Social Democrats (SPD). Lastly, they show the unique role of men like Adenauer and Heuss in their ideopolitical leadership. Unhappily, the considerable volume of these records is little suited to point up their fundamental significance, or to make them readily accessible to the general public.

This fact should be reason enough for considering an inclusive ideohistorical and historicosociological interpretation of these records and the related constitutional documents, a pressing task for political education in present-day Germany. As a kind of manual of the spiritual and political change in Germany, of Germany's ethical and political return to the West, such an interpretation, it may be hoped, will in the near future be ready for the educators and youth of Germany. It would be the best instrument for combating the ideological and political confusions of the neo-German neutralism and isolationism.

All we can do here is to sketch some of the essential features in the return to the ethical and political traditions of Western democracy, as they have found expression in the Natural Law substance of the state constitutions and the Bonn Basic Law. And we can do no more than touch upon the ideopolitical traditions of the individual states and the ethical and political ideas which the political parties have contributed to this work. We can dwell on these matters only in so far as a basic, historicosociological discussion of them is indispensable for an understanding of the new ideopolitical elements in the structure of the Federal Republic. All these problems will be treated more extensively in the two volumes of our comprehensive sociobiographical exposition of Adenauer's personality, achievements, and development.

Let us touch first on the interrelationship which exists between the Bonn Basic Law and the most important individual state constitutions. The essential features, the ethical and political ideas and basic rights of the federal constitution, were already contained in the state constitutions promulgated at a prior time, especially those of Württemberg-Baden and Rhineland-Palatinate.

One fact in particular is of importance here. The Württemberg-Baden constitution served as an especially effective guide for the Bonn Basic Law, in its Natural Law aspects. It is no mere coincidence that Theodor Heuss—who has been called the "father" of the federal constitution—had already taken a leading part in the writing of the Württemberg-Baden constitution, where he was Minister of Education in 1946.

If there is any need for further confirmation of our statement of the deep-rooted Natural Law traditions of Swabian liberalism, it may be found in the fact that thanks to these traditions, Württemberg-Baden was the first German state to promulgate its constitution as early as November, 1946, a constitution most definitely in line with the best traditions of Western democracy. It is especially important that it was the Democratic People's Party (DVP) in Württemberg, led by Theodor Heuss, which, as the leading party of the government coalition, was chiefly responsible for the completion of the constitutional draft. In the other important states, which achieved similar constitutional results, the Christian Democrats were the leading government party. In Württemberg-Baden, the Christian Democrats were able to collaborate with the Democratic People's Party all the more wholeheartedly because the ethical and political requirements of a characteristically Christian Natural Law concept are clearly reflected in this constitution. This was reason enough for the Christian Democrats later to give their consent to Heuss's leading role in the Parliamentary Council debate for the draft of the federal Basic Law, although the FDP at the Bonn level under Heuss's leadership commanded only the infinitesimal minority of five votes.

The Württemberg-Baden constitution, especially through Heuss's leadership in the Parliamentary Council, and therewith the tradition of Swabian liberalism made a valuable con-

tribution to the ethicopolitical reorientation of Germany.
Some occasional differences between the Swabian liberal views
and those of the Christian Democrats, which have appeared
at some points and may manifest themselves again, do not de-
tract from the significance of their contribution in the Christian renewal of political and cultural life in the new Germany. (These differences concerned such issues as the extent
of the jurisdiction of parents over the education of their children, and the establishment of denominational schools instead
of schools for the entire Christian community.)

We find the basic attitude of the federal constitution already expressed in the *invocatio Dei* of its preamble. The deliberate reference of the constitutional authorities to their
"responsibility before God" denotes the serious religious
mood in which the basic rights of the German people were
here molded into an ethical and political framework. The
legislators intended this barrier of religious ethics as a protection against rationalist and secularist dilution, especially
for those basic rights which in the constitutional text are explicitly or implicitly founded on Natural Law. Among these,
the most important are: protection of the law of marriage and
family; education of children as a "natural right of parents";
protection of freedom of religion and conscience; recognition
and protection of religious instruction as a regular scholastic
subject; the right to establish private and public elementary
schools in response to the demands of parents for community
schools, whether of denominational or secular type; safeguarding of the churches as entities under public law; and continued validity of all official pacts concluded with the former
states, including the state concordats with the Vatican; safeguarding of church property; special protection for Sundays
and holidays, religious service, as well as the practice of the
ministerial office in government-owned or public institutions;
legal validity of the religious oath, etc. The federal constitution also contains those universal basic rights of a political

nature—personal liberty, protection of private property and unimpaired exercise of professional and political activities—which are similar to those contained in all the constitutions of the Western democracies.

It is indicative of the new type of thinking in matters of constitutional law and social ethics in Germany today that the preambles of the federal Basic Law, as well as of the majority of the state constitutions, open with an *invocatio Dei*. While this formula is of course without any binding validity in the sense of positive law, and while it appears in various forms in the individual constitutions, sometimes explicitly, sometimes implicitly, stated, it always represents an ethical basis, anchored in Natural Law, for the basic rights. For the time being, it matters little whether this invocation to God has the theistic meaning of a religious and ethical motivation, according to the Christian Natural Law tradition (in the sense of Molina–Suarez–Burke), or the deistic meaning of a metaphysical-ethical motivation, according to the *rational* Natural Law of the Enlightenment (in the sense of Althusius–Grotius–Jefferson). In either case, the unqualified theistic or deistic recognition of the Divine authority as ethical fountainhead of all rights and liberties clearly indicates the common ethical and political basis of the Natural Law point of view. The line is sharply drawn between these views, on the one hand, and the atheistic secularism of *rationalistic* revolu-
legal validity of the religious oath; etc. The federal constitu-
the other hand, and the definite rejection of the latter is
clearly implied.

There are certain extremist Catholic circles in Germany today which feel that the recognition of the rational Natural Law, as we have just characterized it—by no means to be confused with the rationalistic position of revolutionary secularism—does not offer enough of a safeguard for a democratic order of law and freedom. They are therefore urging the official recognition of a theological concept of Natural Law

founded on the Integralistic doctrine. These circles should
realize the common tradition of religious thought which underlies the present-day German constitutions. But there are
also some democratic liberals who need a deeper understanding of these ideas. There is a feeling among these groups that
the mere fact that because Catholics accept a theological interpretation of Natural Law, they fail to recognize the validity of a rational interpretation, or ignore the significance of
the rational school of thought for the ethical underpinning
of law and basic rights. Even when the Natural Rights ideas
are presented in the form of neo-Scholastic realism, these
doubts remain. We shall see how Adenauer's Natural Law
philosophy and that of the Christian Democrats reconcile
both these extreme positions. It is essentially due to this new
Christian movement that the majority of the German constitutions, over the opposition of the Social Democrats with
their traditional rejection of any Natural Law concepts, includes an *invocatio Dei* and therewith a justification of basic
rights in the principles of Natural Law. What has been said
should make it clear that Theodor Heuss, together with many
liberal followers of the rational concept of Natural Law—
primarily the Swabian liberal Democrats—agree with Adenauer's Christian Democratic party on this point.

One of the leading constitutional lawyers of the Federal
Republic, Friedrich Giese, pointedly expressed the significance of this endorsement of Natural Law tradition, implicit
in the new German constitutions, and therewith of the ethical and political traditions of the West (let it be said again,
in the face of the ideopolitical indifference and neutralism of
the Social Democrats), when he wrote:

"These basic rights of the post-1945 constitutions are actually 'human rights,' rooted in the principles of Natural Law.
They were not created by positive law, as was the case with
the basic rights in previous constitutions" (including, one
might add, that of the Weimar constitution!), "but they exist

prior to the positive law. Therefore the authors of the constitutions did not have to justify them on constitutional grounds nor, as a matter of fact, were they able to do so. All that was left to them was to confirm these basic rights by some sort of declaration and, moreover, to recognize them and to avoid their violation. This Natural Law concept did not prevent the authors of the constitutions from specifically stating, or elaborating on, the basic rights in terms of positive law."

Compared with Gerhard Anschuetz' above-cited comment on the constitutional law of the Weimar Republic, these statements emphasize the wide gulf separating the constitutional thought of Weimar from that of Bonn. The Weimar law expresses the purely positivist formalism of a democracy steeped in a rationalistic, secular philosophy. In its so-called "ideological neutrality" the Weimar democracy deliberately avoided the use of any religious, ethical, or Natural Law principles, whether in justification of its political and social basic rights, or in its human rights. That decision was already made during the Weimar National Assembly in 1919 in the preliminary debate on the constitutional preamble. At that time, the Social Democrats—then the strongest party of the government coalition—forced all the other parties, including the Center Party, to omit any religious formula, or otherwise ethical or moral justification, from the constitutional text. It is due to this religious indifference that the *invocatio Dei* was kept out of the preamble of the Weimar constitution. It was the same "neutralism" in questions of basic philosophy which left the basic rights of the Weimar constitution without any foundation in Natural Law.

To summarize these facts in our own terms, we may state that the German Social Democrats, in their moral neutralism and characteristically German secularism, prevented the integration of the Weimar constitution with the ethical and political traditions of the West.

It is hardly surprising that in the constitutional debate

after 1945 the Social Democrats took exactly the same position. They could not do otherwise. In the absence of a truly
new ideopolitical concept they were compelled to stick to the
old ideological concepts of the German Social Democracy,
this unique aggregate of "Marxist method" and positivism in
questions of law. The Social Democrats rejected the Natural
Rights tradition, and held an emphatically secularistic concept of democracy. Thus clinging to the questionable "old"
patterns, the Social Democrats could hardly be expected to
face the "new" tasks in postwar Germany and their historic
urgency with any measure of true understanding. The constitutions of those few states in which the Social Democrats,
as the strongest government party, were responsible for the
conduct of the constitutional debates as well as the final
drafts, are historic proof of this dilemma of the German Social Democrats.

There is, at first glance, one feature which distinguishes all
the constitutions promulgated by states with Social Democratic governments between 1946 and 1951—Hesse, Hamburg, Bremen, Berlin, Schleswig-Holstein, and Lower Saxony; none of these includes an *invocatio Dei,* or any other
reference to religious or ethical principles, or norms of Natural Law. Whatever might be taken as a clear position in
respect to these matters has been studiously avoided. The
constitutions of Bremen, Schleswig-Holstein, and Lower Saxony in fact fail to include any reference to basic rights.

All the more emphasis has been given by the SPD to a codi-
fication of purely positivistic legislative and government procedures. The Lower Saxony constitution, promulgated in
1951, after five years of constitutional debate and experience
in the Federal Republic, is an almost undiluted document of
administrative bureaucracy without parallel in the entire
constitutional history of modern times. There is no need for
evaluating this document; by deliberately ignoring all principles of Natural Law or basic rights, and by excessive bu-

reaucratic formalism, it writes its own damning critique. This constitution, it should be noted, was drafted under the specific guidance of Kurt Schumacher, as the Lower Saxony Social Democrats, under his immediate leadership, commanded 64 per cent of the total vote in the Diet at the time when the constitution was drafted. There is no need for speculating on what sort of "creative" labor might have come forth from the other West German states if the Social Democrats, under Schumacher's leadership, had controlled the parliaments and governments, as in fact they did in Lower Saxony and Schleswig-Holstein. The presumable results may be summed up in one sentence: If the new Germany had been led by the Social Democratic Party, it would have been a retrogression to the centralism and bureaucracy of Weimar days. What is more, an indifference in ethical and religious matters and the political secularism of unhappy memory would have triumphed. This would have put a virtual end to all hopes for a reorientation toward the ethicopolitical tradition of the West.

This is the conclusive result of a close study of the source material on the constitutional activities of the Social Democrats since 1946. The stenographic record of the constitutional debates in all West German parliaments, plus the texts of the state constitutions, provide the most important documentation for any discussion of the question: to what political forces does Germany primarily owe her ethical and political renascence, and what future contributions may conceivably be expected from these forces and what contributions from their opponents? No one who wishes to understand the current ideological crisis of the Social Democratic movement should neglect to study these documents. They throw a light also on the deeper ideological motives of the political neutralism of present-day Social Democracy and its opposition to the Western tradition and the European policy of the Chancellor. The records of the parliamentary debates, in which Social Democratic speakers tried to formulate their opposition to a constitutional draft or advanced their own proposals, are especially important in this connection.

It is enough to read these documents to understand some of the deeper reasons behind the ideological crisis of the German Social Democrats, and that anti-European neutralism in which they seem caught today. And if anyone is still in doubt about the present state of the SPD, it may be suggested to him that he study the three-volume monumental edition of Kurt Schumacher's speeches and writings. In the most varied shades and nuances, these volumes present the creed of this leader of German Social Democracy, who died in August, 1952. His formulations are highly self-revealing. But what they also reveal is the ideological background of Schumacher's passionate opposition to Adenauer.

Let us sample some of Schumacher's political judgments. First, we have the June 8, 1947, manifesto for the conference of the Socialist International, meeting in Zurich, which was drafted under Schumacher's guidance and read to the conference in his presence. It gives a good idea of what would have happened to a Germany led by the Social Democrats.

"There is only one party which is able to give Germany a more fruitful, more democratic, and above all more peaceful future. That is the German Social Democratic Party. Are we willing to assist the SPD in fulfilling this task, which is also our task? Or are we going to refuse our help to the Social Democrats, leaving them alone in their fight against the German Communists, who enjoy the support of Communists in every country; against the German Catholics, supported by Catholics all over the world; and against the German capitalists, who have all international capitalism behind them."

The following statements by Schumacher are quite in line with the manifesto:

"Democracy can be safe only in a socialist Germany. In

contrast to the countries with old and established democratic systems, capitalism and democracy cannot exist side
by side in this country." . . . "Marxism as a method seems
unassailable to me. . . . But in Germany, a labor movement
without the foundation of the Marxist method is inconceivable." . . . "The most serious sins against the German
people were not committed by the Allies, but by the parties
of the present government, when they established the alternative: 'Christianity or Marxism,' as if the two were mutually exclusive. That was tantamount to splitting the people
of the Federal Republic in two parts. The decision, who is
Christian, and what Marxism means, cannot possibly be
made by one side." ". . . What the capitalistic circles of
Europe are seeking is not peace and reconciliation among
the nations, but the transformation of Europe into a joint
stock company." ". . . That's all a lot of nonsense, that business about the allegedly preconceived principles of East and
West. The alleged principle of the East boils down to the
unlimited expansion of power in the specific, changeable
situation of today, the way the ruling clique is now doing
it at your expense. But the principles of the West aren't by
any means confined to the Western world. Those are the
same principles under which, for instance, the German labor
movement came into being; the same principles to which
the international labor movement owed its origins."

It would seem pretty obvious why the Social Democratic
movement became increasingly blind to the true intellectual
and political necessities of the new Germany and Europe,
while following this type of leadership between 1945 and
1952. As a result, the ideopolitical ignorantism and intellectual isolationism of this same leadership is definitely responsible for the current neutralism of the Social Democrats.

But the ideological crisis within the Social Democratic
Party, long in the making, becomes ever more manifest. It
is clearly a reflection of the elementary changes which are

taking place in the cultural and intellectual life of Germany. These changes are pushing the Social Democratic movement beyond its present ideological stalemate, with its moral indifference and political neutralism veiled by dialectics, toward a thorough reorientation of its ethical and political attitude. No one who feels strongly about the consolidation of the new Germany can relish the thought that the Social Democratic movement has so far failed deplorably. The responsible observer of the German political scene must wish that Western Germany's second largest party may soon find the way toward badly needed reform. But there is one thing the current SPD leadership must realize. It will have to find new forms of moral and political orientation; new forms suited to the creation of a social and political order fitted to overcome its present isolation from the European community. Unless it succeeds in this, the SPD faces the danger that its mass following will be disillusioned and undergo a radicalization process, which would only help Russia and the Communists. Thus the question of the basic indifference of the Social Democrats toward the great moral and political issues can become a matter of life and death for the German Social Democrats—if indeed it has not already become one.

The foregoing indicates that the SPD's attitude toward the evolution of a new constitutional law in Germany and its position in the over-all process of moral and political reorientation have little to do with the growth of essentially "new" elements, or profound changes inside Germany. Those who consider the German developments since 1945—as many German and foreign observers do—solely from the standpoint of the SPD and its ideological isolationism and political neutralism are bound to overlook whatever substantially new elements they entail. The same is true if one relies entirely on these quarters as a source of information. In fact, this is probably one of the chief reasons for the widespread distrust of the so-called "miracle" which is supposed to have happened in Germany. At the same time such a perspective is also one of the major blocks to any deeper understanding of Adenauer's personality and work.

The question arises, to what concrete organizing forces and movements does Germany primarily owe her new orientation? There is good reason for putting the question in this way. Any talk about a "turning point in the minds of men," an "ethical and political reorientation," and similar ideohistorical formulations must needs sound obscure in the political thinking of contemporaries, thinking which is always of an eminently practical bent. Such concepts can become understandable only when they are shown in their concrete sociological application, in the practical results of the interaction between ideas and men.

This is why the popular formula "Adenauer and the new Germany" lacks any tangible meaning, until Adenauer's practical achievements are shown in their proper relation to the organizing and political forces which chiefly made his work possible. Wilhelm Dilthey's sociobiographical formula, in other words, must serve to explain what Theodor Heuss has called "the flow of the present in its historic implications." Only thus is it possible to grasp the "miracle" of the new Germany in its historical and personal contexts.

The significant relationship that exists between Adenauer and the neo-German movement of the Christian Democratic Union can be appreciated only in such a setting; for it is this historic force which is chiefly responsible for the emergence of the new elements on the German scene. We shall lay stress on Adenauer's unique abilities which qualify him for the leadership of this movement when we treat the growth of his political philosophy, along with the historic origins and the development to date of the Christian Democrats, together with the structure of their party. For the present it may suffice to point out that there exists an intimate relationship between Adenauer and this movement; indeed, the achievements of the one would have been unthinkable without the close and wholehearted cooperation of the other.

This interdependence has shown itself in a genuine mutual give and take. Adenauer's real and outstanding leadership has not in the least been dimmed by his unceasing awareness, consistently reflected in his actions, that this movement represents a living focus for the best ideopolitical forces and traditions of Christian Germany. This is true despite its relative youth as an organizational entity. Its effectiveness in German rehabilitation is predicated on the fullest respect for the social and regional characteristics and diversities, the religious and philosophical shades, which are inherent in the German character.

Perhaps for the first time in German history, Adenauer has been able to overcome the denominational narrowmindedness of the typical Catholic politician of the old school. He thus established the prototype of a Christian-German statesman for the present, and, it may be hoped, also future situation, for the benefit of the younger elements in the Christian Democratic movement, Catholic as well as Protestant. On the other hand, the movement's confidence in Adenauer, its unhesitating loyalty, are probably without parallel in the history of German political parties, proof that even in Germany a great political and social movement, in its vital interplay of ideas and personalities, may have a positive type of leadership without a centralized party bureaucracy with its notorious hierarchy of "functionaries."

This explains still another phenomenon which is altogether new in German politics, namely, that Adenauer is not a "party leader" in the usual sense. Nor do the Christian Democrats have the usual crop of "indispensable" functionaries and party bureaucrats. Instead, the party presents a decidedly federalistic structure, a fabric of regional units and state party organizations, each with its unique structural and social characteristics, each guarding these jealously, reflecting the different social stratifications and historic traditions of their native regions. One need only compare the CDU state organization for Northern Rhineland Westphalia with the opposing party in Bavaria (the latter insists even on keeping its own name of Christian *Social* Union or CSU) to realize the extent of these freely accepted differences. Even more telling are the marked differences between such forceful personalities as Karl Arnold, the long-time liberal-democratic Minister President of Rhineland-Westphalia, with his eagerness for social reforms, and the former Bavarian Minister President Hans Ehard with his characteristic social conservatism. It illustrates the creative vigor of this new political movement, under Adenauer's leadership, that both these men, despite their emphatic display of their respective Rhineland-Westphalian and Bavarian traditions, have made outstanding contributions to the rehabilitation of the states which they have been heading for years, in the best national interest.

The records and documents of the debates on a new constitutional law cited above offer an objective judgment on the Christian Democratic contribution to the reconstruction of the new Germany. Ever since 1945 the struggles and successes on the road toward political and social reorientation reflect the spirit of this movement, in its many-faceted ideo-political directives and programs. If one seeks an answer to the question, How far has the CDU been able to realize its theoretical program of the "social-minded" constitutional state?, the party may very well refer to the substance of these West German constitutions drafted under its leadership. True, these constitutions, as well as the federal Basic Law, do not represent the total fulfillment of all the demands contained in the CDU program. But the CDU may point to the considerable extent of agreement between the basic points of the program and the actual constitutional texts.

The Social Democrats, on the other hand, will have to admit
a manifest discrepancy between its longstanding programmatic demands for a Socialist constitutional state and the
meager contents of those actual constitutions which owe their
origin to the Social Democratic bureaucracy.

This refutes the allegation that the SPD failed to carry
out its program because of its exclusion from the federal
government. For even in those states where it was virtually
in control of the government the SPD neglected to project
its most important tenets into the framework of the constitutions.

We are not here giving vent to any personal prejudice
against the Social Democratic movement as an ideology or
party. Rather, we are trying to analyze the question, from a
historicosociological angle, how the new type of ethical and
political thinking and its concrete expression in the Christian Democratic movement have been able to match the
ideology and political activity of the SPD. This inquiry involves the fundamental reasons why the Christian Democratic movement represents an ideohistorical and sociological
necessity for the fulfillment of the democratic idea in the new
Germany. From the ideohistorical point of view, it is the
new type of ethical and political thinking based on Natural
Law and the Christian concept of the social democracy as
represented in the philosophy of the CDU. From the sociological point of view, it is the combination of Christian
forces, united in the interdenominational institutions and
party organizations of the CDU, which has been effective in
the realization of these principles within the new framework
of the German social constitutional state.

For the ideohistorical part of this answer, it is sufficient
to refer to the moral and political substance of the new constitutions. The evidence they furnish is particularly telling
because the substance of basic rights and socioethical provisions contained in the constitutions of the Rhineland-Palati-

nate and North Rhineland-Westphalia present an almost in-clusive catalogue of the Natural Law postulates, which in the Christian view ensure the democratic order of society and state. These constitutions deserve to be studied carefully for a deeper understanding of what is truly "new," ethically and politically, on the German scene. In both these consti-tutions considerable pains have been taken to lay down cer-tain basic rights for the social sphere, in addition to the political rights of man. This undertaking accords with the progressive social teachings of Christian realism, founded on Natural Law, the same teachings which have molded Ade-nauer's philosophy. Provisions in which this tendency is especially evident include the right of codetermination for workers and employees; the concept of community property in the framework of social legislation; and the general con-cept of private property as deriving from society and involv-ing certain obligations toward it. The idea of the socially conscious constitutional state has here been applied to the concrete fabric of constitutional law, to a degree unparalleled in any Western democracy. In this way solid constitutional foundations have been laid for a progressive social policy, which may prove to be a most effective instrument in dealing with the utopias of the Socialist and Communist collective state. And they may prove to be a decisive step beyond the liberalist-capitalist concept of the economy and its relation to the state.

It is hardly surprising if the progressive concepts of social legislation established in the constitutions have not yet been fully realized in actual social and economic policies in Ger-many. The reasons for these shortcomings are clear, if one considers seriously the stark economic necessities and demo-graphic problems under which the Federal Republic has labored for years, and may continue to labor for some time to come, in the wake of the 1945 collapse. Still, the record shows—as closer, critical examination will reveal later—that

the Christian Democratic movement has already proved itself
to be a creative force of historic significance in this respect
also. The relationship between constitutional principles and
the actual texts of the constitutions, or, in other words, between ideology and practice, program and deeds, propaganda
and actual accomplishments, provide the ultimate criteria
for the success of the government.

Turning to the sociological side, the CDU movement appears as the most tangible and vigorous expression of the
new need and opportunity for the deliberate application of
Christian political philosophy in postwar Germany. The history of the CDU from its founding during the days of the
collapse to the completion of its organizational structure,
reaching a preliminary conclusion at the first all-German
party conference in Goslar in October, 1950, illustrates the
profound changes which have occurred in the socioreligious
and political life of Germany.

All the efforts for a radical reorientation in the political
and social outlook of German Catholicism and Protestantism
necessitated by the *tabula rasa* of the Nazis, and the utter
breakdown of the old ideopolitical patterns and concepts,
were consummated in this and in the parallel development
of the Bavarian CSU. For a sociology of religion, the documents of these developments which are partly in print, partly
in archives or private collections, represent the most authentic comment on the moral and political reorientation
of Germany. For our purpose, it is sufficient to refer here to
the creative principle, basic to the socioreligious view, which
made this union of Christian forces in the interdenominational movement of the Christian Democrats possible—a principle which, we hope, will save it from any future religious
schism and denominational strife.

It is the principle of realism and personalism founded on
Natural Law, in the sense of Adenauer's above-cited statement, that is reflected in the new German constitutions.

Here, at least in theory, we see the fulfillment of those long-standing hopes for an interdenominational Christian collaboration. From the days of Von Ketteler and Windthorst to the programmatic statements of Adenauer, Stegerwald, and Mausbach, especially at the 1922 Munich Catholic Conference, this hope consistently inspired the best minds of the progressive socially and politically "realistic" wing among the German Catholics.

It was in this spirit that Von Ketteler wrote as early as 1872: "If I am primarily addressing myself to the Catholics, this is because the misunderstandings between ourselves and the Protestants are still much too serious to think of a political union. Perhaps a common emergency might one day lead to such a union. In this sense, the need for an independent Catholic party is merely a temporary one." Similarly Windthorst in 1873: "Let us keep in mind that as soon as possible we must extend the Center Party so as to include all Christian denominations. I am fully convinced that the Center Party's struggle will be over once and for all, as soon as all positively believing Christians are united in their stand against unbelief."

When this actually occurred in 1945, both Adenauer and Stegerwald, together with many others, were able to translate these long-standing hopes into immediate demands. From Wuerzburg, Stegerwald called for "a political party that would build a strong bridge between town and country, between Catholics and Protestants, resting on Christian culture and a positive social consciousness." In a similar vein, writing to the mayor of Munich, Scharnagl, from Cologne on August 21, 1945, Adenauer urged union upon the planners of the new party that was to embrace the entire Christian community. *"I ask you and your friends always to keep in mind during your deliberations that only the union of all Christian and democratic forces will be able to shield us against the threat from the East."*

Later, Adenauer appealed frankly to the conscience of certain denominational and reactionary groups. They were trying to obstruct the positive union of the new Christian political community, and hopelessly clinging to their old patterns and concepts. "Our Christian Democratic Union," the Chancellor said, "rests upon universal Christian foundations and attitudes. It is neither a Catholic nor a Protestant party. We are sustained by that which both these denominations have in common, the Christian concept of man's duty on earth. Whatever unites both confessions has life for its object, and that includes the political life. It is vastly more important, and far more vital than whatever sets us apart. Those seeking to disturb this common effort are in fact committing a sin against Germany."

With his capacity for reducing profound intellectual problems to the simplest possible terms of political reality, and thereby adapting them to the needs of the time, Adenauer was here pointedly applying Natural Law concepts to the crucial issues of a Christian policy. In the same speech, given before the Third Party Congress of the CDU in Berlin, he stressed the significance of the *human effort for the sake of the concrete human being and the concrete community,* which must at all times remain the essential basis for such a policy. *"For us Christians,"* he said, *"man is always in the center of any political or economic development."*

In simple basic terms this expresses the personalist principle of political anthropology and sociology. Its rational justification, in terms of Natural Law, has been the object of the entire Christian development, from the late scholastics, like Luis de Molina (1536–1600) and Francisco Suarez (1548–1617), to Joseph Mausbach (1861–1931) and Peter Tischleder (1891–1947), as far as it was concerned with the safeguarding of political freedom and democracy, based on the sovereignty of the people. On the one hand, this principle leads to unrestricted freedom for everyone, regardless of theological dogma and ecclesiastical authority, to give his allegiance to any political and social doctrine which is not in conflict with the universal moral laws of Christianity. It leads, on the other hand, to the doctrine of the sovereignty of the people, which in turn rests on Natural Law; to the doctrine, in other words, of the natural and moral freedom of the people, as the natural source of government authority, freely to choose those forms of government—if the common interest warrants, even by revolutionary means—which seem most suited to their historic and social individuality.

The application of this principle to historic reality has not only occasioned considerable dispute between Catholics and Protestants. It has even created some heated doctrinal and political arguments within the Catholic camp itself. The most spectacular instance was probably the debate at the Catholic Convention in Munich, in 1922. These discussions appear particularly significant today, because in their speeches at the Munich meeting Adenauer, Stegerwald, and Mausbach already anticipated those Natural Law concepts, which in 1945 became the very basis of the Christian Democratic movement. Adenauer's long-standing and articulate commitment to these ideas would, in fact, suffice to qualify him for the role of leader in the new movement of Christian Democratic unity.

Once more, as in the Munich days, this emphatic democratic interpretation of the Natural Law philosophy and its application to the political realities proved to be a source of dissension in Catholic ranks. But after 1945, significantly, the overwhelming majority of the German Catholics, including many bishops, decided in favor of Adenauer's view. The Christian Democratic movement is, in fact, made up of about two-thirds Catholics. But the Natural Law concept of the CDU has made it possible also for Protestants, especially the followers of the Lutheran confession in Germany, to join the CDU.

For many Protestants this was in fact not a difficult step, because a tradition of Natural Law has been strong among Lutherans, especially during the eighteenth century, and in the southern part of Germany. Added to a number of other factors, mostly based on the religious thought and experience up to the Nazi period, this tradition created for them a kinship with the basic Natural Law philosophy of the CDU.

As for the positive contribution of the Protestant members of the CDU to the ideopolitical program and practical policies of the movement, in the framework of Natural Law, one may again emphasize the fact that purely theological considerations concerning the problem of Natural Law are almost without practical significance. This is especially the case where, as in the CDU movement, the social and political program and practice are based on a *rational interpretation of the Natural Law* concept, deriving its metaphysical justification from the Christian concept of the Divinity. This is fully adequate as a protection against the tendency to assign an absolute role to human reason, as the origin and sole source of law, precisely the tendency which characterizes the interpretations and errors of the *rationalistic* Natural Law concept of the French Revolution. There nevertheless have been certain tensions, resulting from the problem of the Natural Law, within the ranks of the young CDU movement, and there may be more in the future. But that seems unavoidable in view of the characteristic German interrelation of social and political problems with the no less typically German *Weltanschauung* positions.

For a solution of this problem, it seems extremely important that the continued growth and consolidation of the CDU theory and practice should keep itself free from the influence of the theological Maximalism of the Catholic Integralists, just as it ought to shun the theological Maximalism of the sworn enemies of the idea of Natural Law, such as

Karl Barth and many of the followers of the Calvinist concept of the authority of the state as an exclusive "order of sin" (Gogarten). Meanwhile, the experience of the barbarism of the Nazi state has convinced a majority of German Protestants that an exclusively secular foundation of the authority and power of the state cannot afford true security against the political misuse of the natural principles of human and social freedom. It is perhaps this experience, and the insights that have grown out of it, which present the strongest basis for a fruitful collaboration of German Catholics and Protestants for the realization of the democratic idea—the type of collaboration sought inside Germany by the CDU, and which it has already realized, at least in part.

The sweeping statement that Protestantism is basically opposed to the Natural Law philosophy may easily be met with a reference to the great and, in their time, salutary traditions of Natural Law evolved by German Protestants from Althusius to the young Fichte, including many scattered exponents during the nineteenth century.

Even Prussia under Frederick the Great and his successor was still conscious of having strong ties with this tradition, as demonstrated in Wilhelm Dilthey's study *Das allegemeine Landrecht,* now available in his collected works, vol. XII, 1936 (and unfortunately far too little known) or in the fundamental studies of Otto Hintze, now contained in his *Gesammelte Abhandlungen,* 3 volumes, Leipzig, 1941–1943; not to mention the long-forgotten book of the Halle jurist, Carl von Kaltenborn, *Die Vorlaeufer des Hugo Grotius,* Leipzig, 1848, which is still a good introduction to the evolution of Natural Law concepts in Protestant Germany, up to the middle of the nineteenth century. In this literature Protestant members of the CDU will find a significant reminder of a German tradition, at the same time representing one of the most outstanding traditions in Western Natural Law philosophy as a whole which still knew the basic unity of

Catholic and Protestant social and political thought. A closer study of these traditions might enable even many of the Protestant politicians within the CDU to formulate their theoretical position on the social and political Natural Law concepts, now such a timely problem, in a far more incisive manner than has been possible so far.

Thus it is unjustifiable to speak of a "theologically unacceptable choice" facing modern Protestantism in Germany, with regard to the basic philosophy of the CDU. Those who take that view extend unduly the position of Karl Barth and the German followers of dialectic theology to the rest of the Evangelical denominations in Germany. This position, it is true, is based on the Calvinist concept of hereditary sin, and rejects the theological and rational doctrine of Natural Law. People like Martin Niemoeller and many of the ministers of the "Professing Church" may never find their way to the CDU, for reasons related to their views on Natural Law, but also for other very essential reasons.

But against this historical background, it becomes clear why practically all those Protestant theologians who belong to the Social Democrats, with their implicit hostility toward the tradition of Natural Law, are also close to the views of Karl Barth, the Swiss Protestant theologian, and those of his followers among the "Professing Church" in Germany. But this cannot stamp the entire Protestant movement as "traditionally hostile to the concept of Natural Law." Loyalty toward the Protestant church in no way precludes membership in the Christian Democratic Union. Those who feel otherwise are influenced by narrow denominational or else unfortunate political prejudices. The strongest refutation of their views may be seen in the fact that some eminent Protestant clergymen, including the bishop of Berlin, Otto Dibelius, participated in the founding of the CDU. More than a third of the CDU vote is Protestant. Similar proportions hold for the elected deputies of the CDU in the federal and state parliaments. Adenauer's former deputy, as chairman of the CDU party organization, was a member of the High Consistory of the Lutheran Church—the late president of the federal council, Herrmann Ehlers. He was succeeded by the late Dr. Robert Tillmann, a member of the federal cabinet, also an Evangelical Protestant.

It is typical of the new intellectual climate in Germany that for the first time in German history there exists now a joint movement of Catholic and Protestant forces aiming at the application of common Christian principles, founded on a rational interpretation of Natural Law, to the political and social life of the country. This is possible, because Adenauer's realistic vision of the Christian Democratic role, and his trenchant definition of the nature of Christian politics, foreclose any ideological argument. All that highly inflammable mass of theological argument which has accumulated around the Natural Law doctrine has thereby been kept out of the political sphere.

What this means in ideopolitical terms is that the basic CDU program, with its foundations in Natural Law, cannot be affected either by the more one-sided Catholic doctrines, especially the theological Maximalism of the Integralist Thomist school, nor by those of the Protestants and their Calvinist and dialectic rejection of Natural Law. Thanks to this aloofness in questions of dogma, the CDU has also maintained its political independence both from the reactionary Rightist and the radical Leftist forces in the Catholic and Protestant camps, whose ideologies are essentially related to these theological positions.

The CDU thus appears as a political movement in which Catholics and Protestants have joined hands for the realization of Christian concepts of government, the Christian program for the socially conscious constitutional state. This common effort is on the other hand opposed by splinter groups and sects, Catholic as well as Protestant, distinguished by their Integralist philosophy in questions of theology and by the authoritarian radicalism of the Right and Left in political affairs. The sharp line that divides these political camps runs straight across the ideopolitical and sociological structures of Catholicism and Protestantism in Germany. The limitations upon a political collaboration between the two confessions are no longer set by their respective sociological peculiarities, ultimately based on denominational differences, but by the ideological and theological attitudes toward the practical application of the principle of Natural Law.

What was the rule yesterday seems the exception today, such as the mainly abortive attempt to resurrect the old Center Party along strictly denominational lines. This is indeed no more than a practical confirmation of our earlier findings, that there is no longer any ideopolitical necessity for special denominational groupings within the political sphere, thanks to the existence of a vigorous interdenominational movement based on the universal Christian concept of Natural Law. It is, in fact, one of the most decisive marks of the present German situation, in socioreligious respects, that the old forms of theological and denominational influence in the sphere of politics have become obsolete. Only one who is familiar with the internal story of the CDU development knows of the painful efforts of some of the best minds in the German Catholic, as well as in the Protestant, camp in opposing a narrow denominational factionalism. In these issues Adenauer's vigorous leadership proved decisive. The young political movement of the CDU will nevertheless have to be on guard against the ever-latent danger of a renewed invasion of narrow denominational influences into its organization and program.

Yet among the most pressing tasks the CDU faces now is the question of making up for the comparative absence of a new, qualified leadership generation and the *tabula rasa* in the cultural sphere, the twofold heritage of the Nazi regime.

The CDU will have to devote its very special attention to the development of young leadership material within its ranks, as well as to the continued evolution and practical realization of its social and cultural programs. This work will center heavily on the CDU party organization within the individual states and the larger communities. We shall later discuss the very considerable and promising strides which have already been made on this level.

It is only fair to note that the job of organizing the Christian Democratic Union, and its educational work—the primary basis for the success of the Adenauer policy—have been a joint effort, in which each part of this highly diversified Christian movement may claim its own particular share. All the more reason for these various elements and their Catholic or Protestant leaders to recognize the outstanding leadership of the Chancellor. His strong personality, exemplary realism, and intellectual integrity have been the human and intellectual focus for the movement. Without it, the movement could never have been fruitful and effective under present-day conditions in Germany.

In return, the CDU has supported Adenauer's efforts in his domestic and foreign policies—the efforts of the "Chancellor of the Vanquished" for the rehabilitation of the freedom and national pride of the German people, and it has thus become the outstanding spokesman for the European idea in Germany and the best German traditions in Europe. Its manifesto of October 19, 1952, proves to be the best answer of an alert Christian conscience in Germany to all the dubious neutralist arguments.

"The Berlin Party Conference of the Christian Democratic Union of Germany pledges its allegiance to the idea of German unity, peace and freedom. In a sense of brotherhood with all those Germans who are separated from us by the Iron Curtain, the delegates from all over Germany who have convened here are stating their common purpose:

"We shall work with all our might for the reunification of Germany in peace and freedom. As yet, Bolshevist lust for power obstructs the realization of this aim. Bolshevism feeds on the hope that the powers of the free world, instead of working together, will consume their energies in mutual conflict. In the face of this attitude, the task of the free world, of which Germany is a part, is to close our ranks and thus to show the Soviet Union that neither the cold nor the hot war can lead to its success. It is, and shall remain, the outstanding task for the Federal Republic to contribute its share to this common front in its striving for the free reunification of Germany.

"The Party Conference therefore declares its renewed allegiance to the idea of a European Federation, in the knowledge that the Western European nations can maintain their common values, on the basis of Christianity, only through a joint effort, and that only through joint action will they be able to maintain world peace. Freedom at home and abroad, which this policy asserts for the Federal Republic, is the most essential premise of a free order in a common Fatherland, also for those Germans who are still separated from us. This Fatherland must rest on the firm recognition of the inalienable right of man to his native country.

"The Party Conference stands in faith and admiration before Konrad Adenauer and his work."

VII

The Statesman: "Chancellor of the Vanquished"

If the popular legend of Adenauer's Germany has any meaning at all, it can only be taken as a reflection of the eminent role Adenauer has played in the rehabilitation of Germany and the consolidation of her international position. Adenauer's achievements must be viewed as an individual expression and focal point for the intellectual and political efforts which have gone into the remaking of Germany. Adenauer's personality and life are almost ideally suited for any attempt to interpret Germany's recent history and its premises in the "historic and personal environment." The first thing to note in such an analysis is that the impressive impact of the Chancellor's personality lacks any mysterious element. At the root of his extraordinary achievements is solely a felicitous, also sometimes tragic, interaction of ideohistorical and political circumstance.

Foremost among these premises is Adenauer's eminent talent as statesman, his singular moral integrity, and the firmness of his ideopolitical beliefs. Adenauer comes from a background combining the best and most progressive traditions of social and political Catholicism, plus those traditions and experiences reflecting the best in German politics and government administration during the past century, up to 1933. The happy meeting of these elements explains the personal and social bases and therewith the sociobiographical substance of Adenauer's life.

When the Federal Republic attained its full sovereignty on May 5, 1955, with the ratification of the Paris treaties, the first period in the remaking of Germany after 1945 drew to a close. This act may well be viewed as the crowning of Adenauer's life work. At the same time, a chapter in German history found an at least tentative conclusion which, as an instance of a defeated nation working its way back, stands unparalleled in the annals of history.

Konrad Adenauer was especially qualified, morally and professionally, to fill the office of the first "Chancellor of the Vanquished." His moral integrity and ethicopolitical steadfastness had already been tested at the time when he courageously stood up for the democratic idea and the constitutional privileges granted by the Weimar Republic, which no presidential "emergency decree" could invalidate. He was not to be intimidated by any cardinals dabbling in politics, nor by any field marshals making light of the constitution. Adenauer remained loyal in this attitude even after Hitler's ascent. He did not allow himself to be induced to accept compromises of any sort by the threats of the Nazi terror. This record has set him off from the deplorable group of politicians who, by their indirect or direct coresponsibility for the rise of the Hitler system and their legal and diplomatic sanction of it once it had installed itself in power, must be listed in a moral and political sense among the truly "defeated" after 1945.

No wonder that, after the war, these politicians were unable to face the Allies in representing the vital interests and ethicopolitical rights of a defeated nation, with the moral self-assurance of a German of Adenauer's mettle. While fully recognizing the collective responsibility of the German people for the crimes that had been committed in its name, Adenauer was able to present to the Allies an important fact: namely, that he was one of a group of uncompromising foes and persecuted opponents of the Hitler system. Since this group had never morally surrendered to the Nazis, the victors could not possibly question its ethicopolitical attitude and sense of responsibility, much less "defeat" them.

One may well apply to this situation the popular concept of the "clear conscience," which even the Allied Occupation Powers were bound to respect, unless they wanted to deny the basic moral principles of their political actions. Nothing has perhaps strengthened Adenauer's personal impact and the prestige of the new political objectives for which he was chiefly responsible, as much as precisely this "clear conscience," the moral and ideopolitical integrity of the Chancellor.

Wherever Adenauer took a leading hand, wherever he was engaged in executing a policy, wherever he raised his voice in terms of guidance and leadership, or of protest or warning, apology or self-defense, explanation or condemnation; whether speaking in negotiations with the occupation authorities, with foreign statesmen at international conferences, or in relation to domestic affairs of government and party politics, it was at all times the true German and Christian statesman, whose clear conscience and profound faith in God permitted him to carry the burden of the "morally undefeated" "Chancellor of the Vanquished."

The nature and development of Adenauer the statesman

have been pervaded by this force, the clear conscience, the living expression of an unswerving orientation of practical action toward his obligations before the moral order of history. It is, ultimately, an expression of the same moral realism which has molded the attitude of such truly Christian statesmen and political philosophers as Edmund Burke, Abraham Lincoln, Alexis de Tocqueville, and Emanuel von Ketteler, men who were concerned with the genuine democratic substance of a true *res publica Christiana*. Here we have that living expression of a realism founded on the concepts of Natural Law, which does not permit of any schism between moral principles and expediency in the sphere of political action. It is indeed the legitimate expression of a genuine Christian pragmatism, which will always take the world as it is in its changing historic realities only to improve it to the extent that the existing possibilities permit, with a view to upholding the ideals of freedom and the common good. Because this moral attitude is rooted in the ethicopolitical tenets of a definite cultural community, formed by the spiritual and historical tradition, it is in the best sense of the term a "conservative" attitude. In fact, Adenauer's person epitomizes the principle of conservative political realism, whose significance for the present German situation has already been pointed out.

From such a perspective Adenauer's political conscience, over and beyond his indebtedness to the universal moral laws, appear especially bound to the traditional values of his political philosophy, as well as to the historic values of his nature as a German. From this vital unity of moral orientation, spiritual tradition, and historic reality Adenauer has drawn the strength for an ever-vigilant, sober evaluation of any threat to his political philosophy, from whatever tangible historic situation it might arise. When in 1945 he witnessed the utter collapse of the historical realities on which his entire existence as a German was based, the integrity of his philosophy in its religious, moral, traditional, and spiritual components remained intact, so that he was able frankly and fully to face the facts.

For these reasons Adenauer's assessment of the catastrophic plunge into the abyss which the German nation underwent in 1945 was essentially different, and far more susceptible of moral and political interpretations, from for instance Kurt Schumacher the Socialist leader's attitude, discussed earlier. Schumacher, whose conscience, morally and politically, was as clear as Adenauer's, unhappily lacked those ethicopolitical forces, anchored in the certainty of tradition and of an ideo-historical philosophy, which enabled Adenauer to make a realistic evaluation of the catastrophe. The profound personal bitterness with which Kurt Schumacher accepted the disaster is largely accounted for by these deficiencies. Lacking those deeper resources, Schumacher could not grasp the inevitable political and historic consequences which the condition of an utterly defeated nation was forcing upon all German postwar policy.

The most intimate psychological and ideopolitical causes of the unbridgeable gulf which separated Adenauer from Schumacher, and which so unfortunately affected adversely the work of rehabilitation, probably lie in this different potential for evaluating the disaster of 1945, and, as a result, in differences in capacity for drawing moral and political conclusions. This difference explains, too, why Schumacher failed to understand Adenauer's real reasons for his frank admission that the German people had suffered total defeat. It may explain why Schumacher made himself guilty of calling Adenauer the "Chancellor of the Allies," and of similar slanderous statements. Any man who thus casts suspicion upon the Chancellor's patriotism reveals a complete ignorance of the peculiar characteristics of Adenauer's ethical beliefs, as we have discussed them here. There have even been those who questioned Adenauer's integrity in religious and political matters. The fact that Adenauer is a believing Catholic is used to defame him as the "representative of a Fifth Occupation power," an agent of the Catholic Church and in particular of the policies of the Vatican.

It must be taken as an indication of the ideopolitical confusion of our time, if certain non-German quarters have until recently gauged Adenauer's personality and work by similar misconceptions. A discussion of these views may omit any especial attention to the Communist propaganda against Adenauer, since its motives are only too evident. The same holds for all the confusion on German matters which exists abroad as an heritage of the Nazis and the sacrifices involved in the fight against them. One might, however, cite the significant fact that the doubts cast upon Adenauer's patriotism, inside Germany, find their counterpart abroad in precisely opposite suspicions, where Adenauer is painted as the open or disguised exponent of National Socialism, or even of a "neo-Nazi" renascence of German designs for world power. Usually, these absurd ideas rise to a climax in the even more widespread allegation that Adenauer the "Catholic's" European policy is really an instrument of some international conspiracy of the clericals with the aim of realizing the Vatican's "religiopolitical imperialism" within a specifically "Catholic" Europe.

We shall see later how all this anti-Adenauer propaganda completely ignores the necessities, as well as the opportunities, under which a truly German and European policy has had to operate ever since the disaster of 1945. In fact, this entire catalogue of German and non-German misconceptions and erroneous interpretations of Adenauer's policy is proof of the tenacious hold which old and obsolete categories still have on the contemporary mind. Just how obsolete they are, may have become evident from this historicosociological introduction to the problems of the "new" forces and elements. The slanders show also in how pitifully few non-German quarters—and incidentally German quarters as well—has it been possible to appreciate an altogether new type of German and European statesmanship which has come to the fore in the person of Adenauer. This statesmanship is one of the most significant contributions Germany has made toward a solution of the modern problem of political leadership in general. This contribution may be viewed in four possible ways: from the basic problem of political morality as such; from the specific problem of a Christian policy; as the emergence of a new type of professional politician on the German scene; and as that of the new type of European statesman.

Adenauer's policy reveals the creative power of a set of moral values uncompromisingly linked with the ethical and political norms of a Natural Law realism, while at the same time reflecting the intellectual traditions and sociological values among the historical realities of Germany and Europe. For this reason, Adenauer's policy is always a policy of "conviction." It is not merely based on theoretical principles, but its practical expressions are at all times guided by concrete moral standards. In his ethical realism, Adenauer's political action is safe from abstract theorizing and futile ideological preoccupation. All political activity is wholly focused on the practical mastery of the tangible, day-by-day, political problems and tasks. This "policy of conscience" is a realistic type of policy, but it differs substantially from the manifestations of a purely positivistic utilitarian policy of expediency, because at no time does it sacrifice moral principles and spiritual necessities for temporary political advantage, in the name of that threadbare concept, expediency.

Much of the misunderstanding of Adenauer originates in the criticism of Heinrich Bruening, strangely enough endowed with high prestige abroad as the last Weimar Chancellor, who surrendered the Weimar Republic to Hitler. After his return to Germany he criticized Adenauer in a speech at Düsseldorf as "all too dogmatic." Bruening himself found hope in the Rapallo policy of playing East against West and West against East as a legitimate exploitation of Germany's geopolitical position. In Bruening's view Adenauer's European policy is too deeply committed to certain definite spiritual and moral principles to permit the adroit maneuvering required of a "statesman."

We have touched on the subject of the potentialities and opportunities for a Christian policy, which Adenauer outstandingly personifies. One should note that the chief element responsible for Adenauer's evolution against a "new" and changed background, from a Catholic politician of the Weimar days into a leading Christian statesman of European status, has been his realistic philosophy, founded on Natural Law, the very basis of his moral values. He thus overcame all that denominational narrowness which usually restricts the Catholic politician of the old school. He was at the same time realizing deep-seated hopes, nourished especially by his great model Emanuel von Ketteler. The development of the Christian Democratic Union, which we have already discussed, and the crucial contributions of this movement to the establishment of a new order in Germany, prove the significant role of Adenauer's moral philosophy for the realization of a Christian policy within the new Germany.

There are two analyses of the characteristics of a statesman that may be of interest here. One is that of Heinrich Bruening in his essay on the statesman; the other is by Max Weber, far the greatest sociologist and political philosopher of modern Germany. Bruening does not specifically mention Adenauer, although his essay is essentially a negative picture of Adenauer. Max Weber did not have in mind any such figure as Adenauer arising in the future. But his specifications for the quality of a true statesman fit perfectly the character of Adenauer.

In 1947 Bruening published his essay, "The Statesman." In this essay the former chancellor and last leader of political

Catholicism under the Weimar Republic expounded his views about the fundamental qualifications required for the Christian statesman and the calling of true political leadership. What he gives us amounts to a mere positivist definition of the techniques of political action and the diplomatic craft, without even so much as a word for the problem of ethics in politics. The image of statesman he presents is precisely the old Prussian type, accepting the law as enacted without question of its moral quality. The psychological and technical aspects of political strategy are elevated to the role of central problem of statecraft. Most striking is Bruening's association of the qualities of the statesman with those of the general. Bruening is insistent on the participation of the general staff in the work of statesmanship—the old Prussian tradition.

If there is anything to justify Adenauer's warning against clinging to "lost illusions," and his insistence on a "break with what has been," it is Bruening's version of the Prussian philosophy on the nature of the statesman and the arbitrary use of power.

Bruening's conception of statecraft would have sounded plausible in the days of the Kaiser, nor even much out of fashion under Weimar. After 1945 they are incredibly obsolete.

History is replete with examples of political figures returned from exile who had forgotten nothing and had learned nothing. There is nothing remarkable in Bruening's position. What is remarkable, however, is the degree of credit accorded abroad to Bruening's criticism of Adenauer, implied or expressed. Even in the United States, where the "neutralism" of Indonesia or Iceland is viewed with deep concern, Bruening is listened to with respect, although the policy he advocates would not only make Germany neutral, but would use this neutrality as an instrument for playing West against East and East against West. The geopolitical position of Germany, Bruening maintains, makes such a pol-

icy practicable. But the geopolitical position of Germany is
no longer what it was when East Prussia was a salient of
Germany, reaching toward the heart of Russia. Today Germany is half ringed around by Russia's buffer satellite states.
The less said about her geopolitical position the better.

After the First World War, Max Weber gave fitting expression to the German effort to evolve new forms of political thought and statecraft. Under the impact of profound
upheavals, similar to those which Ernst Troeltsch had experienced in connection with that German catastrophe, Max
Weber, in one of his last lectures in 1919, on the subject of
"Politics as a Vocation" (*Politik als Beruf*) discussed the
special qualifications required of the statesman from the
viewpoint of "ethics and politics." They have a particular
significance in view of the new type of professional politician
in Germany as represented by Adenauer.

"Precisely because power is the inevitable means, and the
striving for power therefore is one of the driving forces in
politics, a political force cannot be more fatally wrong than
when it thrives on the self-satisfied enjoyment of power,
gives way to worship of power as such. The mere 'power
politician,' whom an eager cult seeks to glorify even in our
midst, may have a forceful impact, but his actual results are
bound to be futile and vain. The sudden inner breakdown
of typical exponents of this type of attitude before our own
eyes has manifested the inner weakness and impotence which
hides behind the bombastic totally empty gesture. It is the
product of a miserably and superficially blasé attitude toward
the meaning of human action, lacking even the slightest
touch of an awareness of the essentially tragic nature of all
human action, and all political action in particular."

In contrast to Bruening's concept of the characteristics of
the statesman, Max Weber insists that the statesman should
have three outstanding qualities, namely, *passion, responsibility, and a sense of perspective.* "Passion in an objective

sense," he says, "means a passionate devotion to a cause, to the God or the demon behind it. For mere passion, no matter how genuinely felt, is not enough. Passion does not make the true professional politician, unless in the service of a cause; the responsibility toward this cause becomes the guiding light for all his actions. That, however, in turn, requires a sense of perspective, the capacity for letting the realities affect us, while we preserve an inner concentration and quietude, or in other words a proper distance from matters and men."

For Max Weber the moral decision between God and demon, that is, between the power of good and that of evil, becomes the core of the problem of ethical responsibility in politics: *"He who wishes to engage in politics as a vocation must take account of these ethical paradoxes, and his responsibility for whatever may become of himself under their impact. He is involving himself with those demonic powers lurking behind any violent act."*

Weber is here primarily concerned with the tensions, or even contradictions, facing any responsible politician when he attempts to reconcile the ethical and political norms which he represents, with the actualities and requirements implicit in all practical politics. It is the problem of the dichotomy between the morally valid and the politically legal underlying all political action, which Max Weber, too, recognizes as the central issue in the ethical underpinning of any political power. *"The fact that specific means of legitimate violence as such are placed in the hands of human institutions is what presents the peculiar ethical problem in the political sphere."*

Konrad Adenauer's outstanding domestic and international achievements offer overwhelming evidence for the validity of Max Weber's postulate, that ethical responsibility must become "the guiding light for any political action." The course of recent history has furnished a telling confirmation of the views of Max Weber by lending its peculiar weight to the moral and political convictions of that minority which had found no vital response in Germany prior to 1945.

It was for this reason that in 1945 the same minority, now called upon to lead the defeated German nation, felt morally justified in asking the Allies to gauge the "ethical paradoxes" in the political pattern of the old Germany with an objective "sense of perspective" and a "proper distance toward matters and men." This was the only way for a proper differentiation between the *hybris* of the old German power-political ambitions, culminating in the Nazi regime, and the thought and strivings of a minority among this same German nation, which had been without any influence and impact before 1945. Max Weber had expressed their aspirations in his demand for an ethical foundation of professional politics.

Adenauer felt both justified and obligated to state in a radio address in 1945, that "The German people—the Nazi crimes notwithstanding, which the Germans in their overwhelming majority recognize and abhor today—must not be judged according to this period of their history alone."

But this statement implies still another fact which is essential for German history: the historic validity of a type of political thinking in Germany which meets Max Weber's definition. After the war, this tradition legitimated the "clear political conscience" of its exponents, while it became also obvious that these elements would be indispensable for the job of rehabilitation. But the call to leadership in no way dimmed their "sense of perspective," the recognition of the true dimensions of the German catastrophe, and the inescapable necessities which it imposed upon the German people. Adenauer, the primary representative of this mentality, manifested it when on July 10, 1945, amidst the still smoking ruins of the once glorious city of Cologne, he gave his first statement to the international press: "The occupation of Germany will be necessary for a long time to come. Germany is now incapable of ruling herself. But in order to give courage and hope to the nation, we must have as much freedom of action as possible, like a horse to which one gives the reins. The Germans are used to being told what they ought to do. Now, more than ever, they need to be told what they may expect of the future, and what they ought to do themselves!"

Ever since this statement Adenauer, with his characteristic passionate devotion to a cause, his realistic "responsibility toward the cause" of the defeated Germany, has striven untiringly, in countless speeches, private discussions and public rallies, to remind both victors and vanquished of their mutual obligations for a soul-searching, historic insight into the nature of this "cause." With the same passionate devotion with which he represented the spiritual and political interests of the German people before the Occupation Powers, he endeavored to raise the nation under his leadership to a clearer understanding of both the German and the international situation. With the assurance of a clear conscience and the emphatic sobriety of his political intellect, Adenauer reminded the Germans at every opportunity—and there were many— that they had indeed utterly and in every respect lost the war. More than that, he consistently tried to deepen the understanding of the German people for the unique position and responsibilities of the Allies vis-à-vis the new Germany. "We neither can nor should let ourselves assume that others have had a sudden change of heart in their attitude toward Germany," he said during the Federal Council debate about the Petersberg Contracts, on November 24, 1949. "This means plainly that we can only regain their confidence slowly, step by step. As it would be undignified and wrong if we should follow a policy of slavish submissiveness, it would be a stupid and unwise policy indeed if we should suddenly wish to assert ourselves, and I believe it would be a futile policy as well. We Germans must guard especially against the type of speculation that we could gain any benefits from a dissension among the big powers. Let me emphasize again: the method of German domestic and foreign policy must be, to work up slowly step by step; above all it must be a psychologically sound method designed to regain the confidence which we Germans, unhappily, have largely lost thanks to the Nazi system."

With this attitude and this realistic appraisal of the real opportunities and necessities within which the new German policy must work, Adenauer has to this hour served the German people tirelessly. In his policy he has taken the responsibilities toward the German people as seriously as the moral responsibility of the German nation for peaceful relations and cooperation with the outside world. This included in particular the sincere effort to repair the damages and make up for the crimes which the Nazi system in the name of the German people had committed abroad, so far as that was humanly possible. And out of this basic attitude Adenauer, as "Chancellor of the Vanquished," has honestly striven for a mutual understanding, for a reconciliation of all Germans among themselves, and of the German community with the world, with all those nations which after the war were ready to turn a new leaf in the book of history.

Any results which Adenauer was able to reap since those dark days in July of 1945 for the benefit of the German people, as well as for the entire world community, are based on that strange new phenomenon by which a wise statesmanship has enriched the course of German history: the quest for a channeling of the moral and political energies of the people, released or aroused in the great national catastrophe, into the task of creating a new way of life; a new order to be based upon the best traditions inherited from periods of German history which preceded the tragic defection from the Western community, and which attained a last glow in the intellectual loyalty to Europe of Leibniz and Kant. It is the sincere attempt of Adenauer to overcome the fatal *hybris* of German power politics, by tying the political thought and action of the new Germany to the basic moral laws in which any genuine and hence fruitful "policy" must be anchored. The great sage of Koenigsberg has left his own formulation of this principle, almost like an intellectual legacy for the present generation of Germans:

"All genuine politics," Kant says in his *Toward Peace Eternal*, "is unable to make a single step without first having given its homage to the moral laws. Although politics is a difficult art, its union with the moral laws requires no art at all; for the latter cuts the knot which politics is unable to solve when the two are in conflict. Politics must always bend its knee before right, but it may hope, even though slowly, to reach a level where it will shine in a steady glow."

All the analysis of the ideohistorical background and the actual achievements of the Chancellor's policy resolves itself into the basic understanding that Adenauer, as a statesman, has at all times simply and consistently followed the Kantian tenet—followed it with the tenacity that is so characteristic of him, and in profound obedience to the Divine law. This explains why the regeneration of political life in Germany has aroused visible confidence throughout the world, and at the same time has made its impact felt almost equally in the renascence of a genuinely European policy.

Even one so stubborn in his anti-German position as old Lord Vansittart recently had to admit: "My lifelong aversion against Germany is well-known; but now for the first time I perceive a German Government and a trend which might be altered in favor of Christian civilization." Vansittart's own changed attitude also reflects a significant link with Adenauer's achievements. To the extent that the reorientation of German politics toward European principles, under Adenauer's leadership, with its implicit creative regeneration of the best Western and German traditions, leads to the increasing stability of the European order and civilization, the historic role of a Christian Germany within a European com-

munity demands increasing recognition. An English contemporary of Kant's, the great statesman Edmund Burke, had
thus defined that role in 1791:

*"A great upheaval is underfoot in Germany, which in my
opinion will be more decisive for the fate of nations than the
revolution in France. It will be seen that the principles which
characterize the unrest and crisis of our time flow here from
a different source than in France. Does not Europe see that
the independence and balance of the German empire form
the core and being of that system, by which the European
powers maintain their balance? Does it not recognize that it
is of the greatest significance whether the system of public
law or the sum total of the laws, on which this independence
and balance are based, be maintained? If they should be destroyed, the entire European policy of more than two centuries would have been pitifully wrong!"*

What Burke had in mind were the beginnings and implications of Germany's fatal defection from the European
order, of which we have spoken earlier, and which culminated in the 1945 disaster. Vansittart now places his sympathetic confidence in a development which, under Adenauer's
guidance, strives for Germany's return to the same European
tradition and political system with which Edmund Burke was
concerned. One may argue about the historic context of
Burke's and Vansittart's respective positions vis-à-vis Kant's
and Adenauer's deeper ideohistorical understanding of Adenauer's European policy.

In his period of abstinence from all political activity during the Nazi era, Adenauer devoted himself to historical and
political studies. How fruitful these were may be seen in his
subsequent ability to grasp the problem of European unity
in the full depth of its world-wide implications. Its essential
aspects, especially the imperative need, from the German as
well as from the European point of view, for the spiritual
and political community of Germany with Europe, have al-

ready been extensively discussed. However, the world-wide implications of the European problem, especially those related to America's unique role in the European security system, call for at least a sketchy treatment along historicopolitical lines. In his countless statements in defense of the American policy in the Federal Republic, Adenauer revealed a unique knowledge of history and geopolitical understanding, as well as the logic of compelling statesmanship, when he again and again stressed the fundamental historic inevitability of this issue. His historical understanding leads him to the realization that Europe's freedom and security, originally an exclusively continental problem, has in our time grown into an intercontinental problem on the level of the world power relations and tensions between America and Russia. Adenauer's arguments dealing with the military implications flowing from this fact receive substantial support from the views of earlier observers of the historic evolution of this whole complex.

Outstanding among these witnesses is the great Frenchman, Alexis de Tocqueville, whom Dilthey called the greatest European political thinker since Aristotle. It is fair to consider him as the intellectual father of Adenauer's Western orientation and European policy. As early as 1835, de Tocqueville, with his singular knowledge of European history and an almost visionary genius, foresaw while he was engaged in his profound studies of Russia, and especially the development of democracy in America, that a world-wide dualism between America and Russia would arise with historic inevitability. It seems tragic now to note how little attention was given his insights by the statesmen who gave their final diplomatic and power-political sanction to the world-wide antithesis between Washington and Moscow, while essentially neglecting European interests.

"There are two great nations in the world today," de Tocqueville wrote in 1835, "which, while starting from different points of departure, are going toward the same goal: Russia and America. Both have grown up almost unnoticed, and while the attention of mankind was diverted by other things, both have suddenly emerged to a prominent place among the nations. Thus the world suddenly recognized the existence and greatness of both at almost the same moment. All the other nations seem to have reached their natural boundaries, and the only task left to them is the preservation of their power. But these two are still in the state of growth, while all the other nations are standing still, or are advancing only with great difficulty. The American must struggle with the natural wilderness of his country; but the foes of the Russians are men. The former struggles with the wilderness and the barbarism of the savages; the latter are fighting civilization, with all their weapons and artifice. Hence, while the conquests of the one are achieved by means of the plow, the other conquers with the sword. The Anglo-American attains his ends on the basis of his personal interests, and thus gives free reign to the unhampered effort and the common sense of his citizens. The Russian, on the other hand, embraces all authority in society with one strong arm. While the chief instrument of the former is liberty, that of the latter is servitude. Russia's and America's points of departure are as different as their development; nevertheless, each of these two seems chosen by Divine Providence to determine the destiny of one part of the globe."

Even more amazing is de Tocqueville's realization that this development calls for an *entente* between a united, strong Germany and France for a joint defense against the Russian danger. The great French thinker appears as Adenauer's teacher especially in this respect. Already in 1850 de Tocqueville refuted the arguments of a French neutralism which, inspired by fear, opposed the close collaboration of Germany and France. His refutation deserves our attention because of its almost uncanny timeliness.

In trying to allay French fears about the German unity movement of 1848 de Tocqueville pointed to an even greater danger, the Russian threat. His thinking was here completely in line with Adenauer's and that of numerous Frenchmen who have placed their confidence in him. "Should we wish that Germany become a united nation?" de Tocqueville asked. "Or do we want Germany to remain a poor conglomeration of separate entities under separate rulers? There is an ancient tradition in our diplomacy, which aims at keeping Germany divided among a great number of independent powers. Such an attitude was understandable at a time when there existed nothing beyond Germany except a half-savage Russia. But is that still the case in our own days? The answer to this question depends upon the answer to another:

"What exactly is the danger from Russia, which threatens European independence? It is my conviction that sooner or later our Western world will be in danger of falling under the despotism, or at least the direct and irresistible influence of the Csarist regime. That is why I feel that our first aim must be to further the unity of all German tribes, in order through them to oppose the influence of the Russians. The world is in a new and changed situation; we must adjust our old principles, and we must shed the fear that our neighbors will become too strong, so that one day they will be able, together with us, to push back the common enemy."

De Tocqueville thus recognized the historic importance of a close Franco-German collaboration even on the military level. And probably no one has struggled more passionately, ever since 1945, for a universal recognition of this insight, nor more honestly for its realization than his disciple, Konrad Adenauer. Even during the most difficult phases of his efforts, such as the restriction of German economic sovereignty through fusion of the West European mining and steel industries, the restriction of military sovereignty through the Paris treaties of October 23, 1954, and especially during the

Saar negotiations, the Chancellor has always been guided by his belief that "a community of European nations can only be built on the basis of healthy Franco-German relations."

Just as the great Frenchman had seen that the most sensitive spot in Franco-German relations was the French "fears," Adenauer also identified this as the central problem. For centuries such fears have undoubtedly affected an essential aspect of the French national character, and the terrible experiences of the last war have tended to turn the fear into a full-fledged national *neurosis*. The heated debate in the French parliament over the European defense community, in particular Edouard Herriot's gripping and emotional speech, demonstrated how little this whole complex is affected by rational arguments or practical political considerations. After all, we are here face to face with a type of problem rooted in the sphere of the emotional and moral forces of history, and which therefore can only be solved on that level. It is, ultimately, the problem of confidence among individuals and nations, manifestly an essentially psychological and moral one.

The almost miraculous impact of Konrad Adenauer's moral force once more shows itself in the tremendous difference between Franco-German relations at the end of the First and at the end of the Second World War. It is amazing how far Adenauer's name has become widely synonymous with the idea of confidence in the new Germany, even among many of the opponents of German rearmament. The confidence which the strong moral personality of the Chancellor has been able to inspire, particularly in France, a country so savagely devastated by Hitler, borders indeed on the miraculous.

Adenauer's background, the life of an extraordinary German, especially the organic growth from his beginnings as a highly talented administrative official, through his development in the vocation of the Catholic politician, into his present stature of Christian statesman of international repute, vouch for the safety of European peace and the well-being of the nations in Adenauer's hands.

There is an added safety element in the fact that the fulfillment of these lofty tasks is for the German Chancellor not solely a matter of passionate devotion to the hard, sober life of professional politics, but at the same time is a concern of conscience and of the heart. Konrad Adenauer knows that all true politics must in the last analysis be founded on service to man, if it is to live up to its mission. Let us therefore conclude this chapter by citing a simple confession, which reveals something of the feeling German heart under Adenauer's sometimes harsh appearance, and of his personality, so taut with political energies. This vital heartbeat is, perhaps, the most powerful among the resources from which this great statesman draws the strength for his extraordinary achievements.

"I am sometimes said to be too cold, too prone to let the head direct my actions," he said in his concluding speech at the Third Party Conference of the CDU, held in Berlin on October 19, 1952. "Well, dear friends, a man is sometimes different from what he seems. Someone who has to carry such an amount of political responsibility needs to have a warm heart. But he needs a cool head as well. For unless he is cool-headed, and unless he weighs everything very coolly and carefully, his warm heart might easily lead him astray."

VIII

Humanity and Conscience in Politics

Birthdays of statesmen remind us that even the greatest among them are not, after all, "immortals." As inevitably as all other mortal contemporaries, the creative movers and makers of the political sphere are subject to the natural order of birth and death, and therewith to the universal laws of physical and intellectual development, of being human and sharing the fate of common humanity. This is what makes the humanity and conscience of the true man of politics such a crucial factor in his maturing process: in his development from the early call to politics, through the progressive experiences of the years, to the fulfillment of statesmanship in the fullness of life, the decades of mature age.

In Konrad Adenauer's person this development of mind and conscience to the peaks of humanity and statesmanship has attained a unique and spectacular completion. What Germany's Federal President, Theodor Heuss, said, epitomizing the wisdom of the aging process, seems particularly pertinent for the Chancellor:

150

"One must be able to grow older, perhaps even old, with decency," this wise man said not long ago, "in order to retain one's chance to stay young. What that means is to be able to sense the stream of the generations in one's self, from the fathers to the grandchildren, to remain aware, on the long road toward death which we have been walking since childhood, of being links in a chain."

Adenauer's achievements as a statesman in the German and international developments of the past ten years have been so spectacular that in the eyes of most people both in Germany and abroad they have tended to overshadow the more intimate features of his personality. It is nevertheless true that the personality of Adenauer the statesman is nourished by a deep wellspring of genuine religious humanity. Konrad Adenauer's private life rests and still to this day feeds on the creative sources of the Christian family tradition together with the unique democratic tradition of the *Civitas Coloniensis:* while his moral personality and ethicopolitical existence draw their most vital religious energies from his partaking in the fountainheads of the Christian religion and his loyal sense of community with the Catholic Church.

In all these respects Adenauer the man and Christian is distinguished by a singular uprightness and straightforwardness of mind and heart. That for many of his contemporaries he may seem inaccessible and difficult to comprehend may merely indicate the extent to which they have been ready to sacrifice their own humbleness and the straightforwardness of a living conscience to the calculating coldness and unscrupulous pragmatism typical of the political and economic materialism of our time.

One who has the good fortune to meet the statesman, now in his eighty-second year, on a more intimate basis and experiences the living impact of his total personality—not only that of the statesman but of the man as well—realizes how profoundly mind and physique, intellectual faculties and conscience are interrelated and mutually interdependent in this extraordinary personality. And also how completely mind and heart are attuned to each other, evidencing the "wholeness" of the man, Konrad Adenauer's thorough humanity. Adenauer once told his friends, with some embarrassment, that one who must bear a great political responsibility needs a "warm heart," aside from a calmly calculating and soberly thinking "cool head."

Undoubtedly it is this "warm heart" from which Adenauer has always drawn the chief energies for his statesmanship and which has enabled him to grow "old" in the unique way one admires in his ninth decade as an extraordinary capacity for staying young. Adenauer, however, has been able to preserve for himself another inexhaustible source of inner youthfulness in his ability to keep on intimate terms with both family and nature—no matter how exacting the burden of his professional life—together with a deep religiousness and a humble faith in God, and an always stimulating contact with a group of friends. His gift for the preservation and loving care of the private sphere, in the circle of family and friends, has protected Adenauer from surrendering his home and private life to the kind of time-consuming and nerve-racking routine of social and representative obligations, which in every age has proved the undoing of many a political leader and statesman.

Because Adenauer has never been too fond of these things, some busy society circles to which he failed to open his home have accused him of social aloofness, if not outright "misanthropy." But at any genuine human contact Adenauer gives the lie to such accusations; they reveal how much the harassed Chancellor must suffer from the kind of frostiness in personal relations which seems to characterize our political everyday climate more than ever before. It must be this feeling which, on each Christmas Eve, moves him to seek the company of the "lost" orphans of Bonn and Niederdollendorf; in humble words he has voiced his gratitude for the experience of time spent among the children and grandchildren of mothers and fathers who are no longer among the living:

"It is always a great pleasure for me once in a while to find an hour's relaxation, because at all other times my road leads me up and down through a desert. This is why I am grateful for every hour I am allowed to be a human being among other human beings!"

His need, as well as his ability for being a mere "human being among other human beings" and to share their emotions, is probably one of the major explanations of the extraordinary human and emotional impact Adenauer enjoys among the German people. But there is, moreover, the great originality and effectiveness of his oratorical gifts, nourished precisely by this need and ability. Adenauer as an orator seems always intent, over and above the framework of the political debate and the official pronouncement, upon vindicating the true purpose of all political activity, i.e., to uphold morality and justice as a criterion and a means for the realization and protection of humanity and human freedom.

Whenever Adenauer is particularly concerned with these matters—which was probably the case whenever, during the past ten years, he has commented on issues of basic significance, or whenever he took an issue directly "to the people" —Adenauer's speeches appear to be more than a mere sober, rational discussion of the issue at hand; they seem to become a medium for voicing ethicopolitical insights, insights of the conscience and moral concerns. Added to this dual-level quality of content and technique, of motivation and objective in Adenauer's rhetorical performances, especially in certain crucial situations, is often a peculiar perceptiveness and warmth of heart—as he evinced in his Christmas speech of 1956.

From a purely methodological point of view this speech revealed the singular originality of Adenauer's particular brand of oratory. In a sense, his rhetorical performances are

never "speeches" in the ordinary meaning of the term—that
is, they never really belong in the realm of rhetoric, but,
thanks to the combination of all these elements they invari-
ably and in a curiously immediate way give the impression of
a kind of one-sided "conversation." Or, to put it differently:
*Adenauer never really talks "to" the people but seems always
to be conversing "with" them!* The vital harmony of these
dual elements, the practical and rational on the one hand,
and the voice of conscience on the other, or even the trinity
of mind, conscience and heart make the speech something of
a live *dialogue* between speaker and audience, with every one
of the latter feeling that he is being directly addressed, and
that what is said concerns him personally. To anyone who has
heard Adenauer's Christmas speech, or has read the published text—a worthwhile experience when one feels the need
for reflective self-appraisal and meditation—what might
sound somewhat complicated in this sketchy analysis will be
readily understandable: the astonishing fact that many of
Adenauer's public addresses and speeches produce the effect
of an actual conversation which, in its intrinsic seriousness
and cordiality, cannot fail to touch the heart—unless the heart
be supercharged with hostilities and resentments. And yet,
the full impact of this strange gift can only be experienced
if one is granted the privilege of a personal meeting with the
Chancellor, in which this extraordinary man can show himself unabashed as a "human being among other human
beings."

It is a testimony to the genuine imprint of his statesmanship that Adenauer, even in such private conversation, does
not try to conceal his concern for the fundamental political
issues, their implicit personal and ethical element, or, in
short, his own *conscience*. As a matter of fact, it is precisely
in relaxed conversation that the Chancellor, in these days,
reveals a degree of metapolitical motivation in his professional
thinking and searching which is rare for its acute intellectual

alertness in political leaders of the present or the past, who have crossed the threshold of their ninth decade. In a way, this is doubtless the result of the notable gift for politics which Adenauer seems to have received as a gift from God and which, in years of hard work, of self-improvement and service to his people, he has developed to its highest potentialities. But it also reflects that particular sobriety of mind and alertness of conscience which have been the steady companions of his evolution from politician to statesman. Only the combination of their effective, unyielding and therefore often painful and costly manifestations has produced the unique phenomenon of Adenauer's political stature in the eighties— a phenomenon for which Eduard Spranger, with his characteristic insight, has given the explanation that a man must live long with the state, studying its nature, must reflect about it and even suffer for it, before he is ready to take over its leadership.

Adenauer's international concepts have received a telling confirmation through the latest chain of events, beginning with the Polish and Hungarian developments and the crisis in Egypt, and including the return of the Saar to Germany. These events also confirmed the accuracy of his views on the reunification of Germany. What is more, these developments have strengthened the international scope of the Federal Republic as well as the moral and political prestige of the Chancellor to an extent which would have been inconceivable only a few short years ago.

It is due to these facts that the voice of the German Chancellor has attained such an eminent weight, especially recently. His speech on Budapest's "Bloody Sunday" (November 4, 1956); the official Government pronouncement on the international situation of November 8, 1956; his Christmas speech, and his address on the occasion of the return of the Saar (January 1, 1957) may be considered as the expressions of a Christian statesman's sense of responsibility toward Germany and Europe. More essentially, they represent the living voice of conscience, matured in reverence before God and in a genuine wisdom in political matters, reminding the West of the moral bases of freedom and law.

Those whom he thus addressed, primarily the German people and its friends abroad, might look upon the following excerpts from Adenauer's addresses as a wholesome opportunity to open their hearts and consciences once more to the full impact of the exhorting and guiding voice of one who is both a German and a European statesman:

It is true that tomorrow rests on today, and yet both today and tomorrow are founded on yesterday. Nothing in the world can shake this truth. We must all return into ourselves, once in a while, even to that in us which is of the past. And thus we must review our inner development. Only those who become aware of themselves in this manner can lead a life of awareness, a life worthy of the dignity of man. Failing this, one renounces one's very self, one's true personality.

There is certainly much that is good and beautiful, much honest effort and honest work in our time. And yet one thing, it seems to me, has become rare, one thing without which one cannot live if living is to be more than to vegetate through one's days as best one can. We seem to have lost something that was common to most people in the past, a sense of *inner harmony*. But where the inner harmony is lacking there is no inner strength, no equanimity, no calm, no contentment. I would be the last person to live only in the past, to think that all that was good is of the past. Man must strive forward, tirelessly and forever.

But a man must also recognize the peculiar dangers of his age, the age in which he has been placed, and he must take from the past that which was good in it. And it was part of the good things of the past that many, perhaps a majority of people, had reached a certain inner harmony which lent them a firmness, a steadfastness, an inner weight which enabled them to preserve their inner self even through confusing and insecure times.

An inner harmony possesses one who knows the difference between good and evil, and who is firmly resolved always to remain loyal to the good. This sense of inner harmony everyone must acquire for himself. That may take much serious effort, and much firm resistance against untoward influences, whether they stem from one's own inner self, or from without. But unless we possess this inner harmony, neither profit nor pleasure nor outward success can help us to attain an inner balance—and therewith the highest happiness which this life holds in store for us.

The division of our country is particularly painful for us on this Christmas holiday. True, hundreds of Christmas trees have been lit along the Iron Curtain for a common Christmas holiday. They carry our greetings across into the Soviet zone, where the people know only a dim reflection of the Christmas light. But the wound of our mutilated country continues to hurt and the time when reunification will become a reality seems far too long and too cruel to us. And yet, we may hope that the year 1957 will bring for our German brethren in the Soviet-occupied zone, if not the fulfillment of our common heartfelt desire, at least a tangible approach toward this fulfillment, because at last our hope seems to come true—as we begin to discern some movement in the rigid ranks on the other side.

The Germans in the East may consider the return of the Saar as evidence that even a steadfast policy based on truth and truthfulness may overcome grave differences through the medium of international agreements. Like ourselves, they will look upon these developments as a hopeful sign for a settlement in the East.

The Saar solution is in truth a fact of the greatest historical significance. And we may thank God for that; because now the road is open for a real, vigorous cooperation between our two nations in a common effort within their particular joint field of interest, which stems from the fact that they are neighbors, for a sincere common effort toward European integration, for their cooperation toward a free world!

Our world is chaotic and restless. It brims with unresolved problems. Yet the population of the Saar, as well as France and Germany, have shown that it is possible to resolve conflicts which seemed insoluble at first by applying the rights of man, the principle of free self-determination, in a spirit of reconciliation and peace. I do not abandon hope that even in the East solutions may be possible on the same basis—solutions which may turn out to be a blessing and bring well-being for all concerned!

We must overcome all conflicts, to work together in the great vital issues of our nation!

It should be the aim and purpose of any policy devoted to the promoting of peace to restore justice wherever it has been violated, and freedom wherever it is suppressed. And yet, in large sections of the world people have been deprived once more of their most elementary rights. Nations which, confident in their right of self-determination, attempted to restore a free order based on lawfully constituted governments have again been subdued, forced into totalitarian systems in which the concepts of democracy, freedom and justice are no longer recognized. The political picture has become even more confused because in other parts of the world, simultaneously, young nations without a proper share in the technological and cultural developments of the past centuries have applied their prerogative of self-determination, establishing new, influential, powerful political positions in the world. These developments have profoundly altered the concepts which were still accepted at the end of the war, and which found their expression, as in the Potsdam Agreement, resulting from the conferences of Yalta and Teheran.

Although it has been possible to eliminate tensions and conflicts in some parts of the world; although, on the other hand, certain contradictions have become manifest which cannot but further the development toward a healthy balance, there has nevertheless remained chaos in other sections of the world, and this chaos has even arbitrarily and irresponsibly been increased.

Freedom and self-determination ought to be recognized as valid principles everywhere. One would be endorsing a system of lawlessness if any nation were granted the right to interpret these concepts in its own fashion, and to invoke or reject these principles as it sees fit!

Both the written and the unwritten law must be the same for everyone, and all must equally renounce the use of force. Great and small powers must be equally bound by this principle—or else no one will feel bound by it. If the larger nations are not to have a prerogative to misuse their strength against a weaker nation, it must be equally impossible for the smaller nations to break treaties and agreements, in the conviction that the big powers, under present circumstances, will shrink from the risk of military involvement. Justice and law must apply to all without exception, otherwise they lose their binding force for anyone!

PART TWO

The Crucial Task: Reunification

IX

Problems of Reunification

Basic Considerations

It would be a mistake to approach the problem of the reunification of Germany from any one-sided, isolated and specific angle within the German evolution since 1945—whether that be Adenauer's personal achievement, or the domestic problems of the Federal Republic, or such distinctly international and ideological considerations as the possibility of a "Western," "Eastern," or even "neutralist" solution of this whole grave issue. Having attempted in the preceding chapters to understand the German postwar developments through an analysis of Adenauer's policy and of the ideopolitical Western orientation for which he stands, we must now broaden our scope in order to find a more suitable perspective for the specific problems of the German reunification question. The following considerations will show why this is necessary.

The reunification of Germany—notwithstanding its eminent significance for the rehabilitation of the German mind and life—is above all an international problem; the power-political realities of the East European nations, led by Russia, are at least as significant for the solution of this issue, if not actually more so, as the position of the West, including the Federal Republic itself.

Next to this fact any internal German aspect of the reunification problem appears of distinctly secondary importance. This is true even for the understandable national feelings of the German people and their various ideological expressions, the expressions of wounded national pride and their use, or misuse, by the different political parties. Or in other words, no matter how much the reunification question may be a vital, as well as legal, problem for the German nation as a whole, rather than the concern of any single political party; no matter how much it may be an essentially national issue of equal importance for every German citizen, it is at the same time (and possibly even more acutely) a matter of direct and vital concern for all those nations which since 1945 have been holding German territories in the East. Their involvement is due to the inescapable logic of cause and effect in political reality.

The net result of these facts is to rule out any real possibility of a peaceful solution for the reunification problem as long as those who actually wield power in these areas are supposed to look upon it exclusively as a demand raised by the German people; as long as Germany fails to evince the sincere and unmistakable desire to prevent any future misuse of these territories as a geopolitical and strategic basis for German aggression, after the manner of Hitler's aggression against the nations of Eastern and Western Europe. In such a perspective the reunification question appears ultimately as a problem of military security, and as a problem of the new Germany's willingness and ability to give the moral and political guarantees for her democratic organization, based on the principles of law, and her integration with a peaceful international order.

This is the only possible approach to an objective evaluation of what Adenauer, as Chancellor of the Federal Republic, has up to now been able to contribute toward the solution of the reunification problem. And only from such a perspective may we hope to gauge the issues which are as yet unresolved, because their practical solution has as yet been beyond the reach of Adenauer's domestic and foreign policy.

We may thus have to distinguish between Adenauer's actual efforts and achievements on the reunification problem and the things which, in the opinion of certain of his detractors, he failed to do although he would allegedly have been quite able to bring them about. On the other hand, we shall frankly and factually have to face those resistances which have prevented the free, democratic reunification of Germany ever since the Potsdam Declaration of 1945, especially those created by the Russians, which have limited and restricted Adenauer's efforts for the reunification of Germany since 1949.

Such an approach reveals essentially three different aspects of Adenauer's policy, what it has accomplished and its potentialities, which are really tantamount to three different stages in his political efforts:

One, the establishment of the Federal Republic and the recovery of full-fledged sovereignty, its ideopolitical and actual integration with the West—aspects which have been treated in the preceding chapters. Second, the consolidation and extension of the international potential of the Federal Republic, including the solution of at least one fundamental reunification problem in the West, i.e., the return of the Saar. And, third, the specific efforts for reunification in the East which entered a new phase with Adenauer's trip to Moscow in September 1955, and reached yet another level with the revolutionary events in Poland and Hungary of December 1956—a phase which it is still too early to assess in its full significance.

Future historians may be in a better position than we to judge the full scope of Adenauer's political achievements, and to evaluate with greater finality the fundamental significance of his achievements for the ultimate rehabilitation of Germany and Europe. When that time comes, it may be possible to talk with a greater measure of calm objectivity than has been possible under present conditions, both as to the merits of his statesmanship and as to some of the criticism voiced by his political opponents. In the final analysis, the eventual shape and time of reunification in the German East may depend somewhat less on Adenauer's intentions and efforts than on the developments in Moscow. In other words, it may depend on the ultimate triumph of tendencies there involving at least the recognition of Adenauer's basic efforts, i.e., of the peaceful, democratic, German and European spirit now at work in the Federal Republic. Such a full and fair understanding is needed if a free and united Germany in an equally free and peaceful Europe shall become a reality—a Germany with which even her neighbors to the East, above all Russia, may live and work in peace. Moscow cannot possibly hope to achieve such a solution from Europe unless it arises out of a Germany inspired by the ethical fervor of the "Chancellor of the Vanquished," acting and evolving its policies in his spirit. Anybody who is really familiar with, or at least anxious to understand, the Chancellor's efforts and his true attitude concerning the reunification problem at this point will know that this is so.

International Aspects

In the preceding chapters we have tried to demonstrate that the domestic German opposition to Adenauer's foreign policy originated primarily in the fundamental gap which separates the Chancellor and his party, the Christian Democratic Union (CDU-CSU), from the Social Democratic Party

PROBLEMS OF REUNIFICATION

on the issue of the international implications of Germany's position following the collapse of 1945. Adenauer, the political realist, especially since he became the Chancellor of the Federal Republic has tried to steer a foreign policy course aiming at the liquidation of that heavy moral and political mortgage with which the Nazi system had burdened the German people. By contrast, the Social Democrats have to this moment opposed Adenauer's foreign policy on grounds of purely domestic considerations and claims. They have chosen to ignore that mortgage which has weighed so heavily upon the German postwar developments, due to Hitler's policy of aggression and the aggressive warfare of the armies of the Third Reich against the nations of Europe. For the Social Democrats this has meant that they have insisted on viewing the reunification issue primarily and almost solely as a German problem, with the result that they have continuously clamored for the satisfaction of the natural and just demands of the German people for the restoration of their basic unity, while ignoring the equally natural and just demands above all of Germany's neighbors to the West and East which these nations had to raise before being able to consent to reunification. This situation has been at the root of the highly unfortunate dualism prevailing in the Federal Republic to this very day, which has overshadowed all efforts toward realizing the reunification goal. It has prevented the unanimous rallying of parliament and political parties behind Adenauer's international efforts in this field, which would correspond to the basic unanimity that in fact characterizes German domestic attitudes. Undoubtedly, large segments of the opposition, including the most farsighted among the Social Democratic leaders, are well aware of these international implications. Yet, they have so far failed to work with sufficient energy for a realistic assessment—which could only mean the frank and concrete political recognition of the international aspects—of the reunification problem inside the Social Democratic Party, or at any rate have failed to influence the over-all policies of the party in this respect. The deeper reasons for this failure must be sought not only in the ideological blind alley into which the Social Democrats have got themselves since 1945 —in contrast to the attitude of the French, Belgian and British Socialists—because of their obstinate clinging to a vision of Europe and a concept of the European balance of power harking back to the days before World War II. The reason lies just as much in the ideopolitical crisis and the confusion in moral and political values now reigning among German Social Democrats which has prevented them from identifying the moral and political problems of the reconstruction of Europe, including the German reunification problem, with the clarity that has distinguished Chancellor Adenauer's foreign policy.

It seems impossible, in view of these facts, that there will ever be a full and fair recognition of the "German position" on the reunification issue unless and until the international facets of the problem are fully and fairly understood and recognized inside Germany.

History bears out this view by reminding us that the dismemberment of Germany's basic unity and the foreign occupation of German soil occurred, after all, not as a result of some actions on the part of outside powers in violation of international law, or of an unprovoked military assault on the part of foreign armies. On the contrary, far from foreign powers having assaulted Germany, it was Nazi Germany which has assaulted her neighbors, and it was the armies of the Third Reich which originally brought war to these neighboring countries. And it was in the course of the defensive actions of the invaded countries, set off and necessitated by these acts, which led to the *military* fact of Germany's total occupation in 1945, and which at the same time involved the *political* fact of the total obliteration of the former Germany's national and international sovereignty as stipulated in the decrees of the Potsdam Conference. Thereby Germany's territorial and political integrity had been surrendered, both in terms of international law, and in actual political fact, to the unqualified will of the victorious powers. It was now squarely up to these powers to determine both the extent of *compensation* for the damages and injustices they had suffered, as well as the extent of the *guarantees* they felt they would need in the interest of their future security.

This dual claim for physical compensation on the one hand and political and moral security safeguards on the other has been, and still is, the ultimate basis for the international implications of the German reunification issue ever since the Potsdam Conference. Nothing in the fundamental political and moral justice of these claims has been diminished or invalidated by the fact that the victorious powers, immediately following the Potsdam Conference, began to disagree among themselves as to the extent and the methods for the realization of these claims—disagreements which over the years have led to those complexities of the German problem which today are apparent especially in the international implications of the reunification question.

Within the last few years we have obviously seen an at least partial solution of these problems, especially as regards the Western, in particular French, aspects of the reunification issue. And there is now at least the semblance of a possibility of developments in Eastern Europe, which might ultimately cause Russia to modify her position on the reunification of Germany. And yet, no matter how much the Russian, and above all the Polish, attitude on German reunification might change in the years to come, neither Russia nor Poland will be able to forgo a sound solution of the following set of problems and demands. This is why the political parties and their responsible leaders in the Federal Republic, who are seriously striving for a peaceful and fair solution of the problem, will always have to keep them in mind.

To begin with, irrespective of present ideological forms of their political existence and system of government, one must grant the Russians the right to secure for themselves effective international guarantees against any future misuse of a re-united Germany as a basis of military aggression against Russia. Germany's other neighbors to the East, especially Poland and Czechoslovakia, are entitled to ask for similar guarantees.

The Russians furthermore, as well as the Poles, must be given guarantees against the contingency that the wretched spirit of Prussian militarism and power-hungry Pan-Germanism, the Nazi ideology or any other totalitarianism should again take hold of the German people. Therewith, the question of restoring the unity of Germany becomes also and primarily a highly ideopolitical and ethical one. Its solution is conceivable only on the basis of the most serious German efforts aimed at bringing about the kind of atmosphere in Russo-German and Polish-German relations in which it might be possible to approach the problem of redeeming the heavy moral mortgage burdening the German conscience—that mortgage due to the aggressions and crimes against the East committed by the Third Reich. We shall show further on how Adenauer, at the Moscow Conference, managed to make an essential contribution in this respect; and how, on the other hand, the solution of the reunification problem in the German West, as signified by the return of the Saar, must be credited entirely to the Chancellor's prolonged efforts toward generating an atmosphere of moral and political confidence in the Federal Republic among its French neighbors—which proved to be an indispensable prerequisite for a solution of the Saar problem in line with Germany's interests.

German Attitudes

The implicit dualism of Germany's position toward the international aspects of the reunification issue is not confined to the problems which have been discussed so far. It is also evident in the many different ways in which Germans tend to interpret the international responsibilities and obligations jointly assumed by the signatory powers of the Potsdam Agreement, especially England, Russia and the United States, for the restoration of German unity. The same dualism tinges the various German views as to the practical foreign policy course the Federal Republic should steer in relation to the guarantor powers of the Potsdam Agreement, so as to cause them to live up to these obligations. This is precisely the crux of the differences between Adenauer and the Social Democrats, with Adenauer following the road of "Western" orientation, while the Social Democrats chose a deliberate "neutralist" position. Ever since the days of the Bonn Agreements * this attitude has caused the Social Democrats to maintain a totally negative attitude on all those crucial matters of German foreign policy whose positive solution has distinguished Adenauer's international achievements since 1949, marking so many milestones in the rise of the Federal Republic to a place of equality among the nations. Recently one of the Chancellor's closest confidants, Karl Arnold, formerly Minister President of the state of Rhineland-Westphalia, speaking in Essen on January 10, 1957, in words which were directly inspired by Adenauer, has presented a sober balance sheet of the neutralist foreign policy of the Social Democratic opposition, from 1949 to date: "The Social Democratic Party's 'No' to the Bonn Agreements— which after all have brought us the cessation of dismantling operations; the SPD's 'No' to the Council of Europe; the SPD's 'No' concerning the Schuman Plan; the SPD's 'No' regarding the German policy in the Saar question; the SPD's 'No' concerning the German membership in NATO; the

---

* The "Petersberger Abkommen" was immediately dubbed "Bonn Agreements" by the State Department, as I recall from my own work in the Department's Bureau of German Affairs at the time—Transl.

SPD's 'No' on the question of Western European Union; and so forth. . . . And anyone who thought that the bloody Hungarian events would cause the German Social Democrats to change their attitude—which to be sure they did for their Icelandic associates—has been in for a disappointment. For what was the SPD's inspired answer to the Hungarian developments? Merely another 'No,' incomprehensible though it may seem! The SPD now demands that the Federal Republic should quit NATO, that defense community which guarantees the protection of the great power of the United States for more than 50 million Germans in the Federal Republic!"

It might be interesting for Arnold's compatriots to study the balance sheet which he offered in the same speech, in assessing the sober policy of Adenauer and his Christian Democratic Union and its real achievements in German foreign policy since 1949:

"Our policy based on the solidarity with the West—a policy painfully wrested from the Social Democrats—may have brought us closer to reunification than we were some years ago. For the net effect of our policy of solid friendship with the West—rather than the SPD's invariable 'No'—is that, in our negotiations on this issue with Moscow, we do not stand alone, but enjoy the support of the United States and the other Western powers. Thus, our position is far stronger, more flexible and generally more hopeful than it would be if we were left to shift for ourselves. It was our policy—not the propaganda of the Social Democrats—which netted us the Moscow invitation and enabled us to bring the prisoners-of-war back to their native country. It was our policy—not the 'No' of the SPD—which produced the diplomatic note to the Soviet Government of September 1956 suggesting the start of negotiations on the reunification of Germany. And, finally, it was our policy of practical economic and political cooperation and concrete contractual agreements with France—not the SPD 'No'—which produced the diplomatic climate for the return of the Saar!"

Finally, since last year a third position of "qualified neutralism" has crystallized, standing somewhere in the middle between Adenauer's point of view and the position of the SPD. This is the position taken by Thomas Dehler's Free Democratic Party (FDP) which of late has swung into opposition against the Adenauer government. The ideological and psychological effects of this "third" position have done their share in contributing to the confusion surrounding the reunification issue, especially among middle-class groups in the Federal Republic. Perhaps the most representative and valuable expression of this brand of opposition to Adenauer's policies may be found in a book by a well-known newspaper man, Paul Sethe, published on the eve of the Hungarian revolt under the title: *Between Bonn and Moscow*. There is much that is objectively interesting and well worth being taken to heart in this challenging volume. Still, for those who are deeply concerned about German reunification Sethe's book remains disappointing, as the author fails to offer any real solution, in keeping with the political realities, among his many noteworthy "conclusions." The reason is that Sethe is prevented from presenting convincing conclusions, because he does not take the trouble to follow through his half-hearted critique of the Russian attitude, or his half-hearted approval of Adenauer's position—about which he avoids being specific—to the logical end. Nevertheless, Mr. Sethe deserves our gratitude even here, because his perfectly sincere indecision is an accurate reflection of the type of "German attitude" about reunification which has become the rule among certain segments of the German middle classes. For these groups the Chancellor's position is too "Catholic"—or even too "clerical"—while the Social Democratic position is felt to be too "leftist," or even "revolutionary." Thus, Sethe's book will remain a valuable document for the crisis of the bourgeois "center," the crisis of a certain kind of political liberalism which results from a deep-seated inability to meet the crucial problems of a new type of international reality and international thinking, and whose roots must be traced both into the past and into our immediate historical situation.

The Hungarian events should have made it obvious for all the advocates of an "internal German," neutralist solution, how little an isolated, neutralized Germany may expect by way of true reunification in peace and freedom from Moscow's graces, even under its present "destalinized" label. But for all the evidence which the international crisis of the final months of 1956 has supplied, neither the Social Democratic nor the Free Democratic opposition have revised their stand sufficiently to support the Chancellor's policies. As a matter of fact, even the return of the Saar has failed to pacify the opposition although it should have represented a telling theoretical as well as practical justification of Adenauer's foreign policy, especially in his handling of the German unity problem. Actually, the exact opposite happened: to the extent that a majority of the Social Democratic and neutralist arguments against Adenauer's policy were crumbling under the weight of recent developments, the opposition seemed impelled to concentrate on other domestic facets of the reunification problem. Their chief aim was the revival of deep-seated issues of national pride, in particular the demand for resuscitating Berlin as the capital of the Federal Republic— an objective which was publicized with fervor, as if its realization alone would decide the fate of German unity. Early in January, 1957 the Federal President, Theodor Heuss, took the opportunity of a short stay in Berlin to appeal for greater levelheadedness and political realism since he felt this type of agitation might tinge the domestic debate on the reunification problem with dangerous nationalistic emotions. Soberly and deliberately he cautioned his audience:

"Trying to proclaim Berlin already at this time the seat of

government and parliament is not a matter for a decision to be taken overnight, possibly even right now, amidst great romantic excitement; nor is it any mark of true patriotism; on the contrary, in view of the prevailing confused world situation, this is an issue on which passionate feelings must be kept in check by *a sober assessment of the actual power relationships* on the part of everybody—I repeat, everybody concerned. That does not mean that we should once more be 'patient.' Of course not; our inner restlessness is our perennial companion in this age, and the speaker would be as bored as his listeners in forever counseling patience. But the point is *to avoid self-deception!"*

Unfortunately, German public opinion has paid little heed to these words, much as the appeal for sober political judgment and the caution against ideological self-deception seems called for in the current West German atmosphere, and although the Federal President, by common consensus, is recognized to be above party politics. The fact that Adenauer's moral and political prestige rose perceptibly during the international crisis around the turn of the year 1956–57 and that the opposition reacted by mounting a propaganda campaign with distinct political overtones, with the result of creating an almost metapolitical confusion of German public opinion, would have seemed to make Heuss's appeal even more necessary. The propaganda of the opposition conducted on a level of narrow party self-interest, seeks above all to foment the national resentments against Germany's continued division by harping on natural patriotic feelings, from a knowledge that the broad masses are all the more susceptible to oversimplified political panaceas, the less feasible they prove to be in the hard daily realities of practical politics. The visitor from abroad who had the opportunity, during those critical months, to get a firsthand view of the various shades and hues of the German attitude on the reunification question, and to observe its odd composition of genuine patriotic sentiments

and phony nationalistic frustrations had to draw the following conclusions from intimate contacts with a cross section
of all groups in the Federal Republic:

At least half the population in the Federal Republic, all
the propaganda of the opposition notwithstanding, stands
unreservedly behind Adenauer's policy of "the sober assessment of power realities," both in foreign affairs in general
and on the reunification issue in particular. It is, of course,
that same "German position" which Konrad Adenauer has
for years advocated in practice and theory, and which is based
on a realistic assessment of the fundamental factors of the
East-West conflict and their crucial significance for a healthy
policy of European unity and German reunification. In
Adenauer's own words:

"The division of Germany is not due to any dispute among
Germans, but to the East-West conflict. The world is not divided because Germany is divided, but the division of Germany is due to the current division of the world. Therefore the
division of Germany can be overcome only through a universal
relaxation of tensions. We believe that the West, if politically
and militarily united, is capable of bringing about a peaceful
relaxation of the East-West conflict through a concentrated
diplomatic effort thereby solving also the German reunification problem and the problem of the Oder-Neisse line.
Neither peace nor our own freedom must be imperiled
thereby." (March 19, 1953)

And: "The restoration of Germany's unity is only a partial
problem within the great conflict which today separates East
and West. Therefore, it can only be solved within the framework of a universal relaxation of tensions. I am nevertheless
firmly convinced that the German people will recover their
unity." (August 6, 1952)

It is due to this sober political realism that Adenauer has
always considered a united—and, hence, strong—Europe as
the primary condition for Germany's reunification.

"To say that we consider the unification of Europe as a so-called substitute for the reunification of Germany would be absolutely wrong," he said on January 5, 1956. "Above all, the reunification of Germany, in peace and freedom, remains the supreme objective of German policy. What is more, the realization of the European idea is for us, among other things, a means toward this end, a highly important means to bring us closer to the goal of reunification. Lastly, however, to this very day, I remain convinced that our continent must be united for Europe's own sake because this is a question of life and death for the European continent."

With similar clearsightedness Adenauer has always insisted that an isolated German initiative for opening negotiations with Moscow—for which his opponents have clamored with considerable propagandistic vigor—would not bring Germany any closer to the reunification goal, while such a course would lack the responsible and active support of the Western powers.

"The Federal Republic," he said on May 27, 1955, "has ratified the Paris Treaties and joined the Western European Union. According to the London Protocol of October 3, 1954, this step gave effect to the contractual obligations, assumed by the three Western powers, under which the establishment of a completely free and united Germany, by peaceful means, remains a basic objective of their policies. The other member nations of the North Atlantic Treaty Organization have endorsed this aim. This means the contractual obligation that these powers will not agree to any settlement which would establish, or be predicated upon, the division of Germany. In the past the American, British and French Governments have repeatedly expressed endorsement of this principle. The government of the Federal Republic as well has reaffirmed this position at every opportunity." The rather emotional and illusory concept of a "direct solution" through direct, separate negotiations with the Russians—something which certain opposition groups have insistently demanded, and the idea of a renewed, direct initiative for negotiations between Bonn and Moscow—a demand raised at regular intervals, with unvarying monotony as well as vagueness, by the Social Democrats—have always been countered by the Chancellor with the reminder that a successful practical policy may involve some inevitable detours, as well as a great deal of patience and faith.

"We all must realize," he said on July 16, 1952, "that our way toward securing the reunification of Germany in peace and freedom in a free Europe requires a great deal of time and patience, faith and persistence."

And on February 22, 1954: "Wherever anything happens that furthers a lessening of tension in the international conflict, something happens also in the German interest. Within the framework of a universal global settlement a solution of the German problem would be comparatively easy. But even with every partial settlement the solution becomes somewhat easier. Impatient elements inside Germany may consider this as a detour. But it is better to reach one's objective by a detour than not to reach it at all. A successful policy for the reunification of Germany rests to no small extent on the insight that detours are unavoidable, on a realization of the importance of the indirect method!"

And: *"In time, even Soviet Russia will understand that she does not possess unlimited power. We have again made friends among the nations of the free world, and this free world stands on Germany's side. Let us be wise; let us neither jeopardize nor precipitate anything; let us merely stay firm in our resolve that we shall once more be reunited!" (June 28, 1953)*

The Western Solution: The Return of the Saar

The Moral Implications

Some day historians may cite the reunification of the Saar with the German Federal Republic as a particularly telling example of a type of policy and its conciliatory and constructive effects, which flows from a conscientious understanding of the moral obligations implicit in the concepts of law and freedom. Certain significant metapolitical relations between Frenchmen and Germans underlay this event. Without proper regard for these psychological elements, the political act of the return of the Saar on January 1, 1957, and its validity in terms of international law would have been simply inconceivable. The reader of the present volume will have no difficulty in identifying these elements—as far as they may be identified with any single person—with the moral prestige and the policy of Konrad Adenauer. In his role as "Chancellor

179

of the Vanquished" he focused his efforts upon a solution of the Saar problem in the spirit of a genuine Franco-German understanding. What Hubert Ney, Minister-President of the Saar, said during the official ceremony at Saarbruecken may stand as an impressive testimony to this spirit:

"If politics, irrespective of legal claims and prerogatives, may be defined as the art of making the difficult possible, then we owe a debt of gratitude on this day to the foreign policy of the Federal Chancellor, his striving for the reunification of our nation in peace and freedom and, moreover, for a solution of the vital problems of the European nations on the basis of a good-neighborhood policy with France. *It is thanks to his unerring policy of Franco-German understanding that the atmosphere of confidence has come about, in which a fair and just solution of the Saar problem has been possible.*

"And we owe a particular debt of gratitude to the Federal Chancellor for never having abandoned his conviction, practical considerations notwithstanding, that the German population of the Saar must retain its freedom of self-determination, one of the fundamental prerogatives of Western civilization; that we must be allowed to determine our future by means of a free and unhampered plebiscite. We have considered, and still consider this as the due recognition of our right to share in the shaping of our own future, as mature citizens, and of the fact that we have been called upon to share the responsibility for the fundamental problems of our time.

"We have used this right of self-determination with a sense of responsibility before our conscience, before the community of our nation and before the tasks of the European community of nations which we desire to create jointly with our neighbors.

"If France, by recognizing the free plebiscite, has set an example here in the Saarland for the coming community of

European nations, in accordance with her own great tradition of freedom, we Germans living at the French border know how to appreciate the human and political significance of this fact, the recognition of our freedom of self-determination —we who are now the first to extend the hand of friendship across the border.

"While the governments in Bonn and Paris, in tireless and unwavering efforts, have for years walked the road of cooperation, we on our part are gratified that the Saarland has become a milestone on this road toward understanding, at whose end stands the goal of lasting friendship between Germany and France."

It was in the same spirit that Chancellor Adenauer, during the same ceremony, expressed his gratitude to France:

"In this hour our thoughts turn to France. This renunciation has not been easy for France; the war has left its cruel wounds. We needed much patience and readiness to wait, so that France would have the time to acquire the *atmosphere of confidence in the new Germany* which alone permits the spirit of reconciliation, understanding, neighborliness and friendship to grow. For centuries distrust, even hostility, have existed between these two neighbors, to the detriment of both nations and of Europe. Ever since the seventeenth century the Saar problem has played its disturbing, poisonous role. All this is now past! We thank God for that, now that the road is open for a genuine, vigorous cooperation between these two nations, for a common effort in the specific areas of interest growing out of our neighborly relations, for a close cooperation for the establishment of a peaceful world!"

If one views the development of Franco-German relations since 1945 in their entirety, without bias or prejudice, one can hardly blame Adenauer for looking upon the Saar solution as a special reward for his personal efforts, including his personal cultivation of French public opinion. His primary aim was to create a real atmosphere of confidence among the

French in the sincerity of German postwar policies and the aim of liquidating the unhappy debt with which the Nazi regime had saddled the German people.

The first step toward any diplomatic action after 1945, in this sense, was the German recognition of the crimes committed against France; the premise, at the same time, for the practical political means by which Germany might be able to make up for the damage she had inflicted, whether by means of reparations, cession of territories, or whatever else. Such were, of course, primarily questions of practical concern, while the first was a problem of ethical considerations, of "guilt, repentance and atonement"—and, hence, an eminently ethical and metapolitical problem. What further complicated matters was the traditional moralistic emphasis characteristic of French political thinking since the First World War—which hindered a truly "rational" settlement between the two nations. For the solution laid down in the Treaty of Versailles was, as the historical perspective reveals beyond question, an extremely doubtful solution indeed. Its effect was to permit those Germans who bore real guilt to escape a genuine acknowledgment of the moral implication, while preventing the innocent from acknowledging a qualified co-responsibility as a basis for a rational policy of moral and political rehabilitation.

And so the excessive moralism of French politics during that period, plus the moralizing hypocrisy of the Versailles Treaty on the one hand, and German unwillingness to face up to the truth, together with outright nationalistic amorality on the other hand, created a deadlock. Together, these elements prevented the development, during the Weimar Republic, of an atmosphere of confidence in German politics on the part of the French as well as a genuine German understanding for the French desire for moral and political guarantees.

In view of the ethical implications of the Saar settlement

it is important to recall these facts because they highlight the fundamental changes which have taken place in the meantime among the French as well as the Germans, both in the relations of the two neighbor nations and in their attitude toward the liquidation of the results of the First and Second World Wars. Konrad Adenauer's contribution to this particular issue in his role of "Chancellor of the Vanquished" after World War II has been discussed in the preceding chapters. Not impossibly, he might have influenced the course of Franco-German relations with some success even after the First World War if the conditions we have just described had not obviated any genuine rational and moral regeneration in the policies of both countries. This, however, would have presupposed quite a different climate also for the so-called "indemnification" and reconstruction policies of the Weimar Republic, in place of the highly dubious "policy of international understanding" and the inevitable selfishness of the political parties—factors which blocked the rise of so scrupulous a personality as Konrad Adenauer to a position of responsible leadership in the period between 1921 and 1926.

One might recall, in this connection, the dramatic appeal which Adenauer, as President of the German Catholic Conference meeting in Munich in 1922, addressed to the French Catholics: "The German people have been starved and trampled upon. A confession of guilt has been extorted from the broken-down nation, conditions have been imposed upon us designed to stamp out our national and political existence, to destroy our economy, to abandon millions to slow death by starvation, to keep the rest in unbearable servitude and slavery. There is not a single document in European history, whether during the Middle Ages or in modern times, which defies all human and Christian principles as blatantly as does the Dictate of Versailles. I ask, I beg of the Catholics in the United States, Belgium and England, the Christians through-

out the world, all who still confess in the name of Christ:
help us! Remember your faith, your Christian denomination!
Prevent the death of a sixty-million nation!

*"My appeal goes out especially to the French Catholics:
France is torturing us, your own co-religionists! In fairness
to France I believe that France acts as she does because she
believes that this is how she must act! But believe us: France
is mistaken, there are other ways for France to obtain what
is her due! Let us get together, French Catholics, together let
us search for a way which will be helpful for both our nations!"*

For Adenauer the search for a "common road" toward an
understanding between the two nations has always been a
concern of the heart, as much as a question of conscience.
Ever since his great speech at the Guerzenich, at his inauguration as Lord Mayor of Cologne—against the background of
the feverish wartime nationalism of 1917—Adenauer strove
with growing seriousness for a better Franco-German understanding as the moral and political basis for a vigorous Europe united in freedom and peace. The best testimony for
these efforts are his passionate appeals addressed to the responsible political leaders in Europe, as in his acceptance
speech for the office of curator at the University of Cologne,
which he had founded in 1919; or his appeal during the
ceremony for the liberation of Cologne, in the night of
January 31, 1926. In his dramatic warning in 1919 he had
addressed himself to the conscience of all true Europeans,
cautioning them against the fatal implications of the Versailles dictate, then in its preparatory stages: a warning which,
let it be noted, anticipated in precise detail the tragic developments of the European catastrophe up to 1945:

*"Whatever the ultimate shape of the peace treaty, here on
the Rhine, at the ancient international crossroads, German
civilization and the civilization of the Western democracies
will meet during the decades to come. Unless a genuine*

reconciliation is possible between them, unless the European nations learn to recognize and cultivate that which is common to all European civilization notwithstanding the justified preservation of their respective national characteristics, unless it becomes possible once more to unite the nations through cultural understanding, unless in this way we shall be able to prevent a new war among the nations of Europe, European world leadership will be forever lost!"

Speaking on the torch-lit Cathedral square in Cologne, during the dramatic night of January 31, 1926, Adenauer once again appealed to the European conscience. At the same time, he expressed his appreciation for the attempt of the British occupation forces—which had just evacuated Cologne —to accord the defeated German nation fair treatment:

"Hard has been our lot under the heavy fist of the victor during these seven long years," he said then. "But today, in this sacred hour, let us not mention these things; yes, we wish to be fair, despite everything we have gone through; let us recognize that the enemy who has now left our city observed the rules of fair play in the field of politics. Let us hope that the years of suffering have not been in vain for us; that a genuine new spirit will from now on arise among the European nations. The principles of justice and morality, recognized for the relations among individuals, according to which all men are free and equal, must become recognized in fact, not merely in words, also among the community of nations!"

At least two things are obvious from these brief references to Adenauer's earnest, tireless efforts as Lord Mayor of Cologne during the Weimar period in the interest of a better Franco-German understanding and the realization of the European idea. First, that Adenauer, after 1945, was uniquely qualified—unlike most of the leading men of the Weimar generation—to represent Germany's interests and obligations in a Franco-German understanding and in the rehabilitation of Europe. And, second, that his efforts during the Weimar era had succeeded in earning him an extraordinary prestige among many of the intellectual and political leaders of France. Later, his uncompromising rejection of the Nazi system and his self-effacing stand during the Third Reich added a special moral sanction to this prestige.

Here is one of the deeper causes for the astonishing sympathy with which the leading French politicians after 1945 met Adenauer's efforts for Franco-German understanding and practical collaboration. These circles were fully convinced of the sincerity of Adenauer's European idea, precisely because it had its legitimate intellectual and political roots in his earlier efforts as Lord Mayor of Cologne. Several times during the Hitler years, whenever the conversation got around to the splendid "maire de Cologne," I had occasion to hear confirmation of the extraordinary French respect and admiration for Adenauer from such a wide range of political leaders as Léon Blum and Geneviève Tabouis, Herriot, Henri de Keryllis and Flandin, down to Laval and even Charles Maurras. During my visit to Cardinal Jean Verdier, the liberal, democratic and fiercely militant archbishop of Paris, back in 1939, the cardinal produced an extremely interesting newspaper clipping from his files which had aroused his interest in the Lord Mayor of Cologne as early as 1921. It was an editorial from the then leading French daily, Le Temps, dated June 16, 1921, containing an appraisal of the "maire de Cologne"; and it seems memorable today for two reasons. For one thing, the editorial represents a tangible refutation of the myth about Adenauer as the "Francophile separatist." What is more, it contains an almost psychic appraisal of Adenauer's significance and future career.

"The most spectacular thing in Cologne is not the cathedral, but the mayor of the city. This man, or rather this superman, manages to fill with his activity the entire city, the harbor and the surrounding countryside. And nobody in Germany should be surprised if he should one day step into the post of Reichschancellor Wirth. For, as even his foes must admit, he possesses the qualifications of a top-flight administrator in addition to actual leadership qualities, including a knack for giving orders. But in our opinion, it is not merely his valuable qualities and his brilliant future which make this Balzac-type figure, with its half Gothic, half modern features, so interesting. Perhaps he does not always observe the rules of fair play toward us, but play it is nevertheless, and it is fascinating to watch how his well-ordered German brain makes use of the *divide et impera* formula—which has become something of a public utility since the days of Louis XI."

Thus, Adenauer's role in the pattern of Franco-German relations between the First and Second World Wars helps to explain the attitude of the Fourth Republic toward the German Federal Republic. Yet one must also consider the internal factors which have contributed to the profound change in the French attitude toward Germany, from the Weimar Republic to the so-called "Adenauer-Germany." Between 1919 and 1933, the French attitude was determined by the spirit of the Versailles Treaty, including all the devastating implications of the idea of annexation and revenge. Much in contrast, the France of the Fourth Republic has oriented its relations with postwar Germany essentially on the idea of the European community, in terms of both its actual political and its moral implications.

This change has been symbolized by the changed role of the city of Strasbourg. After the First World War Strasbourg was the intellectual center of that specific brand of French chauvinism which, under the leadership of Maurice Barrès, advocated the annexation of the Rhineland and the Saar, with the aid of the Separatist Movement in Germany. After World War II the same Strasbourg became the intellectual focus and administrative seat of the European movement, the stage for the moral understanding and the practical political exchange between the new France and the new Germany represented by men like Robert Schuman and Konrad Adenauer. French Saar policy from 1919 to 1935 had been largely responsible for blocking a genuine Franco-German understanding. But after 1945 it was the Saar which became a mainstay in the reconciliation between the two countries, the test for the moral fiber of the European movement, as well as a practical instrument for a progressive realization of its basic principles—the rights of man and the free self-determination of nations. In this sense the Federal President, Heuss, could celebrate the vindication of these principles through the return of the Saar—a high point in the policy of Franco-German understanding—as an obvious triumph of moral over political concerns, an event in which "the eternal had won out over the forces of our passing contemporary scene."

Political Realities

The history of the first ten years in the fight for a united Europe has yet to be written. When that is done, Franco-German relations with regard to the Saar between 1946 and 1956 will emerge as the core in an analysis of the potentialities and progress of Franco-German collaboration toward the European community. These developments have proven one thing beyond question: the extraordinary reality of the European idea as a political factor in concrete Franco-German diplomatic relations. This is especially true in the sense which Adenauer has so often emphasized, namely that only through close cooperation between Germany and France can the unity, peace and well-being of Europe be assured.

"There is no European policy without France, or against France," he said on July 2, 1954, *"just as there can be no European policy without or against Germany. Franco-German understanding, in the full meaning of the word, is for me a matter of rational conviction, as much as it is a concern of the heart."* (July 2, 1954)

And: "We do not merely intend to safeguard peace in our interest and in the interest of Europe now, but we want to make sure that even in ten or twenty years, when the world might be quite different, and when the European nations might once more have become powerful, the possibility of a European war between Germany and France will have been eliminated once and for all." (February 7, 1952) "In solving the problem of the German contribution to the defense of Europe—a thorny problem in Franco-German relations for years—we should be able to achieve lasting peace between Germany and France. This has been an immutable objective of the Germany policy I have represented during these years, because it is one which the German as well as the French people desire with all their heart." (October 3, 1954) "Germany's relations with France occupy a central place in the history of Europe. The Paris treaties of October 1954, by laying a foundation for improved Franco-German relations, will make it possible to realize their ultimate objective, European unity." (March 29, 1955) "The example of the Saar treaties of October 1956 demonstrates to us that one must always act from a firm resolve to look ahead, rather than backward, whenever one strives for a new, free, peaceful future. This must remain our highest objective. This is also what the Saar population has been fighting for." (October 27, 1956) "The people of the Saar, together with France and Germany, have shown that it is possible to resolve conflicts which at first seemed impossible to solve; to resolve them on the basis of human rights and free self-determination, and in a spirit of reconciliation and peace." (January 1, 1957)

These utterances reflect the tough, long, political and diplomatic struggle, and its underlying convictions, which Adenauer had to wage as Chancellor of Germany and—with as much skill as honesty—as a European diplomat, while searching for a settlement of the Saar problem with France. The starting point for these efforts was a situation in which the

effective representation of Germany's interests seemed to be
a hopeless affair. It was inevitable that both sides tended
continually to slide back from the positions they already
seemed to have reached while these efforts were in progress.
But the ultimate moral and political results and their implications in terms of constitutional and international law
proved to be equally inevitable. In the end, Adenauer's policy
stood revealed as a masterwork of Franco-German understanding and over-all European diplomacy. This statement can
easily be substantiated by a sober enumeration of the political
facts and the successive diplomatic phases in this development—facts which the Chancellor's political opponents unfortunately prefer to forget, out of a narrow political interest
connected with the election tactics of their parties, in de-
bunking any objective appraisal of Adenauer's achievements
as sheer "myths" and political "forgery." This then is the
actual balance sheet, as time has recorded it, soberly enough,
in the annals of the history of the Saar.

To begin with, France in 1945, without consulting her
allies, absorbed the Saar region into the French economy
after the American forces had transferred the area to France.
This veiled political-economic annexation received an important constitutional and diplomatic sanction in 1947 with
the promulgation by the Saar parliament—without a plebiscite!—of a "Saar Constitution," laying down in constitutional
terms the economic and currency union with France together
with complete independence from Germany. The defense
and diplomatic representation of the Saar was simultaneously
conferred upon the French government. At no time did
France pronounce her effective absorption of the Saar area
to be an annexation, but preferred to justify it as a mere
matter of economic reparation and economic and military
safeguard against Germany. First in 1946, and in a more final
form at the Moscow Foreign Ministers' conference in the
spring of 1947, these arrangements furthermore received the

consent of Britain and the United States. In the meantime, the autonomous Saar regime, headed by Johannes Hoffmann, established an administrative and political setup on a strictly anti-German constitutional basis, which prohibited the organization of pro-German political parties as well as any political manifestation of a pro-German nature at all. Therewith the threat of the total Frenchification of the Saar, at least politically, had become a very real possibility, and had in fact even been sanctioned as a concrete political system. This situation was further aggravated by the diplomatic position of the defeated Germany, in particular her lack of international or constitutional sovereignty, which excluded any informal or formal diplomatic discussions of the Saar problem between Germany and France, not to mention the absence of any legal basis for the recognition of German interests in the Saar in the framework of a future peace treaty.

Such was the situation in the Saarland in 1949, when the Federal Republic was established and Adenauer took office as Federal Chancellor. In view of this situation he proposed, in his first official pronouncement, a temporary solution of the Saar issue in the framework of a European Union; with the final decision as to the form, in which the status of the Saar should be determined within a German-French peace treaty settlement, to be reserved to the people of the Saar. Adenauer's proposal was the opening for the Franco-German Saar debate in a European framework. Its gradual extension led to the recognition of the profound European implications of the issue for the two nations, which found its tangible expression in the various contractual agreements, from the European Coal and Steel Community agreement of April 1951, via the Paris treaties of October 1954 and the Luxembourg Agreement on the Saar of October 1956, to the ultimate return of the Saar into the community of the German Federal Republic on January 1, 1957.

In all these negotiations Adenauer proved himself as stanch

a fighter for the Saar population's right of self-determination as he was tireless in his search for devices permitting a genuine European solution involving a fair and viable recognition of the vital interests of both sides, the French as well as the German interests in the Saar. His first success consisted in the official French agreement, coinciding with the ratification of the European Coal and Steel Community treaty, that the final status of the Saar should not be settled before the final peace treaty. Then, as the Paris treaties were being signed, Adenauer obtained French consent for the European status of the Saar, under the auspices of the Western European Union. At the same time, France conceded the admission of pro-German political parties in the Saar and the resumption, although on a limited scale, of economic relations between the Saar and the Federal Republic.

And as the idea of European union was suffering a serious defeat through the rejection of the European Defense Community—largely the result of Mendès-France's handiwork, then premier of France, Adenauer managed to obtain a provision for the special status of the Saar, as an adjunct to the Paris treaties—an interim settlement of the problem, reflecting a truly European concept. The result was "the Saar Statute," now the object of much abuse on the part of Adenauer's political opponents in Germany, which was submitted to a free vote by the people of the Saar on October 23, 1955. The fact that the Saar area was to be considered as temporarily "Europeanized" by the terms of the statute, until a final peace treaty should have been signed, appears neither very important today, nor did it have much of an actual significance at the time. Soon, however, another provision of the Paris treaty proved to be far more important as far as the statute was concerned: the international guarantee for a free plebiscite on the statute by a simple "Yea" or "Nay," without any other alternatives. The right to organize pro-German political parties in the Saar, for which specific contractual provision had been made, lent this free vote an additional importance. With unrestricted freedom of action people of the Saar were allowed to promote the critical discussion and even the rejection of the statute. The actual course of the plebiscite proved that the people of the Saar were to take full advantage of this privilege.

The plebiscite of October 23, 1955, resulted in the rejection of the Saar Statute by a vote of 423,434 (or 67.7 percent) against approximately 202,000. Even more significant were the political repercussions, since the Hoffmann government was now forced to resign, dissolve the Saar parliament and pave the way for a newly elected parliament in line with the changed political conditions. For the first time the pro-German political parties were now allowed to participate in an actual election campaign. The parliamentary elections of December 18, 1955, gave the three pro-German parties, which had joined forces in a "German Patriotic Association" (*Deutscher Heimatbund*), a majority of 64 percent. This outcome meant not only the death knell for the "Europeanization" of the Saar as a viable political solution and an international interim-type settlement. It also raised the practical alternative of the return of the Saar to Germany and indicated that a "German solution" of the problem might mean the best possible "European" solution as well. In fact, it was now evident that this was the only conceivable solution, both from the European viewpoint and in the interest of Franco-German understanding.

In any history of political morality, the deeper implications of the "Saar Statute" may one day be considered as the most crucial event in Franco-German relations and the actualization of the European idea during the first ten years after the war. There are two reasons for this prediction: the Saar Statute story, for one thing, highlights the gigantic difficulties facing any European statesman who insists upon the uncompromising application of moral principles and loyalty to the existing agreements in carrying out his task. And yet, the same story illustrates also the extraordinary creative power of the moral element in a constructive approach to international relations, even in this hectic age of power politics and unscrupulous political opportunism. Immanuel Kant's warning seems to have lost none of its validity, ". . . that no true political action can take a single step before first bowing to morality." More specifically, here was telling evidence that a "policy with ethical overtones," much decried by opportunistic pragmatists (who really resent the insertion of any ethical considerations into practical politics), may in fact be a very wholesome element in the struggle for the European idea amidst the realities of the European situation. It may help to relax existing tensions and unite seemingly irreconcilable interests. Kant had already assigned to the ethical factor this role in creative political action when he said: "Although politics is a difficult art when it stands on its own, its union with morality presents no difficulty at all; for the latter breaks the knot which the former is unable to disentangle, whenever there is a conflict between the two." And, lastly, the thorny road which Konrad Adenauer and the leaders of the French government had to travel with regard to the Saar Statute has proved to have been necessary: for even now the historian must view the Saar solution in the light of another of Immanuel Kant's axioms, namely that ". . . politics must always bow before justice; but in so doing, it may hope to attain a level where it will shine consistently."

The four aspects which have been sketched here may highlight the mutual interdependence of the ethical and the political element. It was thanks to their interaction that the Saar solution was possible—a solution both ethical and political in nature, and thus understandable only in metapolitical terms.

The Solution: Return of the Saar

Adenauer's opponents so far have failed to reach this conclusion. In their view, the solution of the Saar problem began
with the results of the plebiscite rejecting the Saar Statute,
just as automatically as all the following developments had
therewith become "inevitable"—an accomplished fact which
the French could not but accept once the majority of the
Saar population had expressed its desire to be reunited with
Germany. On the strength of such oversimplifications, Adenauer's opponents proceed to deny that he had any share at
all in the actual reintegration of the Saar; particularly since,
on the eve of the plebiscite, the Chancellor had explicitly advised the people of the Saar to accept the statute.

What these comments really reveal is a dangerous hang-
over from the unabashed power-political mentality of the
German past. This becomes alarmingly evident if one studies
the record of the Federal Parliament for the sessions debating
the ratification of the Paris treaties, the Luxembourg treaty
about the Saar, and the official government declarations of
the Foreign Minister, von Brentano, of November 29, 1956,
and January 31, 1957.

What one finds there is that the French consent to the
return of the Saar is treated exclusively as the gratification of
a legitimate German claim, while the meaning of the economic concessions to France is minimized as a kind of wanton
bonus, thrown in by Adenauer, who is said to have displayed
a deplorable lack of "patriotic backbone," and to have made
himself guilty of neglecting vital national interests. (Similar
reproaches were leveled against him when he advised the Saar
people to vote for the statute, in his Bochum speech.) Hence,
Adenauer's patriotic contribution to the Saar solution is supposed to be nothing but a "myth"—fabricated by "juggling"
the historic facts, a skillful interchanging of truth and fiction,

which enabled "the Chancellor," during the January 1 ceremonies in Saarbruecken, to "pass himself off as a veritable
god of the Saar," and to reap once more altogether "unde-
served laurels" for the reunification in the West. This type
of slander was climaxed by a man of the stature of the new
chairman of the Free Democratic Party (FDP), Reinhold
Maier. On January 27, 1957, during the conference of his
party in Berlin, he let his native Swabian rudeness run away
with him to level the following insult against the octogenarian
Chancellor: "The great task of the FDP is to put the German
nation back on its feet. The great old man" —meaning Adenauer—"is completely unqualified for this job. His entire
intellectual makeup resists such a mission. It is time for
Germany once again to become a nation, free both in the
domestic and the international sphere."

This may merely indicate what metapolitical impact Adenauer's achievements in the Saar have had with the German
people and how much this has irked the opposition, so that
it had to resort to abusing a man to whose eternal credit, as
"Chancellor of the Vanquished," it is if the Germans are
today back "on their feet"; under whose leadership the German people have found the inner strength and regained the
confidence abroad to win the French consent for a truly "German solution" of the Saar question.

The particular importance of these matters, which has
warranted our detailed discussion here, lies in their significance for the metapolitical implications of the East German
reunification problem, and especially for the Russian attitude. The fact is that the nationalistic misrepresentations of
the moral and political issues in the reunification of the Saar
with Germany spell definite dangers for a healthy solution of
the problem in Eastern Germany. Adenauer's political opponents do not seem to see that these distortions of the moral
and political realities—and therewith Adenauer's merits—in
the Saar solution can only provide new, powerful arguments

for the Russians, with their native distrust, against a fair settlement of the East German problem. Adenauer's foes overlook the bearing of these issues on any future negotiations, whether the German Federal Chancellor, at such a time, is to be Adenauer or Ollenhauer or—may the Swabian gods preserve us!—Herr Reinhold Maier.

The fate of the Saar Statute is, above all, a testimony to the creative power of the European idea. In the first place, Adenauer could never have agreed to the Saar Statute, unless his concern for a speedier, more effective European union had made this seem an imperative step. And, similarly, the prompt, almost unqualified agreement of the French government and assembly, and of the overwhelming majority of French public opinion, to the return of the Saar would have been inconceivable without a sense that this was indispensable for the progressive realization of European unity and security.

It was certainly not easy for the German Chancellor to accept the Saar Statute as part and parcel of the Paris treaties; especially, since the shrewd Mendès-France had produced this amendment only toward the end of the meetings, as a condition for the French consent to the entire treaty complex. What made matters worse, the same Mendès-France, who thus demanded the complete Europeanization of the Saar, had only a little earlier killed the European Defense Community treaty—mostly because he felt that its European character would infringe upon the national interests and the sovereignty of France. Adenauer thus had the alternative either to accept Mendès-France's Saar Statute "rider" or, by rejecting it, to cause the collapse of the whole Paris treaty structure, including its provisions of full sovereignty, equal status in the community of the free nations and membership in the Atlantic defense community for the Federal Republic.

Adenauer made his inevitable choice for the European community and, therewith, also for the Saar Statute. However, he insisted on having certain crucial amendments in-

cluded in the final version of the statute, in keeping with the
principle of free self-determination, as, for example, the admission of unhampered freedom of electioneering for the
pro-German political parties. With these provisions, he paved
the way for the ultimate downfall of the Saar Statute itself.
Only after these amendments were accepted did the Chancellor sign the Paris treaties, aware that he was committing himself to morally binding contractual obligations in the interest
of Franco-German understanding and the European community.

Adenauer remained unswervingly loyal to these commitments even when, shortly afterward, he faced bitter opposition within the Bonn government coalition and even inside
his own cabinet, with an open revolt by Jakob Kaiser, minister for "All-German Affairs," a man from the ranks of his
own party. And he acted out of the same loyalty when he
stepped before the microphone on the eve of the Saar plebiscite and advised the people of the Saar to accept the Saar
Statute which he had, after all, accepted. There were some
who felt Adenauer should have been "smart" enough to remain silent, at least on the eve of the plebiscite, since there
was certainly no "contractual" obligation for him to speak
up. But the Chancellor knew well that at that moment the
eyes and ears of the entire French nation were on him; that
to be silent at that moment would have meant to renege on
accepted commitments, and that the French—not without
reason—would undoubtedly have interpreted his silence as
an act of disloyalty. Although the dilemma in which the
Chancellor found himself at that moment may not have been
understood everywhere in the Federal Republic, it was certainly appreciated by the Saar population. And it was not a
"calculated game" if the Saar people, from a deep and sympathetic understanding, decided to use the privileges of the
Saar Statute in a way which released the Chancellor from
these moral obligations, while in turn committing the French

government to the moral and political implications of a rejection of the statute.

Thus, it came to pass that the statute was invalidated by the application of its own moral and political implications, because both parties lived up to the letter of its provisions. For now that the statute had been rejected by the Saar people Adenauer's consistent loyalty to the accepted obligations had to be matched by the French. Otherwise, the idea of solidarity in the nascent spirit of the European community, the very basis of the statute, would have been compromised beyond repair.

The French government and a majority in the French parliament have lived up to this responsibility. Unfortunately, the chief author of the statute, Mendès-France, chose to evade this responsibility by seeking, however futilely, to prevent his government and parliament from fulfilling their obligations. His vehement opposition when Mollet as premier and Pineau as foreign minister later redeemed these obligations in the Luxembourg Saar treaty does not seem any more defensible because of the fact that he no longer held a ministerial portfolio at that time.

Yet these events have vindicated the role of his partner across the conference table at Paris, the German Chancellor: because the moral force and the metapolitical logic of the European community idea, as the driving power behind these developments, produced a solution capable of "resolving the knot," according to Kant's formula, which no opportunist power politics could possibly have disentangled. What a unique opportunity for Adenauer's political opponents to put their much-vaunted patriotic feelings to the test, their passionate concern for the proper representation of the national and international interests of the Federal Republic, by expressing their approval of the loyalty to the moral and contractual commitments which the Chancellor had displayed. Was this not an unprecedented chance to demonstrate that the Federal Republic was morally and politically dependable, also in international affairs, in the relations between nations? Instead, the campaign continues unabated in the Federal Republic, questioning Adenauer's role in the Saar solution. On January 31, 1957, Foreign Minister von Brentano felt obliged to reply again to the repeated Social Democratic accusations against Adenauer regarding his position toward the Saar Statute:

"The colleague Ollenhauer," von Brentano said, "has chosen to reopen the controversy as to who should get the credit for our successful policy in the Saar. On October 23, 1954, the Chancellor signed an agreement with the Premier of France. We have accustomed the world to the fact that the Federal Government lives up to its agreements, and the Social Democrats, too, will have to get used to this fact. Their criticism of Adenauer, because he spoke in favor of this agreement, amounts to reproaching him because he failed to break his word!"

It is perhaps through this loyalty toward the accepted agreements in the Saar issue that Adenauer may have done most to promote East German reunification. If we grant the Russians and Poles the right to ask that a Germany, negotiating for a future reunification, should provide definite guarantees of an ethicopolitical nature, Adenauer's attitude on the Saar issue may well be cited as a legitimate qualification.

What is more, the Russians and Poles may have been as much impressed with the generous political and economic solutions inherent in the Saar agreements as with their ethical implications. The most striking feature about these solutions is that they were possible only because both sides yielded some of their widely diverging special interests to further the common good. France obviously made some very substantial political sacrifices in exchange for material economic benefits, which in turn represented serious sacrifices for Germany. Nevertheless, events will certainly show that the sacrifices and concessions of either side are going to benefit both nations, particularly since they will promote the economic and political integration of Western Europe, for which they are indeed indispensable. The coal agreement and the agreement about the channeling of the Moselle may be looked upon as vital German contributions to France's economic recovery and, therewith, further economic integration in Europe. The Saar solution, in this respect, may well be considered as an important preparatory step toward the creation of a joint European market.

The reunification in the East will undoubtedly pose problems, also on the economic level, which will be materially different from those encountered in the West. All the more important is the example of honesty of purpose and intent given in the West. It should help to solve even the thorniest international problems between Germany and her Eastern neighbors if they are approached in a spirit of openmindedness, understanding and mutual readiness for sacrifice.

The world-wide ethicopolitical significance of the successful reunification in the West was well expressed by the president of the German Federal Parliament, Eugen Gerstenmaier, addressing its plenary session on January 10, 1957:

"The hectic fever of nationalism in our century," he said, "has created fear and terror not only among the European nations but among many other nations in the world as well. We must hope that the sufferings of two world wars have immunized us against any further fever spells of this kind. But while nationalistic passions are now being bridled through farsighted and conscientious policies, it must be, and is, permissible to voice basic loyalty to one's country, and to cultivate it as an integral part of the political ethics and spiritual strength of a nation. Even the terrible way in which the dictators and fanatics have misused love of country must never dim that love or make it appear questionable for us. One of its manifestations is a nation's living capacity for reconciliation.

"The return of the Saar to Germany represents a triumph of political morality also as far as France is concerned. It is thus not only an event of national scope but, at the same time, a way to gauge whether new ideas and an improved political morality have sprung up among the nations of Europe following the Second World War. It is not easy for any nation to free itself from the notions and concepts which have dominated it for decades and even centuries. We Germans have had much to learn through serious sufferings. Neither can it have been easy for the French to give up certain of their old pet ideas and ambitions, rooted in their tradition of power politics, aiming at the incorporation of the Saar into the national community of France and the consolidation of the French hegemony in Europe. Against this background we appreciate the decision of the French government and parliament in the Saar question all the more sincerely.

"The return of the Saar has been the touchstone for the vigor of a new type of thinking and feeling, and a new direction of impulses for the free nations of Europe. We may take it as a hopeful sign that the desire for integration and peaceful coexistence, which has arisen among them, shall not be extinguished again. We are aware that the situation in Central Germany and at our Eastern borders is fundamentally different. Nor do we overlook the fact that the problems of reunification which are facing us are of far greater dimensions—global dimensions, in fact. And yet, we may say that the return of the Saar should be a new occasion, a new encouragement and impetus for all Germans to fight for the peaceful restoration of a united Germany, and for the friendly cooperation between our nation, once it is united, and all our neighbors to the west and east, north and south!"

XI

The Problem in the East

The significance of the Saar solution for reunification in the East, despite its undeniable ethical and political bearing on this issue, should nevertheless not be overrated. It is important to sound this warning because there is a deep-seated illusion among certain groups in the West, especially in the German Federal Republic, that Moscow's European policy is committed to the same ethicopolitical principles in international relations as is that of the Western countries—at least so far as basic respect for the integrity of a sovereign nation is concerned.

Czarist Russia may have respected such principles. Thus the imperialism of the czars in its European aspirations never developed into a direct and actual threat to the sovereignty of the European nations—as the Congress of Vienna and all successive conferences for the settlement of Russian conflicts with Europe, the Balkans and the Near East amply demonstrate. In fact, the Congress of Berlin, in 1878, represented a kind of model for the normalizing of European relations with Russia, under international law. A comparison of the record of this congress with the records of the Yalta, Teheran and Potsdam conferences, or the Geneva and London conferences of 1955, serves to highlight the profound change in Russian diplomacy from Czarist to Soviet days, and its respective potentialities for normal diplomatic relations.

The two most crucial factors in this change are, one, the Bolshevist denial of the universal validity of the standards and contrasts of international law; and, two, the principle of the Communist world revolution. Thus, it takes no deep-seated Russophobia to accept all Soviet pronouncements in favor of international order and peaceful coexistence with unqualified distrust. Nor does this skepticism disappear when one acknowledges that contemporary Russia is justified in fearing for her national existence and political and military security, not even if one concedes the particular justification of these fears so far as concerns Russia's Western neighbor, Germany, and the scourge of her brutal aggressive warfare against Russia and its people in the none too distant past— and even if one is ready to exclude, from such a perspective, the role of Hitler and the Nazi regime.

Adenauer may justly claim that he has always been deeply aware of these facts. Few criticisms are less justified than that, as German Chancellor, he has fallen short in his efforts to understand the Russian distrust of German policy. The exact opposite is true. Adenauer was compelled to understand these factors and their wider implications all the more earnestly, since the Russians utilize their justified suspicions, with considerable skill and unscrupulousness, to further their ultimate ends, namely, the establishment of a Communist dictatorship throughout Germany, and therewith the total absorption of Germany into the Russian sphere of influence. Hence, Russia's real aim since Yalta is not peaceful coexistence with Germany as a basis on which Russia would be able to live down her suspicions but the subjection of an isolated and fatally weakened Germany under Moscow leadership.

One has to grasp this peculiar relationship between the psychological motivations of Russia's suspicions and the political aspirations of neo-Russian expansionism if one is to understand that specific mentality of the present Moscow rulers which we may call their "German obsession." It has tinged the Russian attitude since Yalta to such a degree that it has been something of a slogan for Russia's entire European policy during the past ten years—in fact for the Russian over-all attitudes toward the West. Yet one element always threatened to contribute additional fuel to the intrinsic explosiveness of this obsession, a certain readiness among large non-Communist circles in the Western world to meet the Moscow suspicions half-way and with sympathetic understanding, including an insistence on "talks" with the Russians at any price, without any sober appraisal as to whether mere "talking" would be sufficient for realistic progress. Adenauer's critics in the Federal Republic harmed the cause of reunification when they tried to make the Chancellor "activate" his policy toward Russia beyond what was and will ever be possible in the framework of European politics and Germany's very real concern for her security and freedom. We shall see later with what results Adenauer has worked for these interests since he first started "talking" with the Russians at the Moscow meeting in September 1955. For the moment let us merely make the following observations:

Any success for the German reunification policy in the East depends primarily on Germany's skill in meeting Moscow's "German obsession" by differentiating its psychological from its political components, depending on the shifting emphasis in any negotiations—and recent experience has taught us how shifting it can be. As for the "psychological" moment, Adenauer's loyalty to his given word, as demonstrated in the Saar solution and throughout his foreign policy, could hardly be matched by any Western statesman, and certainly not by any other German politician, even in Russian eyes. We shall see how Adenauer achieved an impressive triumph in Moscow precisely because of his moral stature. How else can one evaluate Bulganin's acknowledgment of Adenauer's sincere desire for understanding and peace expressed in a letter to the Chancellor, dated February 5, 1957: "To judge by what the delegation of the German Federal Republic has said during the Moscow negotiations," the Soviet Premier wrote, "we may say that there do not exist any forces or politicians in Western Germany who desire an aggressive war."

The entire Moscow leadership seems to have convinced itself that Adenauer not only desires peace, but is seriously working for relations with the Russians which, through the restoration of German unity, would permit Germany to build friendly relations with her Eastern neighbor; although, of course, not at the expense of Germany's independence and freedom—in the manner of East Germany, the "German Democratic Republic."

And yet the Russians are certain that Adenauer will never permit his understanding of the Russian psychology and security-mindedness to be misused for political concessions—or, in other words, that he will never help to advance the power-political aspirations of the neo-Russian imperialism. They know that he would not accept anything that would in the least degree weaken, not to say seriously jeopardize, the peace and freedom of Germany and Europe. Because of this knowledge, the Soviets direct the full fury of their hatred against Adenauer as the guardian of German and European freedom. From this perspective, Konrad Adenauer—or, rather, the German and European substance of his policy—appears to the Soviets as the core of the psychological and political resistance against their imperialist aspirations in Germany and Europe. And this, too, explains the boundless hatred of Moscow's East German puppets; the periodic, and periodically intensified, attacks against the Chancellor in the Soviet press; and, above all, Moscow's tireless maneuvers to create a favorable psychological climate for "talks," by addressing continuously new "letters" and proposals to the Chancellor. The real purpose of these attempts is, of course, to sow confusion in Germany as to the ways and means of reunification and to injure Adenauer's prestige at home—in which they succeed from time to time. Plainly, the Soviets are not interested in promoting a real solution of the reunification problem—although they might actually benefit from it.

These are some of the reasons why all efforts toward the reunification of Germany—and this goes especially for the various German initiatives—are futile unless they are controlled by the kind of *ethical orientation that pervades Adenauer's Russian policy*. Adenauer had formulated its political and diplomatic aspects as early as 1952 in a statement which is still surprisingly timely:

"Once the Soviets understand that the cold war no longer brings them any advantage it will also dawn upon them that their heavy emphasis upon war production, at the expense of consumers' goods production, is no longer worth while. At that time they will be ready, in their own best interest, for a change in their policy. It is our task, that of the Western world including the Federal Republic, to shape our policies so as to make the Soviets realize these things. We shall then be able to sit down with them for reasonable and hopeful talks, and we shall also see the reunification of Germany in peace and freedom. Much as I try, this is the only way I can see" (October 18, 1952).

Replying to Bulganin on February 5, 1957, Adenauer reiterated this view, and applied it to the most topical issue in Moscow-Bonn relations today:

"You have reminded us of the good tradition of Russo-German relations. But this reminder of a tradition based on an orderly relationship, excluding any interference of one nation in the way of life of the other, makes us all the more painfully aware of all that keeps us apart in our present mutual existence. Let me therefore emphasize once more that a basic clarification of our mutual relations cannot be separated from a settlement of the great, as yet unresolved, problems, above all the restoration of Germany's national unity. If it is our task to give our nation a durable peace, offering greater security to coming generations than we have enjoyed so far, we and all those who share this responsibility must work together in order to eliminate the danger spot which has been created by the division of Germany."

In the first part of this book we have shown why Soviet Russia will never be able to tolerate a "neutralized" Germany, much less a reunited Germany organically integrated in the European community of nations: that she cannot do so without renouncing her design for the control of all Europe, to which a Communist-controlled Germany would almost automatically lead. All the diplomatic verbiage about Soviet respect for a free Europe, and about Soviet efforts for peaceful coexistence between a free democratic Germany and her neighbor in the East, remains as empty as it is insincere. Moscow's aim, with all this talk, is to discredit and paralyze the efforts for a healthy integration of the nations of Europe and the peaceful defense of their freedoms. As long as Moscow opposes these efforts, it must seek to prevent, by all conceivable means, Germany's recovery and the restoration of her national and economic unity. And Moscow must at the same time reject any European security system whose open violation would mean inevitable war for the Soviet Union. To prevent the unification of Europe and the recovery of Germany by diplomatic and political means Russia must strive to keep Germany divided as long as possible. Khrushchev, talkative although at least in this case plainly undiplomatic, was therefore undoubtedly sincere when he told Pineau, during the Moscow talks, that the Soviet regime would not dream of swapping the "pawn" of 17 million so-called "un-free Germans" in the Soviet zone against a reunited Germany of 70 million free Germans.

In point of fact, Khrushchev's aside evidences a far deeper motivation for Russia's "German obsession" than the mere ratio of 17 to 70 million would indicate. The 17 million "pawn" is obviously of an essentially political nature in comparison with which the military potential of 70 million appears perfectly negligible. And it is true that the Soviets, both in the past and now, have viewed the German problem primarily as a political and only secondarily as a military one. The shift of the international balance to the Washington-Moscow level plus modern military technology, including the use of nuclear weapons, have obviated the possibility that the military potential, even of a reunited Germany, can ever again become a serious threat to the Soviet Union. By contrast the Russians, with considerable justification, feel that the human and political potential of a technically and economically highly organized Germany, with a population of 70 million, would present an impenetrable barrier to all Soviet aspirations for control over Europe. Without this barrier, and especially without the power potential of 70 million Germans, the rest of Europe would have precious little hope of stemming Russian expansion. Stalin already had devoted some weighty thinking to this subject toward the end of the Second World War, which resulted in his claim for the dismemberment of Germany, filed with the allies at the Teheran conference in 1943, and approved by them then and there. This is Winston Churchill's eyewitness account of the course of the Teheran negotiations on this particular point.

Roosevelt then explained his plan for splitting Germany into five parts: (1) Prussia. (2) Hanover and the northwest part of Germany. (3) Saxony and the Leipzig area. (4) Hesse-Darmstadt, Hesse-Cassel, and the sections south of the Rhine. (5) Bavaria, Baden, and Württemberg. These five sections would be self-governing, but there were two more that would be governed by the United Nations: (1) Kiel and its canal and Hamburg. (2) The Ruhr and the Saar. These would be under the United Nations as trustees. He was only throwing this out as an idea which might be talked over.

"If," I said, "I might use the American idiom, I would say that the President has 'said a mouthful.' Mr. Roosevelt's plan is a new one to me. In my opinion there are two things, one destructive and the other constructive. I have two clear ideas in mind. First, the isolation of Prussia. What is to be done to Prussia is only secondary. Then I should like to detach Bavaria, Württemberg, the Palatinate, Saxony, and Baden. Whereas I would treat Prussia sternly, I would make things easier for the second group, which I should like to see work in with what I would call a Danubian Confederation. The people of these parts of Germany are not the most ferocious, and I should like to see them live tolerably, and in a generation they would feel differently. South Germans are not going to start another war, and we would have to make it worth their while to forget Prussia. I do not much mind whether there are one or two groups." I asked Marshal Stalin whether he would be prepared to go into action on this front.

Stalin said he would, but he preferred a plan for the partition of Germany—something like the President's plan, which was more likely to weaken Germany. When one had to deal with large masses of German troops, one found them all fighting like devils, as the British and American armies would soon learn. The Austrians by themselves were different, and he described the way they surrendered. All Germans were the same. It was the Prussian officers that provided the cement. But fundamentally there was no difference between North Germans and South Germans, for all Germans fought like fierce beasts. We should be careful not to include the Austrians in any kind of combination. Austria had existed independently, and could do so again. So also must Hungary exist independently. After breaking up Germany it would be most unwise to create new combinations, Danubian or otherwise.

President Roosevelt agreed warmly. There was no difference between Germans. The Bavarians had no officer class; otherwise they were exactly like the Prussians, as the American troops had already discovered.

I said that if Germany were divided into a number of parts as suggested by the President, and these parts were not attached to other combinations, they would reunite. It was not a question of dividing Germany so much as giving a life to the cut-off bits and making them content not to be dependent on the Greater Reich. Even if this were achieved for fifty years, that would be a lot.

Stalin said that a combination would not be able to live, and the Germans would take advantage of this by putting flesh on something that was only a skeleton and thus creating a new great state. Here he asked whether Hungary and Rumania would be members of any such combination. He then reiterated his views about the advantages which it would present to Germany in the future.

It was far better to break up and scatter the German tribes. Of course, they would want to unite, no matter how much they were split up. They would always want to reunite. In this he saw great danger, which would have to be neutralized by various economic measures, and in the long run by force if necessary. That was the only way to keep the peace. But if we were to make a large combination with Germans in it trouble was bound to come. We had to see to it that they were kept separate, and that Hungary and Germany should not be coupled. There were no measures possible to exclude a movement towards reunion. Germans would always want to reunite and to take their revenge. It would be necessary to keep ourselves strong enough to beat them if they ever let loose another war.

I asked Stalin if he contemplated a Europe of little states, all disjointed, with no larger units at all.

He replied that he was speaking of Germany, not Europe.

Poland and France were large states. Rumania and Bulgaria were small states. But Germany should at all costs be broken up so that she could not reunite. (Winston Churchill, *The Second World War,* Vol. V, "Closing the Ring," pp. 401-403.)

It is noteworthy that Stalin's demands contain not only the entire program for the expulsion of the German population from the Eastern areas—later sanctioned at Yalta and Pots- dam—as well as the dismemberment of these territories: here, too, is the formula for the dismemberment of the German East which, like a *leitmotif,* has dominated Soviet policy to- ward Germany to this day. One should remember this for- mula, whenever there are cries in the West, particularly in the Federal Republic, for ceasing to distrust Russia's objec- tives in Germany—cries usually raised by those who are for- ever ready to trust the motives of the propaganda for a Mos- cow-sponsored reunification of Germany.

Next to the *political* objective of permanently weakening Germany's potential, through the lasting dismemberment of her territorial integrity—which Russia has been advocating since the Teheran conference—the strategic aspects of reunifi- cation are obviously of secondary importance. Anyhow, Rus- sia's military security against any contingencies of renewed German aggression has evidently been settled since Moscow has become a nuclear power, so that neither a reunited Ger- many nor today's territorially restricted Federal Republic presents an actual threat to the Soviet Union. The powerful Soviet empire could certainly counter any threat at any time with the total and presumably final annihilation of Germany if she should ever again resort to aggression. One must re- member these facts whenever the restoration of Germany's territorial unity is questioned because of military considera- tions arising from Germany's position in a European or in- tercontinental security system. These solid facts have been obvious to the Soviet government ever since it came into possession of nuclear weapons; in fact, so much so that Moscow has *de facto* acquiesced in the rearmament of the Federal Republic and its integration in the NATO security system— despite all official protests. For while the Kremlin knows that these developments do not spell any immediate danger to its security in terms of possible German aggression they did present excellent propaganda opportunities by way of concealing Russia's political objections to German reunification behind a smokescreen of military arguments. Unfortunately, due to the psychological consequences of Nazi aggression, the argument against the defense efforts and the so-called "remilitarization" of the Federal Republic carries considerable weight all through the Western world. It gives the "neutralist"—and, even more, the Russophile—propaganda a unique chance to use the strengthening of the Federal Republic and its vitally needed integration in the Western security system for discrediting the idea of reunification, and of a possible lasting, peaceful understanding between Germany and her Eastern European neighbors.

Such reflections show how hard it is for the leaders of the German Federal Republic to initiate "conversations" with Moscow. And there is the added complication of the Oder-Neisse line, where just German territorial claims against Poland clash with the no less just Polish security demands in a psychological and political climate in which any rational, peaceful settlement of the reunification issue, fair to both German and Polish interests, looks like an almost gigantic task. This situation naturally tends to strengthen the Russian hand even further—as it raises the serious question whether the road to reunification might not lead to Moscow via Warsaw and, on the other hand, whether any progress at all can be made without active Russian support. Yet both from the tactical and the practical point of view, it seems evident that Moscow has to be the primary partner in any such "conversation."

It is remarkable from more viewpoints than one that Moscow, in the fall of 1955, took the initiative for such direct conversations with the Federal Republic. For one thing, this step demonstrated that Moscow was beginning to consider the political potential of the Federal Republic as sufficiently strong to make a continued ignoring of German interests, as represented by Bonn, appear inexpedient in terms of Soviet over-all interests in Europe. This seemed a fact regardless of the official Soviet estimate of Adenauer's policies as expressed in Soviet propaganda. The sheer impact of Adenauer's German rehabilitation and European policy was sufficiently impressive for the Kremlin to cause it, however reluctantly, to exchange its strategy of aloofness toward Adenauer's foreign policy for one of direct diplomatic contacts and conversations between Moscow and Bonn. But this meant that a first phase of Russian interference in German postwar affairs had come to an end. Adenauer's Kremlin visit in September 1955 ushered in a new phase in Russo-German relations distinguished by the diplomatic and psychological tug-of-war on the reunification issue. True, Adenauer's Moscow visit has not netted much by way of tangible results. Nevertheless, the course of the conference proved it to be a turning point in Moscow-Bonn relations. Many of the later initiatives for direct contacts between the Kremlin and the German Federal Republic would have been inconceivable without the Moscow conference and the results it produced.

XII

Interlude: The Moscow Conference

Mission to Moscow

"I am going to Moscow in the firm resolve to do everything that is in our power to promote world peace, to restore the unity of our country and to achieve the return of the prisoners of war. I repeat what I just said: my aim is to promote peace, not only for Europe but throughout the world."

Those were the words with which Chancellor Adenauer, on September 8, 1955, started on his trip to Moscow, in response to a personal invitation from Premier Bulganin, to make a first personal contact and initiate direct negotiations with the Soviet government. The course and results of the Moscow conference serve well to illustrate Adenauer's unique brand of statesmanship. For a variety of reasons, the personal and ideopolitical realities, the broader national and diplomatic implications of this conference seem to have escaped public opinion in Germany and abroad. The following factors are chiefly responsible for this remarkable oversight:

1. World public opinion approached the Moscow conference with expectations which were entirely out of keeping
with the actual framework of the meeting and the reasons
which had led up to it.

2. Soviet motivations and objectives proved to be widely
different from those of their German partners across the conference table, and from the ideopolitical and national attitudes, and the underlying international realities which Adenauer represented.

3. Even in Germany, large groups, especially among the
advocates of "neutralism" and among Adenauer's political
opponents, approached the Moscow talks with certain expectations and demands which were essentially—if not completely
—unrealistic. Their realization was impossible in view of the
ideopolitical situation in the Federal Republic and its interdependence with international factors, such as the policies of
the Western powers. The expression of these expectations
and demands resulted in a type of sweeping generalities and
pragmatic short circuits which remained typical of the neutralist and some of the newspaper comment in the Federal
Republic.

4. The confusion generated by all these factors was further increased by the sensationalist coverage of the talks on
the part of many newspapermen and their frequently biased
comments. As a result, the Moscow conference and its outcome have been subject to misinterpretations and misunderstandings far in excess of what is customary for international
conferences on Germany since the sad example of the Potsdam conference of 1945.

All these factors combined to create a smoke screen before
the facts and the crucial documents of the conference and prevented their objective evaluation. The German and world
press has by and large judged Adenauer's motivations, position and achievements with the yardstick of common prag-

matism, materialism or outright opportunism without any ethicopolitical criteria at all.

The resulting image of the Moscow conference, its progress and outcome did not help to convey the significance of these negotiations for the ideopolitical conflict of our time. But now that the excitement and the sensationalism surrounding the conference have died down, thanks to the soothing effects of time, it may at last be possible to sketch the achievements of the man who stood in the focus of the Moscow talks and put the stamp of his personality on their progress—in a manner which far exceeds the role of the modern statesman at any international conference.

Both its motivations—the reasons why the Soviets had called the conference in the first place—its substance and its development contributed to make the Moscow talks an "Adenauer conference" in the proper meaning of the word. Most of the speculation, the hopes and anxieties about it in Germany and throughout the West, especially in the United States, were focused on the person of the Chancellor. A deeper understanding of the substance and implications of the Moscow talks, beyond a mere superficial impression, must therefore proceed from Adenauer's moral and political concepts and statesmanship.

We may hope that the first part of this book has provided an adequate introduction for an understanding of these elements and their role in the Moscow talks.

Humanity as a Diplomatic Asset

Two elements emerged during the conference which suffice to set it off sharply from all the other postwar conferences. The first of these was *Adenauer's impassioned appeal to the principles of humanity and morality as the basis of all political action as far as it aims at promoting normal relations between nations, or at least restoring their "normaliza-*

tion," once they have been upset by military conflict. Ade-
nauer's human and ethical stature at Moscow has symbolized
a certain approach and established certain facts which may
well be considered a "novum" in modern international diplo-
macy.

Right at the outset of the talks Adenauer called for "unreserved frankness" and a "clean sweep" of the atmosphere as
the indispensable human and moral prerequisite for successful negotiations, if they were to lead to the kind of "normalization" between the Russian and German *peoples* which the
Soviet leaders professed to desire. Adenauer knew that for
him, as "Chancellor of the Vanquished," this suggestion
meant in basic human terms he must approach the Russians
as a "petitioner"; while it imposed on him the moral duty
to "ask their forgiveness." His petitioning consisted in an
appeal to the Soviets finally, after ten years, to settle the fate
of the German prisoners-of-war still in their hands. The request for forgiveness concerned the terrible German heritage
of the Nazi crimes against the Russian people, and the aggressive warfare of the armies of the Third Reich against the
Russian land. It fell to the "Chancellor of the Vanquished,"
speaking for the German people as a whole, to undertake the
liquidation of this heritage through a frank and spontaneous
soul-searching and a confession of German guilt in the midst
of the Kremlin walls.

The profound impression Adenauer's attitude made upon
the tough-minded Soviet leaders may be gathered from the
fact that a large portion of the German prisoners were indeed
released. On the other hand, even the sober record of the
negotiations reflects and, even more, conveys a feeling of the
dramatic impact of the human and moral principles for
which Adenauer stood, upon the entire conference proceed-
ings, and the very real progress for the idea of freedom and
peace in Germany and Russia which this approach produced,
all the dubious and disappointing elements notwithstanding.

The significance of the release of prisoners cannot be properly appreciated unless one realizes the heavy moral and legal mortgage which had burdened this issue. That Adenauer was able to solve it at all is due, on the one hand, to his profound family feeling and its roots in the Cologne *civitas*, which enabled him to evade all the legal and political complications besetting this problem with great frankness as well as skill. It was due, on the other hand, to his ability to convey to the tough-minded Kremlin politicians at least an inkling of the deep human tragedy in which the prisoners and their kin were involved. For legal, political and psychological reasons Adenauer very wisely preferred to forego any actual "demand" for the repatriation of the "prisoners-of-war." Instead, discarding all considerations of diplomatic protocol or prestige, he made a direct, human, if highly insistent "appeal" to have the "detainees" returned. He renewed this appeal in every public meeting, and undoubtedly with even greater insistence during the secret sessions. He did this with so much self-effacing humility that the Russians persuaded themselves at last of the relative political harmlessness of yielding to this request as compared to the considerable propagandistic value of such a gesture. Because the Russians no longer feared that the release of the prisoners would mean a loss of prestige the sensationalized newspaper accounts as well as the conference record itself evidenced the personal humiliation which a celebrated international statesman had taken upon himself before the Moscow rulers to attain the release of his German compatriots. To meet his request could only appear as a magnanimous human gesture.

Whatever "loss of prestige" the Chancellor may have suffered in the eyes of the Moscow leaders—or, for that matter, of any other cynics wherever they might be—the free world will no doubt gladly accept it in return for the eminent prestige of true humanity which Adenauer won for himself by his stand at the conference.

Politics and Ethics

So sharply does Adenauer's attitude differ from the common practices of modern diplomacy that one cannot possibly appreciate its display at the Moscow talks unless one views it as the expression of an ethicopolitical attitude, for which the uncompromising application of morality and justice is the overriding law even in international diplomacy. In Moscow this attitude compelled Adenauer to face up to those issues frank discussion of which was indispensable in order to clear the atmosphere in Russo-German relations, namely, the tragic guilt, and the coresponsibility for the sufferings and horrors which the Hitler regime had brought upon the Russian and German peoples. Adenauer, in Moscow, found a frankness and precision of expression in characterizing these grave issues which has remained unmatched by any German political leader or international statesman.

"It is true," he said, *"German troops invaded Russia. It is true, many evil, horrible acts were committed. But it is true as well that the Russian armies thereupon, in the course of a defensive action, I fully admit, invaded Germany, and that, as a result, many horrible acts occurred also in Germany as part of the war!"*

With this statement—one may look in vain for a similar admission on the part of the German leaders after the First World War, for instance, toward France or Belgium—the Chancellor clearly established Germany's responsibility for her aggression against Russia; by the same token, he recognized the right of the Russian armies to invade Germany, "in the course of a defensive action" against Nazi aggression and, hence, with full justification according to moral standards and those of international law. At the same time, however, he established the responsibility of these armies for the atrocities committed under their jurisdiction. This was tantamount to creating the moral and psychological premises, both for the Russian and the German peoples, for an earnest soul-searching and a mutual understanding. Otherwise a final settlement of the tragic conflict would be impossible for either nation and the Moscow conference would have failed in its ultimate purpose, the liquidation of the conflict and the beginning of "normal good relations between the Soviet and the German people," according to the hopeful terms of the official Russian invitation to the Chancellor.

It is in the nature of moral integrity that it grasps and expresses a truth in its full scope, in order to avoid partial truths to be passed off as the whole truth. This is why Adenauer, in Moscow, felt obliged to supplement his statement of principle about German responsibility and guilt toward Russia with two further statements. They involve the specific responsibility of the German people—but not of the German people alone—for the rise of Nazism and its crimes. As far as the responsibility of the German people is concerned, Adenauer stated in Moscow:

"I frankly admit to you that the Soviet people have gone through enormous sufferings because of this war; but if you say that the German people have been in a different position, let me call your attention to the fact that one must not equate Hitler and his followers with the German people. There is a very large percentage of the German people which, from a deep-felt inner conviction, condemned the Hitler system, condemned this war and condemned all the atrocities committed by the Hitler regime. Perhaps one may object that it is only possible to speak of the German people as a whole. But our task, Marshal Bulganin, it seems to me, is to make possible an agreement with that part of the German people which always turned against these things in horror, and continues to detest these crimes."

Since Adenauer's attitude under the Nazi regime fully qualified him to include himself among this part of the German people, he had a moral right, speaking in the Kremlin before the world, but especially before the Russian people, to establish the Soviet-Russian responsibility, and that of other countries, for the rise of National Socialism in Germany.

"Foreign Minister Molotov said that the Germans had been unable to free themselves from the Hitler regime. But, gentlemen—and what I am going to say now is not only addressed to the Soviet Union but to a number of other countries as well—why was it that the big powers permitted that man Hitler, after 1933, to become as powerful as he did? This, it seems to me, is a rather crucial question. When I remember how the big powers, for instance during the Olympic games in Berlin, were flattering that man Hitler, then—I hope you won't get me wrong!—I have a hard time trying to control myself! I shall never forget how Hitler was permitted to get away with every single breach of international contract. This helped to make that man look like a hero in the eyes of many a stupid German, while driving other Germans to the brink of despair. One could easily foresee—I myself knew that since 1933—how that man was permitted to grow more and more powerful; and now, we—I am referring to the Federal Government and the men in our parliament—are the sad heirs of all this business. Our task is now to try and rebuild Germany, for Germany, too, suffered greatly from the war; we must try to regain the confidence of the outside world, including your confidence! I know how hard a job that is; but somehow, it will have to be done."

It is ironic that Adenauer had to state these things at the Kremlin and in the presence of Molotov who a few years earlier, at exactly the same spot, had signed Stalin's devil's pact with Hitler. But just this fact, and the silence with which the Soviet leaders received Adenauer's statement, contributed to the importance of the Moscow conference. Adenauer had proven that moral steadfastness and frankness in matters of conscience may still have a cleansing and constructive effect in international relations, if practiced by the *right* man, at the *right* time, and in the *right* place.

The reader may, therefore, find it helpful for his understanding of these issues to glance at some further excerpts from Adenauer's crucial statements in Moscow, so that our concluding analysis of the significance of the Moscow conference may be more readily comprehensible.

Adenauer's Voice in Moscow

"Both the Federal Government and I are well aware of the significance of this visit. This is a first official meeting between the representatives of the Soviet Union and the German people; a first contact, not only after many years in which there existed no official relations between us at all, but also after much has happened that has been apt to generate feelings of alienation and strangeness. Thus, I know how difficult it is for all of us to begin our talks; but that does not alter the fact that these talks are vitally needed."

Peaceful Relations Between Neighbors

"We are neighbors, even though not in the strict geographical sense of the term. There are many matters for which your government and my government bear a responsibility; matters which are not merely of vital significance for the fate of our own peoples, but—and I do not believe I am presumptuous in saying this—for the international situation as well. There is only one conceivable attitude, in this hour, in which to begin and conduct our talks, and that is an attitude of unreserved frankness. I ask you to believe me that I have come here with the honest intention to conduct these talks in a spirit of frankness. Even if we can do no more than make a beginning, let us try to get to the root of the matter nevertheless.

"I see my first and foremost task in describing to you the basic attitude which determines the political actions of the German people and its government, as well as the motivations and impulses and the ultimate objectives by which we are guided. The highest good to preserve for all Germans is peace! We know only too well how much the Soviet and the German peoples have suffered from the last war, and I think I will therefore meet with your understanding when I say that the horrors of the destruction of modern warfare, the millions of human victims, the destruction of residential houses and places of work, the devastation of towns and countryside have deeply impressed themselves on all our minds.

"Besides, also in Germany it is known that scientific and technological progress since the last war, in the field of nuclear fission and related areas, have endowed man with destructive potentialities which we can only visualize with terror. And, finally, everybody in Germany knows that the geographic position of our country exposes us to particular danger in case of armed conflict. Thus, you will not find anybody in Germany, not only among the political leaders but among the people as a whole, who would even remotely toy with the idea that any of the great political problems now awaiting a solution could be solved by means of war.

"That longing which has now won such a power over people's minds—that war may have outlived itself through its own awesomeness—is deep and strong in the hearts of the German people. We must find new ways for settling our differences and conflicts; ways based on a sense of international solidarity and international cooperation. This is the highest task for today's statesmen to cope with. All this is not just a matter of dreaming or theorizing for us. Wherever my government has found an opportunity to act according to these principles we have gone ahead and done so. I may recall that the Federal Republic has voluntarily renounced the manufacture of nuclear, biological and chemical weapons. But peace, if it is to be fully beneficial, must not be imperiled at any time; it must be guaranteed forever."

The East-West Problem

"It is the tragedy of the international situation, of which we are a part, that our newly formed state has been placed in a world which bears the imprint of the great East-West problem. If in this situation we have found support through the establishment of the Western European Union and our membership in a larger commonwealth of nations, in the North Atlantic Treaty Organization, we have been guided solely by our desire to strengthen peace. At no time have our actions been guided by any notion that this Western organization might be used as a tool of aggression. Both treaties are totally unsuited, due to their very structure, to serve as instruments of aggression. Besides, the treaty serving as the basis for the Western European Union includes specific clauses involving effective sanctions against any aggressive tendencies to a point where they are practically excluded. I myself am so thoroughly convinced of the importance of these clauses that I pointed out years ago that they represent potential elements for a security system, which might be applied to broader conditions as a possible contribution to a more comprehensive security system.

"What I have in mind is above all the renunciation of the use of force, as I already mentioned; the application of treaty privileges for victims of aggression; as well as the type of armament limitations and controls which we have imposed upon ourselves under that treaty. Whenever the circumstances shall prove ripe for establishing such a security system, which might bridge the gulf between East and West, the Federal Republic will certainly not withhold its cooperation.

"Mr. Premier: In your note of June 7, 1955, which contained our invitation, you emphasized, as your objective, the 'normalization of relations between the Soviet Union and the German Federal Republic.' I think in this wording you have aptly expressed what is also our own hope for the future development of our relations with the peoples of the Soviet Union: peace, security, economic cooperation and the prevention of tensions; it is therefore certainly correct when you say in your note that 'the interests of peace and European security, as well as the national interests of the Soviet and German peoples' 'necessitate' such a normalization!"

The Problem of the Prisoners

"Yet, what can be done to make this normalization come true? I don't believe it is enough to banish war, create security systems and establish diplomatic, economic and cultural relations in a kind of mechanical fashion. On the contrary, I am firmly convinced that true normalization can only be achieved if one goes after the deeper causes which tend to make our situation abnormal, and only if one makes every effort to eliminate them. This brings me to two major problems.

"Let me begin with the question of the release of those Germans who are still detained in the territory or within the spheres of influence of the Soviet Union or are otherwise prevented from leaving these areas. I purposely begin with this problem because this is one issue which probably affects every single German family. I wish with my whole heart that you will understand the spirit in which I would like to deal with this subject. My sole concern is with the human aspect of this problem. It is surely an unbearable thought that, more than ten years after the cessation of hostilities, people who in one way or another have been drawn into the maelstrom of military events should be kept away from their families, their country, their normal peaceful occupations. I hope you won't see anything provocative in my saying that it is

inconceivable to restore 'normal' relations between our countries as long as this problem remains unresolved. It is precisely normalization I am talking about. Let us draw a firm
line under an affair, which is a daily source of memories from
a painful past, apt to keep alive deeply antagonistic feelings."

Germany's National Unity

"The second problem concerns Germany's national unity.
I believe we are in agreement that the division of Germany
represents an intolerable situation, and that the unity of Germany must be restored. I believe we are also agreed that the
restoration of this unity represents an obligation for the four
powers which, after the Nazi collapse, have assumed supreme
power over Germany—an obligation growing out of their
joint responsibility toward Germany as a whole. I know, especially in this matter, that I am speaking for all Germans,
not only the population of the Federal Republic, when I ask
you to devote all your energies to a speedy solution of this
issue.

"In line with this responsibility you have reached an agreement with the three Western powers to include this problem
in the agenda for the Geneva conference. It is not my intention to confuse the procedures designed to produce reunification by opening up any separate, bilateral negotiations.
But it is my inescapable duty to use the opportunity of this
meeting to impress upon you the extreme gravity of this
problem and to discuss it with you, in order to further and
facilitate your task at the coming Geneva conference. Once
the four powers shall have paved the way, the German people
will have the task of furnishing the house of the over-all German state, inside and out, in free self-determination and
aware of their responsibility for creating good-neighbor relations throughout Europe, and for strengthening world peace."

German Unity and the Security of Europe

"The division of Germany is abnormal, it violates divine and human law and the laws of nature. Nor can I see any point in arguing from an assumption that the division of Germany is a given reality, for what is most crucially real about it is everybody's conviction that it neither can nor must be permitted to last.

"Let me try to advance the problem by at least one step during our conversations. Otherwise, the danger will remain that a high-tension area of the first order will continue to exist in the heart of Europe. There simply cannot be any true security in Europe without the restoration of German unity. We must clean out this critical source of danger, which so easily inflames the passions, and we must take care, in good time, to satisfy what is an elementary desire of the German people.

"I am aware of the objection that a reunified Germany might develop into a threat to the Soviet Union. Let me answer, first of all, that in the unanimous opinion of all the signatories of the German treaty, the Federal Republic, the United States, Britain and France, it must be left to the free decision of an all-German government and of an all-German parliament whether they wish to join a treaty system, and which system it should be. If the Soviet Union, as a result of the reunification of Germany, should feel that its security is being threatened, we shall be quite ready to do our share by collaborating in a security system which will be qualified to allay these fears. To me, it seems a proper approach to consider a European security system simultaneously with the deliberations on the restoration of German unity.

"You mentioned the fact that there is talk in Germany about a 'position of strength.' I think here we encounter a major misunderstanding. There is no one in Germany who has the slightest illusion about negotiating with the Soviet Union from a position of strength. I think in all these matters it is important to consider the over-all world situation and the over-all situation in Europe, not merely the relations between the Soviet Union and the Federal Republic. And one should also keep in mind the defenseless and insecure position of our country. The Federal Republic has been in a state of total disarmament, it was occupied and was the prey of all manner of insecurities and threatening conflicts. Even small countries, such as the German Federal Republic, need to be able to defend themselves—a need to which, incidentally, the German Democratic Republic has given recognition.

"Let me add a word about the German Democratic Republic. Foreign Minister Molotov has mentioned, and Mr. Bulganin has stated as well, that the Germans themselves must take the initiative to get together again. There is something to this, I admit. But we, gentlemen, are of the opinion that the government of the German Democratic Republic cannot claim to speak for the 17 or 18 million Germans in the Soviet zone because the people of the Soviet zone fail to recognize it as their representative government. Believe me, it is not as if, as we are sitting here facing you, we feel vastly superior to these people. Not at all! As soon as we can feel sure that they are the real representatives of the people of the Soviet zone, recognized as such by the people, we would not hesitate for a moment to sit down with them to talk. In that case, I am sure the German people would know what they have to do."

Releasing the Prisoners

"You, Mr. Premier, have mentioned the prisoners-of-war. May I point out to you that the term 'prisoners-of-war' has been absent from my statements. I deliberately avoided this term. If you will look closely at the record of what I said, you will notice that I have instead talked about 'detained persons.' You have spoken of 'war criminals' and of sentences passed by the Soviet courts. There have been similar cases also in our relations with the United States, Britain and France. But in these countries an understanding has taken root that the sentences passed by the courts of those countries during the earliest postwar phase were not free from emotional bias, such as was characteristic of the atmosphere of those days; that witnesses had been subject to these influences; that the whole atmosphere was unsuited to pronouncing sentences of the kind which would have been handed down after sober examination of all the facts. Hence, the proper conclusions were drawn, and in most instances amnesties have been issued, shortening the prison terms.

"Let me add one more word in all frankness: we believe that we are informed about instances—and it is not a small number either—where Germans, captured as members of the armed forces, have been sentenced for crimes allegedly committed after the cessation of hostilities. The Soviet Russian people are a people with a great deal of feeling and heart. I may say the same for my own people, and that is why this question is so immensely important to us.

"What we would like is merely that you reexamine this issue together with us. Let me ask you from the bottom of my heart merely to open up the discussion of this matter. I beg you not to let us return home saying that the Soviet Government has refused even to discuss this question with us.

"*Germany wants peace! And still one more word, Mr. Bulganin: please, remember that we Germans are perfectly aware of our geographic position, and that you cannot conceivably have a stronger factor obstructing any attempt, at any time, to unleash war in Europe, because we would be the ones to suffer most acutely from it!*"

Justice as a Political Force

Perhaps the most striking feature of the Moscow conference was the tenacity with which the Chancellor was able to maintain the integral unity of his human and moral position with the legal interests of the German people which he was to represent. In this way he managed to develop the legal position of the German Federal Republic, at the Moscow conference, into an established and universally recognized fact of international law.

Assuming political action has retained its function of creating law—in this case the function of an international conference to evolve international law of a kind which even the Soviets are forced to recognize—Adenauer's diplomatic success at Moscow must be considered on a par with his human and moral triumph. What he achieved was a clarification of the question which government is to be recognized as the duly constituted and legitimate government of the German people; and, hence, who is to represent Germany's international and diplomatic interests according to international law.

The record of the conference shows how persuasively Adenauer, in Moscow, was able to resolve both these issues in favor of the Federal Government. The record also reveals his diplomatic skill in extracting this recognition from the Soviets, partly directly, partly by implication. In the following we are citing his three key arguments. They should indicate that a study of the conference record—which has lost none of its timeliness—is still worth while, and that it serves to highlight Adenauer's diplomatic strategy and actual achievements on the reunification problem.

(1) Reminding the Soviets, on a level of equal partnership in the negotiations, that the division of Germany is both morally and legally untenable: *"The division of Germany is*

abnormal; it violates divine and human law and the laws of nature. Nor can I see any point in arguing from an assumption that the division of Germany is a given reality, for what is most crucially real about it, is everybody's conviction that it neither can nor must be permitted to last!"

(2) Stressing the legally untenable and illegitimate existence of the Communist government of the "German Democratic Republic," and explaining to the Soviets in frank and unmistakable terms, before the international forum of the conference, why the Federal Republic is not able, for these reasons, to negotiate reunification with this regime as a partner: *"Molotov has mentioned, that the Germans themselves must take the initiative to get together again. There is something to this, I admit. But we, gentlemen, are of the opinion that the government of the German Democratic Republic cannot claim to speak for the 17 or 18 million Germans in the Soviet zone, because the people of the Soviet zone fail to recognize it as their representative government."*

(3) Establishing the national and international conditions for reunification, by clarifying the causes and realities of Germany's dismemberment, and obtaining Soviet recognition of these facts. Since the Soviet government failed to refute, or formally reject, Adenauer's arguments on this score during the negotiations, much less to issue any formal protest, one must conclude that Moscow has, at least by implication, recognized these arguments. This may have little direct bearing upon the actual status of the reunification issue. Yet, it is nevertheless significant for the legal clarification of the issue, as well as for any future diplomatic decisions, especially if the German reunification problem should one day come before the United Nations.

At the conclusion of the conference, Adenauer undertook a further step, connected with the resumption of diplomatic relations between Moscow and Bonn, which may serve to confirm our interpretation. I am referring to the letter which the Chancellor addressed to the Soviet premier, Bulganin, before his departure from the Soviet capital. As an official communication by the Federal government it possesses a binding character in terms of international law—especially since the Soviet government failed, either then or at a later point, to reject the statements and reservations of the letter by a similarly official Soviet communication to the Federal government. The communication written by the German Chancellor in Moscow, and transmitted to Premier Bulganin before his departure, on September 14, 1955, reads as follows:

"On the occasion of the resumption of diplomatic relations between the Government of the Federal Republic and the Government of the USSR, I wish to make the following statement. (1): The resumption of diplomatic relations between the Government of the Federal Republic and the Government of the USSR does not represent any recognition of the present territorial situation on either side. The final settlement of the German borders will have to be decided by the peace treaty. (2) The resumption of diplomatic relations with the Government of the Soviet Union does not represent any change in the legal position of the Federal Government regarding the right to represent the German people in international affairs, and regarding the political conditions in those German areas which are at present outside the effective sovereignty of the Federal Government."

In his official report on the Moscow talks before the German Federal parliament on September 22, 1955—accepted with unanimous approval by the Bundestag—Adenauer explained the meaning of this communication according to international law. He explained at the same time why the subsequent unofficial comment by TASS failed to carry any official weight and, of course, was totally without validity according to international law—in short, why it did not alter anything in the facts. Both during the Moscow talks and during the diplomatic follow-up, the Soviet government did

exactly *nothing* to challenge Adenauer's position, that the
Federal Republic is the only legitimate representative of the
German people, in terms of national, constitutional and international law, and hence represents the German people also
in matters of German reunification. In any future international negotiations on the reunification question, especially
on the level of the United Nations, this fact may prove to be
of considerable significance, at least from a formal and legal
point of view.

Moscow Balance Sheet

The critical analysis of the documentary record, as un-
folded here, shows how unfounded were the expectations that
the conference would bring a tangible solution of the reunification problem. And the documentary evidence suggests as
well that any criticism evaluating Adenauer's Moscow performance on the basis of these expectations was equally unfounded; just as it is inadequate to use as the sole criterion
the actual political achievements, the resumption of diplomatic relations, while overlooking the moral and legal implications. Only the examination of the documentary record
is apt to dispel these misinterpretations and decide whether
our own interpretation is justified.

But let us summarize our analysis. There were some fundamental reasons why the reunification problem could not be
treated as a specific subject in the negotiations. For one thing,
this is an issue which belongs to the jurisdiction of the four
victorious powers which in the Potsdam Agreement had
assumed the responsibility for the division and reunification
of Germany. "One-track" negotiations between Bonn and
Moscow would only have served to thwart the diplomatic
assistance which the Federal Republic may expect, and actually enjoys, from the three Western powers. Because of this
Adenauer in Moscow preferred to concentrate his efforts on

those aspects of the reunification problem which were certain not to affect the diplomatic prerogatives of the Western powers. By achieving certain fundamental legal clarifications Adenauer could, in fact, hope to assist the Western powers in the ultimate fulfillment of their obligations.

What Adenauer did achieve at Moscow was a clear definition of the reunification problem in terms of national and international law, and the diplomatic sanction of this definition. He thereby established a fundamental fact: his definition cleared up the internal German aspect of the reunification problem in definite and presumably final form, and in a manner that was to be binding in terms of international law, in favor of the Federal Republic. We may consider this the decisive success of the Moscow conference. Its fundamental significance is not lessened by its manifestation, at least at the present stage, on the invisible level of the law—a level admittedly difficult to grasp for a type of thinking that is exclusively committed to the positivistic and pragmatist view.

Also on the invisible level—this time the level of psychological reactions and feelings—Adenauer scored a further success, hardly less significant, whose effects may yet prove to be vitally important in the future development of Russo-German relations. I am referring to the manifestations of Adenauer's human and ethical stature which undoubtedly helped to create an atmosphere in which a painful phase in the recent past of both nations might give way to an era of better mutual understanding between the German and the Russian peoples. Of course, this would presuppose that the good will, which both sides demonstrated at the Moscow conference, will be translated into reality. It ought to be duly recognized that the Soviets contributed to this new beginning the considerable human asset of releasing the German prisoners-of-war. Unfortunately, it must also be noted that the Soviet government, to this day, has not completely fulfilled this obligation —which it had assumed of its own free will. Nevertheless, every single released prisoner—and there are already many thousands of them—adds substantially to the human credit side of the Soviet ledger. For the Germans this would suggest considerable caution, so that this asset might not be misused for political passions.

The resumption of diplomatic relations itself has implications reaching far beyond the formal establishment of embassies in Moscow and Bonn—which has meanwhile taken place. First of all, as far as the domestic situation in Germany is concerned, Moscow has by this action in effect recognized the Federal Republic as a free and sovereign nation. This is true even though the latter has never recognized the Soviet-sponsored "Democratic Republic" in the Soviet zone; and although Bonn emphatically insisted that its position that it is the sole legitimate representative of the German people should be an integral part of the Moscow record, by way of a reservation under international law.

Moscow's formal recognition of the Federal Republic furthermore involved definite international prerogatives, as compared with the East German Communist Republic, because the Soviet government neglected to insist on the diplomatic recognition of the Pankow regime by the Western powers, as a *quid pro quo* for their diplomatic action. Thus, the positive achievement of the Moscow agreements is that the Russians are from now on obliged to recognize the Federal Republic as Germany's legitimate representative even on the over-all international level, including the United Nations. This is true regardless of whether other nations, especially the Western powers, shall ever accord identical privileges to the "Democratic Republic" in the Soviet zone—which seems a fairly unlikely prospect.

On the other hand, the presence of the Soviet embassy in Bonn is an undeniable liability for the smooth integration of the Federal Republic in the community of the West, as well as for the NATO security system. This could conceivably lead to disastrous developments at a time when another political leader might have succeeded Adenauer while reunification had not yet been realized—a contingency on which the Soviets are certain to count. The presence of a Soviet embassy in Bonn might also encourage the advocates of a "neutralist"-type settlement of the reunification question, and, of course even more, the friends of a pro-Russian, Rapallo-type solution, in a way which could create new serious tensions on the German domestic scene.

But all such disadvantages are decidedly outweighed by the very real benefit of a direct diplomatic contact between Moscow and Bonn for the prospects of the reunification issue, especially in the context of the policy of European integration and German security for which Adenauer stands. The failure of the Geneva conference—which was still viewed with considerable hope at the time of the Moscow talks—has certainly heightened the importance of Adenauer's Moscow achievements, both for the German domestic debate and the diplomatic efforts, as the further development of Russo-German relations has already shown. For since the Moscow conference we have witnessed not only a substantial but also a methodological shift in the whole approach to these problems. By now the Moscow conference proves to have been far more than a diplomatic "interlude"—the beginning of a new chapter in Russo-German relations. The Moscow conversations have been continued in a kind of running dialogue between Moscow and Bonn. And the record seems to show that the reunification of Germany has become the actual object of the diplomatic tug-of-war.

Up to now the German Chancellor has continued to play the leading role in these dramatic developments. The reason lies presumably in the absence of any other German political leader able to express views and take practical positions which would even remotely approach the depth of political insight and diplomatic skill with which Konrad Adenauer has treated Soviet-German relations and, closely linked with these, the problem of German unity. Thus, at the Moscow conference, Adenauer once more proved himself a master in the art of responsible statecraft. Yet his profoundly human approach and the obvious impression he thus made on the Soviet leaders, his ability to thaw out an atmosphere of rigid initial antagonism and to transform it into the vitality of a continuous exchange point to still another facet in his versatile personality. The presence of hidden, possibly unconscious and at any rate deeply instinctive resources—the instinct of the true *"homo politicus,"* the born "politician" who knows how to cut through the most formidable objective obstacles and to pierce the most adverse atmosphere by means of a straightforward appeal from man to man. Like only a few truly great political leaders anywhere in the world, Adenauer vindicates the elementary "knack" of the politician for "dealing with the people"—not by psychological trickery but from a basic human warmth, as a vital asset, a living wellspring in the makeup of the great statesman.

It is an unfortunate fact that this has become a rare faculty in "politicians" today—which may explain why this term, especially in American usage, has acquired its dubious overtones. Adenauer's genuine political wisdom exemplifies what we, in this book, have called *"metapolitics."* Its sustained exercise, we may state axiomatically, is what characterizes the true politician, i.e., the real statesman!

XIII

The Crucial Task: German Unity

As the leaders of the four big powers were breaking up after the Geneva conference of July 1955 they issued a final communiqué containing the following sentence, which proved to be significant for Germany: "Recognizing their joint responsibility toward the settlement of the German question and the reunification of Germany, the heads of the four governments have agreed that the settlement of the German question and the reunification of Germany must be brought about through free elections, in accordance with the national interests of the German people and in the interest of European security."

Thus, Soviet Premier Bulganin had once more committed his government to the obligation, assumed and universally recognized since the Potsdam Agreement of 1945, to work for the reunification of Germany. That Bulganin had not forgotten this commitment by September 1955 was obvious from his reply to a remark by Chancellor Adenauer during

239

the Moscow talks: "It has just been mentioned," Bulganin said, "that the four powers have assumed obligations for the settlement of the German question. I cannot help voicing my agreement with this point of view."

By putting his signature to the final communiqué of the Geneva conference, Bulganin had agreed that the solution of the German problem, and therewith the reunification of Germany, had to be brought about through free elections. But the hopes raised by these developments inside Germany and abroad proved to be in vain. During the second Geneva conference, in November, 1955, it became apparent that Molotov was oblivious of the promises of his premier, for he now declared that the "mechanical" fusion of the two halves of Germany through so-called free elections would violate the basic interests of the toilers in the German Democratic Republic, and was inacceptable therefore.

This change in the Soviet position between July and November 1955 meant a plunge from the summit of the first conference into the lowlands of reality: and the reality was, and still is, that the Soviet Union is not ready to give up its zone of Germany. In fact, ever since the Soviets found themselves unprepared to discuss a "price" for the relinquishment of their occupation zone, assuming they ever seriously had been contemplating a bargain of any kind.

It is instructive to trace the course of German-Soviet relations since the two Geneva conferences and the intervening Moscow visit of the Chancellor.

The starting point for the Soviet thinking seems to have been the fact that Soviet policy—despite the military victory of 1945, the Berlin blockade, the fight against the Marshall Plan and all the other threats and maneuvers of the Cold War —had failed to prevent the establishment of the Federal Republic and its integration in the Western world. Part of this unhappy balance sheet was the Soviet failure to absorb Western Germany into the Soviet sphere, by cold war methods, and in this way to prevent the European consolidation, as the core of the coalition of the free world.

Against such a background the Soviet Union decided that the time had come to introduce new methods in order to realize its unwavering objective—i.e., to upset the unity of the West, and above all to isolate the Federal Republic from the Western community. The new approach became evident as Molotov, during the second Geneva conference and, again, during his visit in East Berlin, coined the phrase of the "achievements" of the Soviet occupation zone which needed to be defended. Ever since, Moscow has taken the line that there exist two equal, sovereign governments in Germany, and that therefore the only thing the big powers could do to bring about German reunification was to place representatives of the two governments at the two sides of a conference table and let them negotiate, "in perfect freedom," as to the manner and timing, in which reunification should be brought about. But before reaching this position the Soviet government first had to jump across its own shadow—by reversing a policy which had been advocated especially by Stalin for a number of years. The Soviets had to grant full recognition to the Federal Republic of whose existence they had so far refused to take notice; to whose representatives they had refused to listen in any international forum. Here, probably, is the deeper reason for inviting the German Chancellor to Moscow, which culminated in his visit of September 1955.

The Federal Government is aware—as it always has been—that Germany cannot be reunited in peace without the consent, if not the active cooperation, of the Soviet Union. Although without a hope that the Soviets would ever voluntarily give up their occupation zone—the futility of any such hope having been demonstrated by the events since 1945—the Federal Government was nevertheless anxious, ten years after the war, to stabilize its relations with the fourth of the big powers sharing responsibility for German unity. Hence, and

because of the opportunity to repatriate a majority of German soldiers still in Soviet hands, the Federal Government
accepted the invitation. The release of about ten thousand
former members of the armed forces from Soviet captivity
proved that the government had done the right thing. Moreover, the Moscow visit produced the resumption of Soviet-
German diplomatic relations, without the simultaneous Soviet recognition of the "government" of the German Democratic Republic.

But that there might not be a shadow of a doubt that the
official Soviet recognition of the Federal Republic might in
any way jeopardize the position of the Pankow regime, Moscow hastened to reaffirm the sovereignty of its East Berlin
satellite. Simultaneously, the Soviets launched their new
"line," foreshadowed by Molotov at the Geneva conference
and repeatedly stressed by TASS, the Soviet news agency.
Thus, when the new German minister arrived in Moscow on
March 1, 1956, TASS noted that the rise of two sovereign
states in Germany left only one way to achieve German unity:
by direct negotiations between the German Democratic Republic and the Federal Republic. Again in June 1956 TASS
observed that a settlement of the German problem, under
existing conditions, depended on the readiness of the Federal
Republic to negotiate about ways and means toward this end.

By contrast, the Federal Government maintained that it
would be an irresponsible act to recognize the so-called German Democratic Republic, and was therefore out of the question. This happens to be a stand on which all German political parties and the German people as a whole, including the
17 million Germans in the Soviet zone, are completely agreed.
To them, the recognition of the Pankow regime would be
tantamount to an endorsement of the terroristic methods of
the Soviet zone Communists (the "Socialist Unity Party");
it would mean the betrayal of the Soviet zone people, as well
as of all the basic values of the Western world. It would,

what is more, mean the recognition of the partition of Germany—inconceivable for anyone with a knowledge of German history, and the centuries-long struggle for national unity. In short, to recognize two separate German "states" would mean to turn the clock back to the days of the German Confederation of 1815–1866—a relapse into a political past which was abnormal even while it lasted, and which would be a complete anachronism today, a threat to a sound European order and international stability. It is not surprising that the Soviets have repeatedly tried to revive the memory of that German confederation of states. Their attempt to "sell" such a German confederation, between Pankow and Bonn, to the present-day Germans as a "preliminary" or "transitional" stage toward an ultimate German unity clearly indicates the real danger which it involves.

The position of the Federal Government was stated by the foreign minister, Dr. Heinrich von Brentano, in a programmatic foreign policy address before the German parliament, in June 1956.

"In the past," he said, "the Federal Government and all political parties represented in this assembly have always rejected the idea of negotiating with the Pankow regime about German unity. The Federal Government therefore questions any proposal for initiating direct negotiations with the Pankow regime, and is not prepared to consider it seriously. The same is true for some more or less modified proposals which would bring about negotiations on condition that the Western powers authorized the Federal Government and the Soviet Union authorized the Pankow regime to initiate such talks.

"The Federal Republic wishes to make its position perfectly clear. In the last analysis, these proposals amount to relieving the Western powers, and particularly the Soviet Union, from their joint political, legal and moral responsibility for the reunification of Germany—a responsibility

which the Western powers have never denied, and which
even the Soviet Union has explicitly recognized at the Moscow and Geneva conferences. Direct negotiations would furthermore involve the express recognition that the Soviet occupation zone represents a sovereign state, with the right to
act according to international law. . . . The reunification of
the German people, if it is to take place in freedom, will be
brought about by the decision of the German people itself.
What that decision is going to be cannot in the least be
doubtful. Neither the Federal Parliament, nor the Federal
Government, as the organs and institutions of a free democracy, have anything to fear from such a decision. Whatever
the results for the various political parties, groups or individuals, we all know that the German people would vote
with an overwhelming majority for the principles of a free
and democratic government based on the rule of law. No
matter what the detailed results, such a vote would in any
case be tantamount to a rejection of the persons and methods
ruling in the Soviet zone.

"I have already mentioned the unanimous attitude of the
Federal Parliament on this question. Let me remind you, by
way of confirmation, of a speech which the late chairman of
the Social Democratic Party, Dr. Kurt Schumacher, gave
before this assembly, and from this exact spot. I am not citing
it in order to produce a cheap and convenient argument; I
merely want to remind you of the unity of conviction and
resolve which pervaded this assembly then and which I am
certain still exists today.

"On March 9, 1951 Dr. Kurt Schumacher said:

" 'The administration of the East zone is merely a part of
a satellite system in which there is only one will, namely,
the will of the central boss and ruler, the Soviet Union. The
Pankow regime means the total de-Germanification and Sovietization of the political life. The alleged German initiative

for unity, coming from the East, is part and parcel of the national foreign policy of the Soviet Union.'

"Dr. Kurt Schumacher then went on to discuss the subversive role played by the satellite political parties in the Soviet occupation zone, saying that it was their task to generate rumors and whispers among some groups in the Federal Republic to the effect that the Soviet Union was planning on certain extraordinary measures which would bring great benefit to the Germans. And he added this appeal:

" 'It has been an ancient tragedy for our country that in the hour of greatest danger our most extreme nationalism has never been patriotic enough, in the literal, decent meaning of the word.'

"We have often struggled hard and passionately in this assembly for the right decision. I feel that the memory of these common efforts justifies me in reminding you of this statement."

Because the Federal Government must try in every way it can to keep alive the obligation of the four big powers for the reunification of Germany—always recognized by the Western powers, consistently put off by the Soviet Union—it had to forgo the opportunity to negotiate directly with the Soviet Government on this problem during the Moscow talks. All the final communiqué of the Moscow conference had to say on this point was that "both sides assume that the establishment and further development of normal relations between the German Federal Republic and the Soviet Union shall contribute to the solution of questions concerning all of Germany, which have not yet been resolved, thereby helping toward the settlement of the chief national problem of the entire German people—the restoration of a German democratic state." Almost exactly the same wording can be found in the first letters exchanged between Bulganin and Adenauer, while the latter was still on Moscow soil.

I may be permitted, at this point, to digress for a moment

to deal with the type of arguments which are continuously raised by the German opposition against the reunification strategy of the Federal Government. Reduced to a simple formula, the opposition insists that one should finally start negotiating with the Soviet Government to find out under what conditions it might be ready to give up its occupation zone. To this day—so the opposition maintains—not even an attempt has been made to get such negotiations under way, not even after the establishment of diplomatic relations with the Soviet Union, including the exchange of diplomatic representatives, would have made direct negotiations possible. But what this line of argument overlooks is that the only basis of hope for German reunification lies in the obligation of the *four* powers. Hence, if the Federal Government initiated direct negotiations with Moscow, the other powers would have to put in their veto—which would end any negotiations right there and then. Or else the Western powers would simply consider themselves relieved of their responsibilities, so that the Federal Republic in negotiating with Moscow would be left to its own devices. The fallacy inherent in this type of thinking is obvious.

The concern for holding all four powers to their responsibility for the reunification of Germany caused the Federal Government on September 7, 1956, to present to them a memorandum on this issue. The memorandum served to remind the world once more of the significance of the German problem; there was an implicit understanding that Washington, London and Paris would consider it merely as a confirmation of their own views, while the actual addressee was the Soviet Government. In this sense, the memorandum might be taken as the first direct exchange of views between the Federal Government and the government of the USSR since the establishment of diplomatic relations.

The memorandum represents a full summary of the problems relating to German-Soviet relations. The context also called for a brief sketch of the German position in Europe and in the world, and a discussion of the interdependence of the German reunification problem with the international situation. The core of the memorandum was an offer to discuss plans for a European security system, referring to the proposal of the then British prime minister, Sir Anthony Eden, to create a demilitarized zone in Europe, and to offer guarantees to the Soviet Union against any threat from a future all-German government, under any shape or form, either alone or in conjunction with other nations. The Federal Government was thus taking up proposals which had substantially influenced the course of both Geneva meetings while leaving open the possibility of negotiating also about other similar proposals designed to satisfy the security requirements of the Soviets—as long as they involved reunification in freedom and peace. Essentially, the memorandum restored the connection of the two large complexes, "reunification" and "disarmament"—a connection that has been consistently recognized by the Western powers in dealing with the Soviets.

The memorandum, which includes a thorough discussion of all the political, economic and military aspects of the reunification problem, is distinguished by its careful and conciliatory tone. But it shows remarkable forcefulness on one point: by once more rejecting decisively the Soviet thesis of the existence of two German governments and pointing out that the Soviet zone regime has obviously failed to obtain the consent of its own people. By way of evidence the memorandum points to the revolt of June 17, 1953, and to the yearly flight of thousands from the Soviet zone.

The three Western powers, in their replies, expressed their complete agreement with the substance of the memorandum. On the other hand, it took the Soviet Union more than five weeks to formulate its answer. When the Soviet reply finally came forth, on October 22, 1956, it contained a sharp attack on the policies of the German Federal Government, the Western defense pacts and Federal Republic membership in NATO. The reference to the revolt of June 17, 1953, was rebuked with considerable vehemence. And there was the renewed suggestion for negotiations between the Federal Republic and the German Democratic Republic, while the proposals for a demilitarized area and for improved mutual relations, especially in the fields of trade and cultural exchange, were noted with interest.

The abrupt tone of the reply seemed to spell the end of the efforts for improved diplomatic relations between Moscow and Bonn. Indeed, one might consider the fall of 1956 as a low in the budding German-Soviet relations. For the moment it looked like merely a question of time until the diplomatic representatives would return to their respective homelands to be replaced by chargés d'affaires and nominal officials. The situation was aggravated by the bloody events in Hungary, the Polish crisis and the severe repercussions throughout the Soviet satellite sphere—proving that the Soviet government, regardless of the will of the people, is unwilling to relinquish any fraction of its power. A phase of "coexistence" had evidently come to an end—or, at any rate, been interrupted for an indefinite period of time—the phase to which the German memorandum owed its origin. Yet, after a few months the Soviet Union renewed its efforts to resume the exchange of opinions with the Federal Republic. A new Soviet minister was dispatched to Bonn who, on February 8, 1957, handed the Chancellor a written message from the Soviet Premier, Bulganin, stating:

"More than a year has elapsed since broad and frank discussions took place in Moscow between the government delegations of the Soviet Union and German Federal Republic, resulting in the establishment of diplomatic relations between our two countries. The delegations of our two countries agreed that this would be the beginning of a new chapter in the relations between the Soviet Union and the German Federal Republic, in the interest of peace and security in Europe. We felt convinced that the establishment of normal diplomatic relations would further the growth of mutual understanding and cooperation between our two countries, and that it would contribute toward the solution of the unsettled problems of the postwar period, which are of concern both to the Soviet Union and to the German Federal Republic, as well as to other nations.

"With the same frankness which has characterized our talks in Moscow, I would like to tell you, Mr. Chancellor, that my colleagues and I are not satisfied with the way relations between our two countries have developed, following the establishment of diplomatic relations and the exchange of diplomatic representations. It is our impression that many favorable opportunities for the further development of mutual understanding and cooperation have been permitted to slip by."

Bulganin went on to restate his objections to the rearmament of the Federal Republic and to NATO, and to warn of the dangers of nuclear war. On the problem of the German reunification, Bulganin wrote:

"The reunification of Germany will not be furthered as long as there are continued attempts to ignore the fact that there exist two German governments. Life itself teaches more convincingly every day that a solution for the German problem can only be found through a rapprochement between the German Democratic and the German Federal Republic. It is equally obvious that the movement toward the remilitarization of Western Germany, the restriction of the democratic rights of its population and the policy of continued antagonism to Germany's peace-loving neighbor governments are not calculated to promote the cause of German reunification.

"There will still be many difficulties to overcome before we shall be closer to the day of German reunification. All the nations concerned must cooperate toward this end. And the earlier this cooperation develops the better. The Soviet Government, for its part, is ready to lend its assistance to the governments of the two German states, when they try to solve the problem of German reunification."

Bulganin then goes on to say:

"It is our opinion that the time is at hand when the two governments, in full accordance with the joint decisions made during the Moscow conference of 1955, should take concrete steps designed to bring about a real improvement in the relations between the Soviet Union and the German Federal Republic by building on the useful, if modest, experience which we have already accumulated in the cultivation of mutual relations in various fields.

"Questions which might be studied include chances for a substantial increase in the exchange of commodities between the two countries, the signing of a trade pact, signing an agreement for cultural and technological-scientific cooperation, signing a consular convention which would establish the respective rights of the signatory powers for the protection of the interests of their citizens and which would facilitate the settling of problems connected with the repatriation of citizens.

"It is no exaggeration to say that there are great opportunities for a substantial development of economic relations, in all the various areas between the Soviet Union and the German Federal Republic, of considerable benefit to both.

"The Federal Republic possesses a highly developed industry which may expect large-scale and lucrative orders from the Soviet Union. The Soviet Union in turn might have a wide range of commodities to sell to the Federal Republic, which might be of interest to its industry and agriculture.

"One reason why we are suggesting the expansion of trade relations with the Federal Republic is that the Soviet Union

considers the development of such relations as a reliable basis
for an improvement in the political relations between the
nations."

Bulganin concludes his letter by stating that the Soviet
Government would carefully consider all proposals which the
Federal Government "feels it could present, in the interest
of stabilizing the mutual relations and of serving the vital
interests of the two nations."

With this letter the direct exchange between Bonn and
Moscow, silenced for half a year, had once more been re-
sumed; by the end of February 1957 the "conversation" was
continued with a reply of the Chancellor, transmitted through
the German minister in Moscow, Haas. In it Adenauer firmly
rejected Bulganin's aspersions against NATO by saying:

"I was happy to note in your letter that you did not question the peaceful intentions of the Federal Republic toward
your government. This causes me to regret all the more
keenly that you chose to misunderstand the nature and aims
of the pact system, of which the German Federal Republic
has become a member, when you said that the Federal Republic would be forced, by its partners in the pact, to enter
upon the road of aggression. May I remind you, Mr. Premier,
that both you and Mr. Khrushchev during our Moscow talks
said to me: 'We were not happy to see you join NATO; but
the fact is that you have joined NATO, and, as realists, we
accept that fact.' I would welcome it indeed if you would
maintain this realistic approach. Above all, however, I wish
to state emphatically that the defense pacts of which the
Federal Republic is a member are of a purely defensive nature, and that they cannot be utilized for any purpose not in
keeping with this defensive character. The loyalty with which
the Federal Republic adheres to its treaty obligations includes the loyalty toward the principle by which these treaties
are pervaded—namely the principle of love for peace and
readiness for the common defense.

"You, Mr. Premier, may be convinced that I have spoken for the German people as a whole when I sounded an impassioned warning during our Moscow talks against new military conflicts, pointing to the grave consequences of the last war. From this experience the Federal Government has always emphasized its interest in disarmament, and we shall be ready at any time to share in efforts toward this goal. But I cannot be silent about the fact that, in the view of the Federal Government, disarmament talks can only be promising if all the nations concerned unconditionally accept an unlimited and effective control, in particular of nuclear weapons, and if above all the political causes of the existing tensions are eliminated."

Adenauer once more rejects the Soviet thesis of the existence of two separate German governments:

"In your letter you say that one must take the existence of two separate German governments for granted. As you know full well, I am unable to share this opinion.

"I ask you to understand my feelings when I say to you, seriously and emphatically: during the Moscow talks, you, Mr. Premier, and Executive Secretary Khrushchev, expressly recognized the obligation of the Soviet Union to work together with the three Western powers for the restoration of German unity. The Soviet Union does indeed have such an obligation which must be fulfilled, if the cooperation between the Soviet Union and Germany, in which we, too, are concerned, is to become fully effective to the advantage of both our nations and of peace in Europe and in the world.

"The three Western powers are ready for a settlement of this problem. In its reply to the note of your government of October 22, 1956, the German Federal Government will discuss in detail the problem of the restoration of Germany's national unity in freedom. Nevertheless, Mr. Premier, I would ask you now, in this personal letter, as sincerely as urgently, not to evade this responsibility for the restoration of Germany's national unity on emphasizing the existence of two separate German governments and by stating that the German problem could only be settled through a rapprochement between the German Democratic Republic and the German Federal Republic. Nothing would contribute more effectively toward German-Soviet relations and peace in Europe and the world than the evidence of a genuine respect for the sovereign right of self-determination of nations—evidence which you and your government could give by your consent to the reunification in the near future of both parts of Germany on the basis of free elections in all of Germany. *By giving freedom to 17 million Germans, Mr. Premier, you would do an outstanding service to the friendly cooperation between our two nations.*"

Adenauer then turned to the problem of the Germans still detained in the Soviet Union, expressing his regret because the Soviets had not made any efforts, beyond the repatriation of the ten thousand former members of the German armed forces, to permit the departure of German civilians still in the USSR. He reminded Bulganin of his promise during the Moscow talks to repatriate also those German nationals detained in the USSR against their will, and went on:

"I do not believe that you are satisfied with the nonfulfillment of your explicit promise, but I cannot conceal from you that there is disappointment and even bitterness about this fact among the German people. I beg you to put an end to these difficulties and to give the necessary instructions, so that the Moscow agreements may at last be honored in the spirit in which they were conceived. You, my dear Mr. Premier, understand the significance of. problems which affect the personal sphere. May I therefore entreat you to relieve many German families of the burden of sorrow which is weighing upon them."

Thus, having spoken his mind with unalloyed frankness, Adenauer left only one point for practical negotiations.

"As regards those questions which are still open since the Moscow conference," he said, "I should first like to discuss our mutual trade relations. This development has been quite favorable. Imports into the Federal Republic from the Soviet Union have risen from 93.1 million marks in 1954 to 185.8 million marks during the first eleven months of 1956. Exports from the Federal Republic to the Soviet Union have risen from 52.8 million marks to 267.1 million marks for the same period. With this as a prelude, it will certainly be possible to develop our trade relations even more fully; I suggest that we initiate discussions about this matter between our governments in the immediate future. I share your view that the expansion of trade relations will serve to improve the political atmosphere.

"For the same reason I would suggest treating matters of scientific and technological cooperation, for the time being, through diplomatic channels. I shall eventually instruct the German minister in Moscow to submit to you certain proposals for an agreement concerning consular privileges."

Official discussions about trade relations—that was the essence, for all practical purposes, of Adenauer's letter to Moscow. Addressing the Chancellor for a third time, Bulganin took up this idea.

"As I see from your letter, we are now in agreement that official discussions on the regulation and extension of trade relations between the Soviet Union and the Federal Republic should be initiated as soon as possible. I take this opportunity to inform you that the Soviet Government is ready to start such negotiations, in Moscow or Bonn, in April, assuming that this date should be convenient for the government of the Federal Republic."

Otherwise, Bulganin stuck to his old views on the reunification question.

"We very much regret," he wrote, "that the government of the Federal Republic continues to be unable to reach a realistic and unbiased appraisal of a situation which has been created by the existence, for more than seven years, of two separate German states, each with its own constitution, parliament and government. It is not difficult to understand that the German Democratic Republic does not intend to accept an extension of the system practiced in the German Federal Republic to its own sovereign territory. After all, the government of the German Federal Republic has stated that it, too, would not agree to seeing the social system of the German Democratic Republic extended to the area of the German Federal Republic. This should suffice to demonstrate that a reunification of Germany presupposes negotiations and agreements between the two German Governments and, in fact, that there is no other way to achieve this end. However, I can see no purpose in going into these matters in detail now, since the Federal Government, as you have pointed out in your letter, intends to explain its views in a special diplomatic note. This should give us an opportunity to continue our exchange of opinions about these vital matters."

Here, then, was the same old story, despite the changes in the Soviet foreign ministry from Molotov, to Shepilov, to Gromyko; and despite the change of the Soviet minister in Bonn from the highly unpopular—and presumably rather clumsy—Sorin, to the more elegant, smoother and more conciliatory Smirnov.

Adenauer had no choice but to drive his views home with considerable forcefulness.

"The desire of the entire German people for the restoration of its national unity," he wrote in his reply of April 17, 1957, "cannot be brushed off with a reference to the alleged existence of two separate German states. It is unrealistic to call the German Democratic Republic, which owes its authority to illegitimate means, and which the overwhelming majority of the people rejects, a reality in the life of the German people. There is, however, one reality which has its roots deep in

German history: that is the fact that *the German people is
one nation. All it asks for is its natural right to live as one
nation, under a freely elected order—a right which the Allies
of the last war, including the Soviet Union, have always
recognized.*

"My dear Mr. Premier, in writing as frankly as I do, I am
guided by the serious wish to serve the cause of peace and
understanding between our two nations, through an honest
discussion of the facts as they are. We would only injure our
common effort if we were to close our eyes to the crucial questions. The tensions and the estrangement which have come
between our nations can only be overcome if we eliminate
their basic causes.

"I ask you to accept my statements in this sense, and to
believe me that the German people have the sincere wish to
live, as a free nation, in a peaceful order with the peoples
of the Soviet Union."

At the same time the Federal Government handed the Soviet Government a *note verbale* in which it stated its readiness
"to enter negotiations with the government of the USSR
about a settlement of the problems concerning German-Soviet
relations. [The Federal Government] desires to reach agreements in these negotiations about the future development of
trade relations between the two countries, and about effecting
the repatriation of the German nationals from the USSR
into the German Federal Republic, as promised by the head
of the Soviet delegation in the official German-Soviet negotiations of September 1955. [The Federal Government] furthermore will propose simultaneous negotiations with a view
to an agreement about consular rights, which should serve
to guarantee orderly communications between the officials
charged with the devolving of consular functions, on the one
hand, and the authorities of the host country, on the other
hand. The Federal Government suggests that the negotiations
shall take place in Moscow."

Negotiations on the extension of trade relations and the repatriation of German nationals from the Soviet Union—these were the subjects to which the exchange of letters between Adenauer and Bulganin had narrowed down, after having grown increasingly more terse. A phase of stubborn but factual negotiations seemed about to begin between Moscow and Bonn—when the diplomatic preliminaries were interrupted by the bombshell of the Soviet note of April 27, containing an unusually—even by Soviet standards—sharp warning against the planned equipment of the Federal defense force with nuclear weapons. The Soviet note stated in part:

"Some recent statements by representatives of the government of the Federal Republic indicate that the government of the German Federal Republic intends to undertake the equipment of the West German army with nuclear weapons. The highly dangerous nature of such a step is further heightened by the fact that the territory of the German Federal Republic is utilized for the stationing of nuclear weapons on the part of the Western powers.

"The concentration of atomic weapons by the Western powers in the territory of the Federal Republic and the preparations for equipping the West German army with nuclear weapons amount to the transformation of the Federal Republic into NATO's chief staging area and chief body of shock troops for nuclear warfare in Europe.

"It is evident that the nuclear armament of the army of the Federal Republic—the only European government which insists on a revision of the existing boundaries in Europe—must inevitably lead to a rapid increase in the international tension for our continent, and must intensify the danger of war.

"This presents a peril for the security of Germany's neighbors. It is easy to visualize how these nations, which have been exposed to repeated German aggression in the past, will react to the nuclear armament of the German Federal Republic. As a matter of course, these European nations would be compelled to take countermeasures in kind, by strengthening their own defenses. The government of the Federal Republic, through this action, would thus be unleashing a nuclear armaments race throughout Europe.

"The policy of nuclear armament of the German Federal Republic is sometimes defended on the ground that it is needed for the security of the country. However, such allegations have nothing to do with the actual facts. Instead of reducing international tensions and helping to achieve an agreement for disarmament and the prohibition of weapons of a mass annihilation nature, the attempt is made to ensure the security of the Federal Republic through a 'policy of strength.' However, the equipment of the West German army with nuclear weapons, and the transformation of the territory of the German Federal Republic into a staging area for American atomic missiles not only fails to strengthen the security of the German Federal Republic but actually exposes the Federal Republic and its population to extreme dangers, far beyond anything which the German people have experienced in the past.

"To this day, twelve years after the end of the Second World War, the wounds of the war have not yet healed in Germany. Countless ruins in many German cities present an unforgettable testimony to the catastrophe which Germany has just gone through. And yet, only conventional weapons were used during the last war. It is perfectly obvious that the transformation of the German Federal Republic into an atomic base for NATO would make Germany, in case of war, the immediate target of a counteroffensive employing all types of new weapons, including nuclear weapons. There is no need to spell out in detail the consequences of such developments for the people and the economy of the German Federal Republic, where population and industries are so densely concentrated that the vital centers of the country could be paralyzed by the effects of a single hydrogen bomb."

And the Soviet Government hastened to add some more gruesome details to this threat. "It is equally obvious," the note went on, "that no outside assistance—of which the advocates of atomic armament like to talk so as to inspire themselves with courage—could protect the Federal Republic from these grave dangers. Indeed, of what possible use could such assistance be to the people of the Federal Republic, even assuming it materialized? It is not difficult to foresee what would happen: *if nuclear weapons should be employed, Western Germany, whose area would undoubtedly be hit by the heaviest and most concentrated impact of this weapon, would be reduced to a cemetery.*"

Anyone familiar with the thinking of the Kremlin leaders will not be astonished to hear the reunification issue linked with the atom and hydrogen bombs in this context.

"One cannot overlook," the note continues, "the repercussions which the equipment of the German army with nuclear weapons would have for the reunification of Germany. If the policy of remilitarization launched by the Federal Government, its participation in aggressive military blocs, the suppression of democratic freedoms and the consistent ignoring of the realities of the German situation have already raised serious obstacles for the reunification of Germany, the arming of the Federal army with nuclear weapons and the transformation of Germany into a source of atomic conflict in the heart of Europe could mean an irreparable blow to the prospects of national unity for the German people. How could one seriously discuss reunification while atomic arms barriers are being raised along the border which divides Germany into two separate states?

"The drift toward nuclear armament in the Federal Republic is irreconcilable with the restoration of German unity, and the statesmen who are now at the helm of the Federal Republic have therewith taken on themselves a grave responsibility."

By way of a counterproposal, the Soviet note then revives the old idea of a "demilitarized" zone: "It might be hard to find another country whose interests require the speediest realization of disarmament and the outlawing of nuclear weapons with the same urgency as is the case for Germany. Germany today has been turned into the scene of a completely abnormal concentration of armed forces and military materiel in time of peace—all belonging to different military groupings. In the view of the Soviet Union, no step should therefore be taken which might add to the existing complications in the situation of Central Europe; on the contrary, everything should be done to reduce the tensions and further the recovery in this area.

"The Soviet Government, as you know, has addressed a proposal to the Western powers this year to proceed with the reduction by one third of the armed forces of the United States, the USSR, Britain and France which are stationed in the area of Germany. Still another proposal of the Soviet Government might be worth mentioning in this context: the proposal to dissolve the military, naval and air bases located in foreign territories."

The Soviet note ends with an attempt to bring in its East German satellite: "The government of the USSR wishes to give its unqualified support to the proposal of the German Democratic Republic, that nuclear weapons should be altogether excluded from German territory, whether they be of foreign or German origin. The effective realization of this proposal would substantially improve the political situation for the whole of Europe. It might above all protect the German people from the danger of atomic war. The Soviet Government, for its part, is ready to reach an agreement with the Western powers excluding nuclear weapons from German soil. A positive reaction from the German Federal Republic to this proposal, needless to say, would certainly assist its success."

The note, handed to the Bonn Government on the eve of
the NATO ministers' conference, had the effect of a thun-
derbolt. Once more, Bonn-Moscow relations seemed entirely
up in the air. Speaking for the Federal Government, the foreign minister, von Brentano, replied on April 29:

In its introduction, the latest Soviet note states that the
German Federal Government intends to equip the Federal
defense forces with nuclear weapons. The entire note is based
on this assumption. The assumption is wrong. Moreover, I
should like to point out that the Chancellor, already at the
London conference, has solemnly declared that the Federal
Republic renounces the manufacture of the so-called ABC
weapons—atomic, biological and chemical. This renunciation
of the Federal Republic has been incorporated in the Paris
treaties. As far as we know, there exists no other government
in the world which has voluntarily assumed such a self-limita-
tion as an effective contribution toward nuclear disarmament.
It is furthermore alleged that the Federal Republic has
placed its territory at the disposal of the Western powers for
the purpose of stationing nuclear weapons. I should like to
comment on this as follows: we, of the Federal Government,
have placed nothing at anybody's disposal in any unilateral
way. All the nations joined in the NATO pact constitute a
common unit, whose territories are to be jointly defended.
The Atlantic community is based on the principle of equality
and mutual assistance in case of attack.

The allegation that the Federal Republic has become the
chief marshaling ground and chief striking force of NATO in
Europe for purposes of nuclear war is completely incomprehensible to us. On the territory of the Federal Republic there
are stationed, as of this moment: six American, four British,
two French and two Belgian divisions, plus one Canadian and
one Danish brigade. By the end of this year, five German divisions will be added to this total. This is the equivalent of a
total of approximately twenty divisions. In the Soviet occupation zone of Germany, there are, on the other hand, about
400,000 men belonging to the various branches of the Soviet

armed forces, plus approximately 8,000 tanks and about 1,500 airplanes. In addition, there are about 150,000 men belonging to the people's army of the Soviet zone. And behind this human and arms potential there stands the military might of about seventy-five divisions in the satellite belt, and of 153 divisions, including about 20,000 planes, in the Soviet Union proper. In addition, the Soviet Union has more than 500 submarines. It is altogether beyond our comprehension how, in the face of such superior forces, one can say that the Federal Republic has been turned into a military staging area.

The Soviet note alleges that the Federal Republic is the only European government which insists on a revision of the present European boundaries. I cannot help noting that it was the Soviet Union which, after the last war, has used all the means at its disposal to establish certain facts in Europe and maintain them by force. On the other hand, the Federal Government and Parliament have stated on countless occasions, undoubtedly within earshot of the Soviet Union, that, although unable to recognize these forced boundaries, they would never work for their change through the threat or actual use of force, but always and solely through peaceful negotiations. In the situation in which the divided Germany finds herself today, the Federal Government cannot be expected to take any other attitude.

The continued forcible changes of the European boundaries in favor of the Soviet Union and its satellites, on the other hand, have only been stemmed by the establishment of the Atlantic community and its defense forces. Nevertheless, the threatening attitude of the Soviet Union toward the free Atlantic world continues unabated. I need merely refer to the dramatic events in Hungary, where the desire for freedom of a small nation has been brutally crushed by Soviet troops.

Only the other day, the Federal Chancellor invited the Soviet minister, Mr. Smirnov, in order to assure him in my presence that the Federal Government does not possess atomic weapons of any kind, nor has requested the allocation of atomic weapons of foreign make. And the Chancellor also stated to the Soviet minister that he does not favor nuclear armaments for any additional powers, as that might make a controlled nuclear disarmament program more difficult.

These conversations took place on April 25; I am unable to understand how the Soviet Government in its note, of last Saturday, could have overlooked these formal commitments, made by the head of the German Government, and why it fails to make any reference to them. My only explanation is that the Soviet note aims at provoking domestic repercussions inside the Federal Republic.

The Federal Government is furthermore charged with laxity in its efforts for reducing international tensions. But the Federal Chancellor has stressed again and again over the past few years, and most emphatically during the past months, that only through an agreement about controlled disarmament and the abolition of weapons of mass destruction could peace be furthered in the world. Since these were no mere words, the Chancellor has seized every opportunity to drive home this concept in his conversations with other statesmen. He has been able to observe in these exchanges that the statesmen of the Western world completely agree with him.

The Soviet Government notes that outside assistance cannot provide adequate protection for any nation in case of war—including the Federal Republic—so long as such help must come from a considerable distance. It is precisely this indisputable fact which explains the presence of NATO forces in the Federal Republic and in other European nations. Let us face the fact that, if anything has been able to stem the Soviet expansion, it has been the stationing of American forces in Europe.

Speaking about reunification, the Soviet note states that the rearmament of the Federal Republic presents a serious obstacle, and that the equipment of German armed forces with modern weapons would be the death blow to the efforts of the German people to be reunited. Let me therefore state here that the Soviet Union, during all these years, has not made a single serious attempt to solve this problem on a basis acceptable to a freedom-loving people.

During these past weeks the Soviet Union has addressed countless threatening letters and diplomatic notes to the various

European powers, asking them not to engage in nuclear armaments. In none of these statements did the Soviet Union as
much as hint that, in case these powers would make such an
express renunciation, the Soviet Government would cooperate
in a fair solution of the existing European problems and would
relieve the European nations of the threat of its own hyper-
trophic power. I feel that the Soviet Union aims primarily at
ensuring a monopoly in nuclear weapons for itself, so as to
keep the European continent in a constant state of alarm.

The Soviet note concludes with the proposal for renouncing
the stationing of atomic weapons in either part of Germany.
But does the Soviet Government feel that European security
would be in any way strengthened if atomic weapons were
transferred a few hundred miles further West or East? Obviously, modern technology has wiped out the practical value
of such minor distances.

A peculiar difficulty for understanding the Soviet note is the
fact that any nuclear armament of the European continental
powers is technically impossible for the next two or three years.
The Federal Government has emphasized that this respite which
has been given to us, during which the nuclear armament situation in the world is going to remain stable, must be utilized to
reach an agreement for controlled disarmament. No one would
be happier than the Federal Government if such an agreement
could be worked out.

It is entirely up to the Soviet Union to restore peace in the
world, by accepting a comprehensive disarmament program,
including nuclear weapons. If the German Federal Government
should be called upon to help reach this objective at any time,
or in any way, we shall be found ready in the interests of the
people for whom we are responsible, of Europe and world peace.

Only a few days before the arrival of the Soviet note Foreign Minister von Brentano had outlined the Federal Government position in an address before the Ernst-Reuter Society in Berlin, given on April 25, 1957. It was a summary of
the policy which will immutably remain in force so long as
Konrad Adenauer is the Federal Chancellor.

Freedom and Neutrality

"Freedom and neutrality may well be compatible," von Brentano said, "at least under certain circumstances—I need hardly name the Swiss Confederation—but the fact is that these circumstances do not apply to our situation, at any rate not for the moment.

"An isolation imposed, or forced upon us in our position between the big power blocs, would not be compatible with our freedom—and I am not referring to our sovereignty. It would reduce us to a hapless object of international politics, an easy prey for the unscrupulous. The very concept, moreover, involves discrimination, the revival of that old difference between victors and vanquished, the good and the bad. It could not promote peace, as we are stanchly opposed to anything which might foster a disastrous new nationalism among the German people, a dangerous kind of revisionism.

"This is certainly not meant as a threat, for we all know that Germany could not, nor would want to ever again play the role she played under Hitler. Yet a Germany unstable in her domestic affairs, in doubt about her own freedom, could only remain neutralized as long as the big powers are in agreement among themselves. For a no man's land Germany is far too vital an area. Let me emphasize here and now our efforts for the integration of Europe, that close cooperation among all the European nations which are ready for it, in all the areas in which this is feasible, and in all the organizational forms suited for this purpose. This policy is a matter of life and death for the German people, and conceivably just as much for the other European nations. Our efforts toward European unity are not motivated by any wish to establish a new basis for power politics—all these dreams have, fortunately, come to an end; they merely reflect a development which has reduced the nations of the European continent to a political and economic stature in which they no longer can compete with the big powers, so long as each nation shifts for itself. This is as true for Luxembourg as it is true for Germany. The question is, should we be prohibited from working toward these goals?

"We are keenly aware that the Soviet Union opposes the European integration idea and thinks it is an expression of an evil spirit of aggression. Strange: the East has established a formidable, centralized system of economic and political cooperation, excluding any free expression of individual interests. Hardly a day goes by without an official visit to some satellite government, with visitors and hosts vowing eternal cooperation under the Soviet system, persecution for anybody who dares to evade these commitments. If anyone dares to break out of this vicious circle, he is subdued by the Soviet power—allegedly upon his own request.

"It is a strange world we are living in, where the spontaneous allegiance to the community of the free is branded as criminal aggressiveness, while the forced allegiance to the community of the slaves, on the other hand, is exalted as a contribution toward peace. That similar reactions may sometimes be observed also in the free countries may give us pause for thought.

"Hardly anyone in Germany today is going to question our feeling that we belong on the side of the free world. And there is no conceivable basis for a membership in this community other than partnership among equals. However, the argument is made that even on such a basis one might accept voluntary restrictions; and that neutrality chosen under such conditions may be desirable, especially if it should prove to further other objectives, such as the reunification of our country. Here we seem to be face to face with a serious argument —perhaps the only serious argument on this score—and we had better face up to it. However, it is an unrealistic argument nevertheless.

"Effective neutrality—to use the term—would have to meet at least two conditions. First of all—and this is a mere hypothesis—it would have to be alluring enough for the Soviets to consent to reunification through free elections in exchange for German neutrality. And therewith we are on a level of pure speculation, for no one knows what proposals the Soviet Union might make, accept or reject tomorrow. Still, we have enough official statements to doubt that the Soviets would be satisfied if we should leave NATO. But there is that other condition, so crucial for us, without which neutrality could never become an acceptable instrument of our policy: that neutrality must never imperil the freedom and security of our people. And that would presuppose, above all, that our Western allies, especially the United States, would consent to our neutrality, rather than turn away from us, with the feeling that they had been betrayed. And, moreover, our neutrality would have to fit into a pattern, a constellation of interests which would ensure us that our allies would be ready to defend our territorial integrity with their lives—not only now or tomorrow, but for years to come, without our offering them anything in return.

"The leader of the British opposition, Mr. Hugh Gaitskell, declared in Rome that if one might cause the Soviets to withdraw their troops from Poland and Czechoslovakia, Hungary and the German Soviet zone, the neutralization of Germany would seem worth while. Of course, such a neutralization to be accompanied by armament controls and a security pact, guaranteeing all these countries the integrity of their borders. What is more, NATO would have to continue under such a setup, and United States troops would have to remain in Europe.

"All very well! I won't go into the practical consequences of such a settlement, such as the exclusion of these countries from the community of the free, equal nations; the permanent tutelage and—to use a fashionable term—discrimination

that would involve; because I am frankly prepared to make
some rather painful sacrifices for the reunification of our
country and the preservation of peace. Yet it seems highly
utopian to assume that some countries, situated in the heart
of Europe, might be placed in a special status under the trus-
teeship of the big powers, among which there is so pitifully
little agreement in political principles. And, furthermore,
such an arrangement would not eliminate but definitely increase the existing tensions, because this political no man's
land would really represent a vacuum which others, following
the law of the *horrorvacui,* would wish, in fact would be compelled to fill. And in their isolation these "uncommitted"
powers themselves would be looking around for new commitments as a simple matter of survival. How could the big powers give their effective, permanently binding guarantees for
the establishment and support of such an artificial structure?
Let us face it: guarantees for peace, exchanged among friends,
may be meaningful. But guarantees for peace given to some
outsider—by whom and against whom should they be given?
Germany need not fear today, nor in the future, that she will
be attacked by France, Britain, the Netherlands or the United
States. Therefore, we would not jeopardize our security by
foregoing a guarantee against such attacks—which the Soviet
Union would be quite ready to give us. But how can we
imagine that these nations would be ready to guarantee us
against threats to our freedom and security, while at the same
time abandoning this part of the world, this part of Europe
to an uncertain fate?

"And, as a final condition, our neutrality must not only be
of a kind not to impair the readiness of the other powers to
grant us their protection, but also their ability. In other
words, by 'neutralizing' ourselves we would have to guard
against causing any actual dislocation in the political and
strategic position of the free world. The possibilities for the
successful defense of Germany, from the first day of a con-

flict—which God may help us to avoid—must never be injured.

"The hard fact is, to put it briefly, that there is no such neutrality. This is why the Federal Government has sought to protect its security against an undeniably real threat by its membership in the North Atlantic community."

The European Policy of the Federal Government

"Nothing would be further from the truth than to think that the integration of Europe, which has found its first tangible expression in the European Coal and Steel Community and which, I hope, will reach its second and third stages with the ratification of the treaties for a joint European market and the EURATOM, should merely serve to promote material well-being in the Western world. On the contrary, we are sure that this policy promises crucial elements for our future. For Europe will never be able to negotiate successfully with the Soviet Union from a position of weakness and disunity. But a Europe with a strengthened economic potential, thanks to the emergence of a great economic community, in which the living standard no longer leaves room for old-fashioned class struggle theories; a Europe for which political integration will be a tangible prospect, the true objective of all our efforts—such a Europe would not only have better chances of survival in freedom; it would also be taken more seriously, its voice would carry far greater weight in the world, including the Soviet Union.

"The development toward European union serves also, in the literal sense of the word, the cause of peace. Many have grasped the fact—although no such understanding has yet arisen in the East—that a Germany bound by mutual commitments toward her treaty partners need no longer be considered a threat by the Soviet Union. As Germany becomes progressively more integrated with the outside world the danger that she will abuse her potential is lessened. The Soviet Union need no longer fear Germany. The Soviet Union should know that the German people desire nothing more urgently than to preserve peace and to establish good relations with the Soviet Russian people, based on mutual recognition and respect. Assuming that their apprehensions are genuine—let us suppose for a moment that they are—the Soviet Union must know that Germany's partners would never launch an attack upon the Soviet Union, so that even a misruled, misguided Germany, brimming with evil intentions, could not possibly realize such insane designs.

"We have always kept in mind that we must never make a decision in our European policy which might hamper the reunification of Germany; and that, whatever is left of common bonds between East and West Germany—such as interzonal trade, no matter how clumsy and imperfect a bond that may be—must never be injured by our policies. This was why the treaty for the European economic community was amended by a protocol about internal German trade. It contains the provision that, even after the treaty comes into force, trade relations between the Federal Republic and the Soviet occupation zone shall be considered as internal German trade relations. Hence, zonal boundaries have not—as the Soviet zone press likes to allege—become a customs barrier. The government retains its free hand in supervising interzonal trade; it always stands ready to explore any possible channels for extending this trade.

"The wording of the treaty makes allowance also for the unique position of Berlin. The six Western European governments issued a joint declaration from Rome that, 'in view of Berlin's special position and need for support through the free world, and wishing to reaffirm their solidarity with the people of Berlin . . . [the governments] will jointly use their good offices . . . to the end that the necessary steps will be taken to ease Berlin's economic and social position, promote the well-being and ensure the security of the city.' The declaration established a basis for possible further steps, beyond the specific provisions of the treaty, in contingencies which could not possibly be foreseen today, so that Berlin's unique requirements would be duly satisfied, also in the framework of the European community.

"There is an intimate connection between this policy of freedom—which urges us to walk the road toward European integration—and the policy of peace. Where there is no peace, freedom cannot thrive. And where there is no freedom, peace is certain to languish. The Federal Government does not pursue a single objective by other than peaceful means.

"A success of this policy of peace and understanding has been the settlement of the Saar question, and therewith a lasting reconciliation between Germany and France. It has not been an easy road. Both sides had to make sacrifices, but the results have justified the efforts and the pains. And if we may say today that relations between Germany and France have never in our common history been as good, as sincere and amicable as they are now, we are simply showing Franco-German relations in their proper light, and trying to express our gratitude.

"We have searched for an understanding also with our other Western European neighbors, and it turned out to be a tough job—may we never forget it!—to eliminate all those mountains of distrust, or to overcome all the understandable resentment. You know that only a few months ago we signed a Belgian-German agreement; that negotiations are under way with the Netherlands; and that all these efforts are aimed at lifting the problems and tensions left by the war.

"Our attitude toward our neighbors in the East, they may be sure, is no different."

Germany's Eastern Boundaries

"The problem of our Eastern boundaries can only be settled by the peace treaty, and the peace treaty can, in turn, only be concluded by a free government acting for the whole of Germany. No one in the Federal Republic has the authority to anticipate such future decisions. It is for this reason that we have never renounced any German territories, or advocated any such renunciation. The only kind of renunciation to which the Federal Government has committed itself again and again is the renunciation of the threat, or actual use of force in settling boundary issues—together with the renunciation of the pipedream of a 'Greater Germany.'"

The Problem of Nuclear Weapons

"A problem closely connected with the policy of peace is the problem of nuclear weapons. It is not a physical or scientific, but a political problem.

"Any German has the right to express his opinions about matters of Germany's foreign policy, and we all have a profound respect for science and are aware of the great responsibility of those who have dedicated their lives to the development of technology—which may affect the well-being or misery, life and death not only of the German people. If eminent and well-known German nuclear physicists indicate their concern for protecting the world from threatening disaster, nobody will dare to contradict them.

"If a man like Albert Schweitzer in moving terms appeals to the conscience of the world, he may be sure that men of good will everywhere are on his side. And if Pope Pius XII, in these days, warns of the end that threatens mankind, no one will turn a deaf ear to his appeal, coming as it does from a profound sense of responsibility.

"Nevertheless, to make a terrible but indisputable observation, for the time being peace, perhaps human life itself, can only be protected by a balanced development in this field. Here we are face to face with the tremendous tension and danger under which we live today; while our very existence is at stake, our only security rests perhaps in the fear that prevails on either side.

"We all know what war is like, because we all have lived through this experience, even though, perhaps, we lack the imagination to visualize what an atomic war would be like. Therefore it must be our common duty again and again to appeal to the world to desist from this terrible game. The United States proposal at the London Disarmament Conference, to place the entire production of fissionable material into the service of nonmilitary purposes, under effective controls, commands the wholehearted consent of all who are sincerely working for peace. It would indeed be effective if all the nuclear physicists in the world would ask their governments to accept this proposal. I think they would find an understanding echo throughout the free world—while it is doubtful how the other side would react. So long as one nuclear explosion follows another in that other part of the world; so long as the Soviet Union is busy dispatching diplomatic notes to its neighbors, threatening them with atomic extinction, we have cause to fear for our security and lives, and to distrust the statements of that power. There can only be one kind of disarmament: universal disarmament.

"It is a matter of course that Germany will remain loyal to her voluntary commitment to abstain from the manufacture of nuclear weapons; and that there will never be any question of equipping German armed forces with such weapons, if the disarmament discussions are successful."

Reunification Policy

"Our reunification policy is really an integral part of our policy of freedom. Because all we want is that 17 million Germans across the zonal boundary shall once more enjoy the freedom to choose their political and economic system, and to live under it in peace, without outside pressures. Reunification without freedom would not be a goal to hope and work for; and therefore our condition is: freedom!

"The Soviet Union and the so-called government of the German Democratic Republic are taking turns in announcing all kinds of conditions for reunification. But at no time have they shown the least readiness to grant the freedom we demand. And even though it is true that politics, and foreign policy in particular, is the art of compromise, I believe that here we are up against an exception. There is no compromise for freedom!

"The fact that the Federal Government has so far been unable to effect the reunification of Germany does not prove that our policy is wrong. So long as the Soviets refuse to grant reunification at a price other than freedom, there exists no practical way toward national unity. However, the Federal Government has tried again and again, by all possible means, to make reunification acceptable to the Soviets, and we shall continue to try.

"In fact, these efforts date back to a rather early phase. And since I am speaking here before the Ernst-Reuter Society, I should like to recall that time in December 1951 when I was summoned, together with Ernst Reuter, to appear before the special committee of the United Nations, which was studying the problem of free elections for the whole of Germany. Speaking for the Federal Government, I said in part: 'The reunification of the four occupation zones and of Berlin can only be effected through the free, unbiased decision of the

German people. Over-all German talks, discussions between the representatives of the Federal Republic and the administration of the Soviet zone cannot possibly lead to this end. Those with whom we are supposed to talk are after all responsible for the destruction of civil liberties—although not human freedom itself—in the Soviet zone.' Mayor Reuter explicitly endorsed this statement, and reaffirmed his support for the Federal Parliament and Government resolution to ask the United Nations to set up a subcommittee for the preparation and actual holding of free elections.

"That was in 1951, and ever since we have constantly tried to convince the world, in East and West, that what we ask is fair, and that we ask for nothing that is not commonly possessed by others."

Relations with the Soviet Union

"By initiating diplomatic relations with the Soviet Union we wanted to begin an exchange of views with the fourth of the powers responsible for the division and reunification of Germany. Through this medium, we wanted to straighten out the misconceptions which may easily originate in a totalitarian system, where the corrective of public opinion is missing. We shall not abandon the hope that the exchange will be helpful, and that it contributes to a perhaps slow growth of understanding. The exchange of diplomatic notes and the exchange of letters between the two heads of governments serves the same purpose. I have already stated that we are ready to make concessions and submit proposals. We have even tried to meet the security requirements, without exploring whether they are genuine or not. Even in our latest note we offered to discuss an all-European security system, including a military 'fade-out' zone in Central Europe. But the only reply all these proposals have evoked was that any security system would have to include the two German states—or, in other words, would have to be predicated on the division of Germany. And that is just about the only condition which is inacceptable for us, since such a system would reinforce rather than eliminate the causes of tensions. Hence, our relations with the Soviet Union have not yet developed to our satisfaction. We do not consider the Soviet citizens as enemies, and I would be happy if one day we could say that there is understanding and friendship between us and the Soviet people, instead of antagonism. But we cannot feel any friendship toward a government which withholds the most elementary rights from 17 millions of our compatriots; which calls what goes on behind the Iron Curtain by the name of freedom; and which chooses to call the Federal Republic a land of slavery, aggressive militarism, social oppression, and reaction.

"As long as the Kremlin does not change its opinion about freedom, there can be no question of normalcy or friendship between us."

German Foreign Policy Prospects

"I cannot outline to you a specific, long-range foreign policy program—because I do not claim to possess any panaceas which I could produce by a magic trick, and I know that others who give serious study to these matters do not claim either to have such solutions. But we may say that we are firmly convinced that this unbearable tension not only must but shall be eliminated, and that in the end Germany will recover her unity and freedom. It is our conviction that the idea of freedom is stronger than the idea of slavery. We all have witnessed a powerful confirmation of this faith during these past months, when we saw that even a brutal system is unable to kill the spark of freedom which lives in man's heart. By slow evolution the idea of freedom will win out. I would not have it otherwise! But we have seen—or we sensed

—that this kind of development has already set in in the East, for what were the events in Poland or Hungary but reflex phenomena to the internal developments of the Soviet Union. This chain of events was set off by the twentieth congress of the Communist Party of the Soviet Union, and this is a fact which ought to be recognized. The Soviet leaders had come to feel that they had to make some concessions to freedom, and give a little more material security. Unwittingly perhaps these concessions have kindled doubts and provoked discussions about freedom. And perhaps those who unleashed these developments were quite unaware that discussions about freedom in a totalitarian system are dangerous, and that even a strong power is never strong enough in the face of this force.

"We believe in the ultimate power of free men, and we feel it is up to us to bring about its triumph. Let us realize that the solidarity among free men, among the great free nations of the world works as a creative power, not through our actions, but simply through the fact that we exist and, by the example of our lives and our creative activities, are demonstrating how much more worth while is life in freedom than a life in slavery.

"And we also believe in the power of reason. We believe that the time will come when the emotional reactions which we detect in many of the actions of the Soviet Union will be corrected by reason. For even behind the Iron Curtain reason must tell them that they suffer no less from international tensions than people anywhere in the world; that they are unable to fulfill even the most elementary and legitimate duties toward their own people; and that it takes but a joint decision to overcome the tensions and free enormous energies for tasks which are more worthy than military preparations.

"One achievement of German foreign policy over the past years is that our claims have the moral and political support of all the governments of the free world. We have succeeded in convincing them that the partition of Germany is the symptom and expression of a tension which is a threat to the world.

"Five or ten years ago, if I had spoken before such an audience, I could not have said that our demands enjoy the support of all the big nations. When we first raised this issue we met with a complete lack of understanding, and were told that this was one consequence of the war—a tragic one perhaps—which we would have to overcome ourselves. It has taken many years until we were able to arouse this degree of understanding, this friendly and convincing support for our policies. I think this is a highly encouraging fact. I believe it justifies our faith that by consistently explaining to both East and West that all we ask is a secure future in peace and freedom, we shall in the end convince the world that the fulfillment of our demand may mean a crucial contribution to world peace."

The Last Phase: Security for Europe

Developments during the coming months may prove decisive for the fate of Germany and Europe. The results of the elections for the German Federal Parliament, on September 15, will decide whether Adenauer will continue as Germany's political leader. And the elections will also decide whether German foreign policy will continue to pursue European integration and therewith a progressive consolidation of the West, in the framework of NATO. The official Social Democratic pronouncements make it clear that if the leadership in the Federal Republic should pass to them some rather basic changes may be expected on the level of German foreign policy, which would inevitably shake the alliance between Germany and Europe.

In a pamphlet entitled "Erich Ollenhauer in the US and Canada," issued by the National Committee of the German

Social Democratic Party, and containing a report about the opposition leaders' American trip, we find this passage:

"Ollenhauer stated clearly—as so often before he has stated in the Federal Republic and in West Berlin—that, if the Social Democratic Party should be called upon to share in the next Federal Government, as a result of the Federal Parliament elections in September, there certainly would be no breach of the 'Paris Treaties,' which have gained the force of international law.

"Yet, it is obvious that the Social Democratic Party, in accordance with Germany's treaty partners, would try to utilize any possibilities for revising the treaties which the Federal Government has concluded since 1949, with a view to creating more favorable conditions for the reunification of Germany. Erich Ollenhauer had to repeat these self-evident tenets of Social Democratic policy again and again, because the atmosphere during the last few years has been so poisoned.

"But Ollenhauer chiefly wanted to emphasize that every effort will be made to initiate discussions with the Soviets, so that one may finally investigate under what conditions they would give their consent to reunification. So far, not a single serious offer has been presented to the Soviets.

"It is, of course, impossible to predict whether there is any chance at all to reach an agreement with them which would make reunification freedom possible—which, in other words, would not only preserve freedom for the 50 million in the Federal Republic, but would also bring freedom to the 17 million in the Soviet zone.

"However, all the arguments against the Social Democratic position collapse before the statement that no serious attempt has yet been made to investigate the chances for reunification."

Manifestly, implications of an application of these ideas to the foreign policy of the Federal Republic, reunification, and

European security are so dangerous that all serious political thought will simply have to rest till the elections are over. On the other hand, it is perfectly clear how the final phase toward reunification would shape up if the Federal Republic continues to be guided in Adenauer's spirit. The Chancellor summed up his views during the NATO conference in Bonn, on May 2, 1957, in a way as forthright as it was indicative of the spirit of responsibility toward Germany and Europe, which seems the best guarantee for a future of peace and freedom inside the Federal Republic.

Russian and German Unity

"The leading statesmen in Soviet Russia advise us at every turn to face the realities. All right then, let us face the basic realities of our time.

"It is only too real a fact that the Soviet Union has been maintaining a standing force of about 5 millions rather continuously since 1945: that 22 divisions are stationed in the Soviet occupation zone of Germany, with about 7,500 modern tanks—almost three and a half thousand more than two years ago. I can only consider this as a permanent threat, and I am sure that any responsible statesman at any time would view such a formidable troop concentration in a neighboring country as a threat to his own country. I could add some further impressive figures about the Soviet air force, submarine fleet or the Soviet atomic potential, to stress that I consider the maintenance of such a force as a very grave threat indeed.

"A further reality is that the Soviet leaders have not abandoned their faith in their own mission to convert the whole world to communism. They have reaffirmed this faith in numerous speeches. And to this day, Lenin's works are taught throughout the Soviet Union. Lenin has said:

" 'If the proletariat makes war, in order to strengthen or expand communism, it is a justified and holy war.'

"Or, in another passage:

" 'We Marxists have always been and always will be in favor of a revolutionary war against the counterrevolutionary nations.'

"We are still waiting for the Soviet leaders to disavow this doctrine. It is true that Soviet leaders, at the Twentieth Party Congress, declared that the process of subjugating other countries might, under certain conditions, occur by peaceful means. They mentioned examples of countries where communism has been introduced in such a 'peaceful' way, namely the Baltic countries and Czechoslovakia. But the fact is that the Baltic countries were invaded by Soviet troops without significant opposition, while the crucial factor in the communist *coup d'état* in Czechoslovakia—according to communist party literature—was the role of the Soviet troops. Hence, the process is peaceful only whenever the victim fails to resist!

"But if a people does resist, if it revolts against the communist oppressor, the communist regime is restored with the help of tanks and bloody terror. Even if the Soviet Union should follow up its current policy of intimidation with another offensive of the big smile, we shall be unable to forget the Hungarian example or the events of June 17, 1953, in the Soviet zone of Germany.

"And what about the third reality? We merely have to glance at the map or into the history books to find it. Where were the boundaries of the Soviet Union in 1939, and where are they now? 1940 saw the fall of Estonia, Latvia and Lithuania. The attack on Finland proved abortive. At the end of the war, the Soviet Union, which formerly used to brand any territorial expansion as imperialism, proceeded to annex parts of Finland, Poland, Rumania, Czechoslovakia and East Prussia. The Soviet Union continued to expand further and further into the West. Wherever Soviet troops were stationed, communist governments were established: in Poland, Rumania, Bulgaria, Albania, Hungary, Czechoslovakia and the

German Soviet occupation zone. This is the third reality we discern.

"In 1948 Berlin was marked for annexation. The Soviets imposed the blockade upon the Western sectors, and it took no prophetic powers to see that Berlin had been marked as the next victim of the Soviet march to the West. However, the Western powers frustrated this scheme. Berlin was supplied by air, and then, in April 1949, the Atlantic treaty was signed. The Soviet Union was warned—according to Articles Five and Six of the NATO Statute—that any attack against a member nation, or against the Western occupation forces—and therewith against Berlin—would be considered as an attack on NATO as a whole. One month after the founding of NATO, the Soviets lifted the Berlin blockade. Since then, the Soviet sphere of influence has ceased to expand. This, then, is reality number four."

Under NATO Protection

"I don't suppose anybody is naïve enough to assume that it was a mere coincidence if precisely from that moment on, since the establishment of NATO, bolshevism has failed to achieve any further successes in the West. I am convinced that we owe the quiet and security in which we have been able to build up Europe and the German Federal Republic to the NATO shield. It was under its protection that we were able to proceed with the European Coal and Steel Community, and OEEC, and will go on to the common European market and the EURATOM.

"NATO's firm attitude has demonstrated to the Soviet Union that any further advances would evoke military countermeasures by the Atlantic alliance.

"Two years ago the Federal Republic joined the North Atlantic Pact. We then assumed the obligation to raise our own armed forces for the protection of our area, because it seemed natural to us that the Federal Republic, as a sovereign nation, should contribute with its own troops to the common defense of its territory and the West.

"If it is sometimes argued that NATO is powerless against the tremendous number of Soviet divisions, one makes a mistake. For aggressive warfare, it is true, NATO would be a futile instrument. But it is not intended as a tool of aggression, but an instrument of defense against aggression, and it is very well qualified to play this role. Let me merely point to the size of the potential, indispensable for modern warfare, upon which our defensive strength is based. Fifteen nations, with a population total of 450 million, have joined forces in NATO. More than two-thirds of the world's steel production and electric power, and more than half of the oil output of the world are within the area of the NATO countries."

Faith in Our Defensive Strength

"These facts suffice to inspire us with confidence and faith. During the last meeting of the Western European Union, in London, a proposal was submitted in my name for reviewing our economic and defensive potential once again, and I am grateful to NATO that it accepted this proposal. I am sure that the results of the investigation will serve to further strengthen our self-confidence and our faith in our defensive ability.

"The Federal Republic desires to contribute its full share. We must strengthen our security to prevent the apocalyptic catastrophe of a modern war. We all know that a modern nuclear war would indeed be an apocalyptic catastrophe, not only for the people of the Federal Republic and the entire Western world, but for all mankind, including the peoples of the Soviet Union.

"It is with growing apprehension that we observe the Soviet

attitude toward this gravest problem, with which history has confronted our generation. I am afraid the Soviet leaders have not yet recognized it in its full magnitude. How else should we explain that they continuously emphasize the dangers of such a war to us and to some of our allies in a way which only seemingly reflects their concern, but actually is meant as a threat; while on the other hand omitting to inform their own people of these dangers, reassuring them instead with the false theory that a third world war would merely lead to the extinction of the capitalist system and the triumph of communism."

Dangers of Nuclear War

"The Soviet Government has found it necessary, shortly after executing a series of nuclear explosions, to alert the Federal Republic to the dangers of nuclear war. But in its note to the Federal Republic the Soviets choose to ignore certain facts;

"(1) That such a war could only be provoked by the Soviet Union.

"(2) That I had already notified the Soviet Government that the Federal Republic neither owns, nor has ever expressed the wish to own, atomic armaments.

"In the Protocol to the Brussels Treaty of 1954 the Federal Republic assumed the commitment to produce neither atomic nor bacteriological nor chemical weapons. Voluntarily, we have assumed the imposition of strict, permanent controls in these fields, plus certain conventional arms categories, such as heavy bombers and long-range missiles. Why does not the Soviet Union, which is supposed to feel threatened by our aggressive attitude, assume the type of commitments we accepted in 1954? I am sure that every nation would follow its example, thus eliminating the danger of nuclear war once and for all. But the Soviet Union is not prepared for this, either. On the contrary, all the Western disarmament proposals break down over the Soviet unwillingness to submit to armament inspection and controls. Years ago I cautioned against atomic armaments and their dangerous implications, and I like to repeat today my earnest warning, addressing it to the Soviet leaders:

> " 'If your concern for the dangers of atomic war is serious, then you should agree to the world-wide effective control of atomic disarmament which the West suggests. Stop resisting such a system of international control!' "

German Reunification

"Aside from the questions which we have just discussed, and which trouble the entire human race, the Federal Government has one particular concern, namely the reunification of Germany.

"Much as we are longing for the day when the Soviet Union will raise the barrier which separates us from our compatriots in the Soviet zone, we must insist on two indispensable requirements: A reunited Germany must be free and secure, so that aggression or threats cannot produce such a condition for the whole of Germany as exists in the Soviet zone today. The fact is that the reunification issue is not a German problem alone. The elimination of the partition of Germany would mean a crucial contribution to the elimination of tensions in Europe and throughout the world.

"Let me add a word about the proposals for the neutralization of Germany. These proposals may be well-intentioned, but they fail to get at the root of the evil. By neutralizing Germany today we would not reduce any tensions. In an age of supersonic speed and shrinking distances a neutral area in the heart of Europe does not make sense, it seems to me.

"Regional tensions might be eased through the device of a demilitarized zone. But we are not concerned here with any regional differences or conflicts between neighboring states as the cause of the present tensions. We know that the terrible conflict comprises entire continents, even half the world. Such a condition cannot be checked by regional measures. A neutralized Germany, in case of war, would have the surest prospect of becoming a battlefield.

"It has been said that our membership in NATO is an obstacle to the reunification of Germany. I must reject this argument. May I cite, in support of my view, Mr. Khrushchev and the correspondence published by the Soviet Embassy here in Bonn, called 'Soviet Union Today,' Number 12, of April 20. Mr. Khrushchev said to me during my Moscow visit:

" 'We were not happy about your joining NATO, but now you have joined, and as realists we accept this as a fact.'

"And the publication of the Soviet Embassy of April 20, 1957, states that the Soviet Union cannot want the Federal Republic to leave the community of the West because that would intensify, rather than reduce, the international tensions. *To bring peace to the world is solely up to the Soviet Union: all it needs to do is give its consent to the controlled disarmament proposal. Once that happens, the world may devote its energies to peace.*"

Germany and the Western World
by Chancellor Konrad Adenauer

So much has been said in recent years about the so-called German "miracle" that the subject has become somewhat tedious. Let me be frank and confess that I never had much liking for this term—which, incidentally, did not originate in Germany. For the fact is that there has never been such a thing as a German "miracle," merely the successful initiative, the self-effacing devotion and energy of millions of individual Germans from all walks of life. To attribute exclusive merits for the rehabilitation of Germany to any particular sector, class or political organization would be grossly unfair: all political parties have shared in it, the worker as much as the employer, the farmer and craftsman as well as the civil servant, or the member of the creative and intellectual professions. And yet, one fact ought to be noted with equal certainty: the major responsibility for the rehabilitation of

287

Germany during all these years, the successes as well as the risks, has been borne, before God and history, by the German government coalition, in particular the Christian Democratic Union (CDU-CSU).

To bear such a responsibility involves more than the mere exercise of governmental power; it means also the persistent awareness of the duties and obligations which this responsibility implies. Only he who never, not even for a moment, loses sight of this essential interrelationship, who continuously weighs these two components of true statesmanship, in sincere scrutiny before God and conscience, forever attempting to strike the proper balance between them, can hope to resist power's thousandfold temptations.

During the last eight years the CDU-CSU has borne the major share of the day-by-day business of government in the German Federal Republic, and during the past four years has even commanded an absolute parliamentary majority. For the first time in German history, a democratic party has succeeded in establishing itself in such a position by unquestionable democratic means, as an impressive testimony to the basic soundness of its political principles. Yet the CDU-CSU has not once taken advantage of its majority position in parliament for selfish party-political ends.

Already at the time of its founding in 1946 the Christian Democratic Union gave programmatic expression to its basic political principles by stating: "For the first time in the history of Germany we have rallied for a union of all Christian and democratic elements, firmly rejecting the political division of our nation. Many have been led back, by the voice of freedom, to those values of Christian civilization whose vitality has survived the centuries, guiding and inspiring the course of mankind with an ever new vigor. In returning to these imperishable values we shall once more find the strength to release the hidden wellsprings and to make our full and significant contribution towards human happiness and progress on a par with every other nation.

The Christian Democratic Union proposes to build a new, a different Germany. Let there be an end to that period in which German intellectual life was based on a materialistic spirit pervading civilization and government. The roots of National Socialism reach deep into this philosophy; in fact, National Socialism represents the most consistent application of this philosophy. We have seen the results of this development, which started before the turn of the century, with our own eyes: the total disregard for the law, the adulation of power, the denial of the dignity of the human individual and its freedom, the deification of the state, and the unbridled expansion of its control. The end is the disintegration and destruction of government, the collapse of the economy, the utter spiritual and material impoverishment of the nation.

To be able to bear the tremendous burdens which have been imposed upon every individual German and to balance the resulting tensions we need a moral regeneration. In place of materialism, we must return to the Christian view of life, the views and principles which grow out of the materialistic philosophy must be replaced with the principles of Christian ethics. These must be our guiding criteria in the reconstruction of government, in delimiting its powers and the rights and duties of the individual, our standards for the economic and social life, for the conduct of our own civilization, as well as the relations of the nations among themselves. The Christian view of life is the sole guarantor for law, order and self-restraint, the dignity and freedom of the individual, and therewith a true and genuine democracy not limited to the outward manifestations of government but apt to guide and permeate the life of the individual, as well as that of the nation and the nations of the world. We consider Christianity's profound view of human dignity, of the value of the individual, as the basis and guiding criterion in our efforts for the political, economic and cultural rehabilitation of our nation.

In the process of reconstruction we have taken stock of these commitments, always reminding ourselves of the Christian principles upon which our party was founded at that time. Again and again, we have asked ourselves—as we are still asking ourselves each day—whether we have kept faith with these basic tenets. But, in a mood of serious reappraisal, we ask ourselves yet another question: whether we still, at this point, have the spiritual power and the strength of mind required to continue our work.

It would be pharisaical conceit to answer such a question with an unflinching "yes." And yet, these principles are no doubt as firmly rooted in our minds today as they were then, just as it is certain that we are trying everything humanly possible, again and again, to translate them into reality. For this is what essentially distinguishes our party from all other political organizations. We are committed to a genuine universal concept, independent of all the passing whims of the rapidly changing *"Weltanschauungen,"* a concept which is deliberately based on the immortal values—and here we may find one of the reasons why the CDU, together with its sister party, the CSU, is as vigorous and as aware of its responsibilities today as it was when it first started.

However, in sketching the achievements of the German rehabilitation effort, I may be permitted to focus the attention, flash-like, once more on the situation as it existed at the very start.

In 1947—i.e., ten years ago, two years after the end of the war—the official food consumption in Germany was 1,000 calories per capita per day. In the long run, that was just about too much to die and too little to live on. Nor was the supply situation for other vital commodities any better; according to the production rate of the German economy in those days, every German would have been lucky to get a new suit every forty years, a new shirt every ten years, and a pair of socks every four years. One has to recall this absurd situation in order to grasp the extent of the change that has taken place in the German Federal Republic within a period of less than ten years. At that time, we undertook the job of reconstruction against a background of total destruction of our productive facilities, isolated from all our links with the international economy, and without a genuine currency. In this situation, we received precious help from nations, some of which had faced Germany only a few years before as enemies at war; most important among these the United States, thanks in particular to the Marshall Plan. This "primary ignition," together with the currency reform of 1948, gave us the opportunity to restart our economy; and when we made a bold break with the cumbersome restrictions of the planned economy, reasserting the power of free initiative in a socially conscious market economy, we had finally managed to pave the way for those achievements of which only a few examples shall be cited here: more than three million apartments built since 1949; steel production—amounting to a mere 6 million tons in 1949—raised to 22 million tons by 1956. Within a short time it was possible to restore a normal labor market situation, integrating into the economy even those millions of Germans who had been driven from the territories in the German East, the area beyond the Oder-Neisse line, and from Southern and Eastern Europe. We have long reached a state of full employment.

We all know that, notwithstanding this economic recovery, there are still great tasks confronting us especially in the field of social reform, representing a challenge particularly in view of the ethical foundations of our party. Much has already been accomplished in this field—for the war victims, the recipients of pensions, the expellees—but a great many problems are still waiting to be solved. In this field it is important to realize that no successful social policy is possible without a vigorous, sound and lucrative economic life. And both are impossible without a sound, solid currency—and I suppose I am entitled to say that the German currency now is solid and will stay solid, as long as nobody is going to subject it to risky experiments. *We* shall most certainly not indulge in such experiments.

Important tasks are, moreover, awaiting us in promoting the creative intellectual endeavor in research as well as teaching. There can be no economic or social progress in the long run without a vigorous development in the sciences. This is true not only for the technological disciplines but is the same, perhaps in an even greater measure, for the humanities. The word that man does not live on bread alone has eternal validity. This is why we must and shall do more than hitherto for the humanities—we of the CDU above all, who build on humanistic foundations.

Only a few years ago, many people outside of Germany feared that the Federal Republic might turn into an element of unrest and concern in the world because its own indigenous forces did not seem to suffice for a lasting stabilization. I think it must be evident by now that such fears were unfounded, since the Federal Republic has become one of the most stable factors in the free world, in every area.

One day, future historians are going to single out the fifth of May, 1955, as one of the most crucial dates in German history, the day on which our national sovereignty has been restored, and with it our unhampered self-determination in every field, together with a heightened degree of responsibility of which we must never lose sight. On that day, we were also reaping the fruits of our efforts in the field of foreign relations, beginning with the Bonn Agreements and distinguished by clarity of purpose, firmness and self-restraint. Here are the pillars of our success: these must remain the foundations for our policy, in time to come. Let us beware of dangerous experiments in our foreign affairs as well, since they would drive the German people back into the abyss and into the policy of adventure. It is our determination to remain firmly committed to the policy of European integration and the North Atlantic Pact.

Let me say a few words at this point about our attitude toward the German Social Democratic Party and why, in the extremely critical situation through which Germany is going, it has not been possible to work out a common foreign policy approach between these two great parties. To me, this is a profoundly painful fact which has caused me very real suffering over all these many years. Even now, in the midst of an election year, I cannot cease hoping that the Social Democrats will one day realize that, if they would control a majority in the Federal Diet, they would have to follow precisely the same foreign policy course as the one we have steered.

From the very beginning, the fundamental tenet of our foreign policy has been to follow a course of firm solidarity with the West, and thereby to guard our own freedom. Guarding our freedom seems, after all, a worthy objective, without which all of Germany would have to surrender to slavery. Yet the Social Democrats, denying that the solidarity with the West will lead to reunification, want the Federal Republic, as well as a future reunited Germany, to occupy a position by itself, in the middle of the two big power blocs. In point of fact, the notion that a reunited Germany would be able to hold her own in between the two big power constellations— prior to a universal relenting of tensions and a consequent over-all change in the international situation—is so thoroughly utopian that one is surprised to see anyone expound these ideas seriously before the German people and the world. Germany stands after all in the very focus of the European high-tension area between East and West—but some people talk as if we were situated in the stars.

The Federal Republic is a member of NATO, which has been established primarily—but by no means exclusively!—as

a military instrument for the defense of freedom. It may be
that the Soviets have deferred the threat of "hot war" for the
time being: in the long run the danger remains nevertheless
real! One can hardly deny that the Soviet Union is ruled by
a dictatorship, whether the dictator is Stalin or somebody
else. We Germans should be the first to realize the extent of
stupid errors and hasty decisions of which a dictatorship is
capable—stupid mistakes even in the face of its own selfish
interests. If it is true that Soviet Russia remains under a dic-
tatorial rule; that she continues to arm and to cause ever new
upheavals throughout the world; that she remains obsessed
—as I firmly believe she does—with the idea of world rule:
would it not seem advisable to guard against possible attack
from that quarter? Some people, both in and outside of Germany, like to call such cautious wisdom a "policy of strength."
I do not happen to favor this term because it is subject to so
many dangerous misinterpretations; nevertheless, I much prefer a policy of caution and "strength" to a policy of weakness!

In becoming NATO members we have assumed, as a matter
of course, the obligation to share in the defense of the West;
and, equally as a matter of course, we shall fulfill this obligation, and would not even dream of abandoning a basic
defense concept which not only serves to strengthen NATO,
but at the same time increases our own security. Now it so
happens that the task which for us grows out of this obligation, i.e., the establishment of a modern defense force, coin-
cides with a revolutionary change in the armament and defense thinking throughout the world, due to the breathtak-
ing development in the field of nuclear weapons and missiles
technology. What that means for us is that the need to rebuild our military establishment out of nothing, following
the vacuum of these last years, amounts to the tremendous
opportunity of a "zero hour," a new beginning; and even if
that appears to spell certain delays in the establishment of a

Federal defense force, we may look forward to the certain prospect of an up-to-date, highly effective Federal defense force which will measure up to its tasks.

Twice during the first half of the twentieth century, the German people has experienced the horrors of war; perhaps better than any other nation we know that a third world war would jeopardize the existence of Europe and of large portions of the world. It is this knowledge that compels us to make every possible contribution to the preservation of peace; this is why neither the Federal Republic, nor a reunited Germany, will ever again present a threat for any other nation in the world, because we shall always respect the honest security interest of all our neighbors, including our neighbors to the east.

In September 1955 I said in Moscow: "The highest good for all Germans to safeguard is peace. You will therefore find no one in Germany—neither among the responsible political leaders, nor among the population as a whole—who would even remotely play with the idea that any of the great political problems, now awaiting solution, might be resolved by means of war." The view I expressed at that time continues to be the guiding principle of our policy.

Notwithstanding all our achievements in the Federal Republic, we cannot forget for a moment that 17 million people are living and suffering in the Soviet zone of occupation in a state where they are totally unfree and oppressed by a regime resting solely upon the support of a foreign power. The supreme objective of our policy therefore remains the preservation of our freedom and the restoration of German unity in freedom and peace. Its realization is predicated upon the holding of free elections throughout Germany and the establishment of a government, freely elected by an all-German parliament, able to determine Germany's future legal and political place in the world. This position has been recognized by the entire free world, together with the fact that already at this time the Federal Government, as the only freely elected German government, has the right to speak for all of Germany. This is an issue on which we are unable to compromise, lest we relinquish our goal of reunification in freedom.

Even in these matters, it is impossible to separate the German interest from that of the entire free world. The restoration of a free German commonwealth is conceivable only insofar as the free world seeks to restore freedom for all of Europe by means of a universal peace offensive. Only an all-European freedom policy, in which the German problem is duly recognized in accordance with its Central European position, can lead to freedom and peace for all. On the other hand, as long as the German problem is treated as an isolated issue, the 17 million oppressed Germans will not come any closer to achieving their freedom, and a dangerous source of unrest will continue to exist in the midst of Europe. It helps to recall the warning which Salvador de Madariaga, the great European liberal and friend of Germany, voiced in Munich in 1956: "Reunification is not a German problem because the Iron Curtain extends from the Baltic to the Adriatic Sea. If Germany should embrace nationalism, the future of Europe would look dark indeed. But if Germany should rise to the level of what she can attain, she will achieve the place, within a united Europe, to which she is entitled, thanks to her intellectual vigor. . . . The time demands great decisions of everyone, most of all the Germans."

Madariaga's words recall that the chief aim of our efforts, next to the reunification of Germany, is the unity of Europe —and that the two aims are mutually interdependent. When I was first elected to the Federal chancellorship, I said in September 1949: "European integration hinges on the relations between Germany and France. I have advocated this view as early as twenty-five years ago." The ratification of the Paris treaties, the acceptance of the Federal Republic in the Western European Union and in NATO have made us the allies of France, and any future war between these two nations has therewith become unthinkable. These facts indicate the extent to which Franco-German relations have changed since the Federal Republic has come into being. The settlement, in a spirit of friendship, of the Saar issue has eliminated the last of the differences which used to divide Germany and France; the end for which I had been hoping eight years ago, in the interest of both our nations, in the European and world interest, and for which I have since striven as best I could, has at last been realized.

But let us view the European problem from a broader perspective: the idea of the nation state has been one of the primary causes for the division and the fraternal strife which have brought our European continent so close to the abyss. We will have to shake off this idea if Europe in the future is to develop as an organic whole, carrying the political weight it deserves due to its history and achievements. This is why we have done everything possible in order to expedite European unity; why the Federal Republic is now a member of the Council of Europe in Strasbourg, as well as of the European Coal and Steel Community. Still, these are no more than beginnings; the ultimate goal is the establishment of a genuine European political community—which should be flexible and lithe, rather than rigid, finding a form which permits each nation to make its own contribution. We therefore welcome the fact that Great Britain, too, has demonstrated her willingness to cooperate in the efforts toward a common European market—representing a substantial extension of the Coal and Steel Community in the mere range of the commodities to be included—and in the establishment of a European atomic community.

Yet, since the end of the war, certain political developments and changes have made us aware not only of the internal European aspects, but also of the world-wide implications of the European integration problem. The concept of a European political and economic hegemony in the world is probably a thing of the past. However, our concern for European civilization, with all that it has given to the world, and including its well-nigh inexhaustible sources of cultural inspiration, demands that we adjust to the changing international conditions, as it requires our active defense if it is to retain its place in the world.

Those days were a test also for our German policy, compelling us to subject the basic assumptions as well as the objectives of our political action to renewed scrutiny. Today, we may say that our German policy has stood the test, at a time when everything seemed to hang in the balance. None of the events of 1956 has forced us to change our course; on the contrary, some of these events have borne out our expectations and justified our fears with an almost tragic consistency.

In the first place, there was, inside the Soviet sphere, the so-called "de-stalinization" process with all its implications and results, the growing unrest throughout the Soviet orbit and the popular revolts in Poland and Hungary. In a most heartbreaking and shocking way I was confirmed in my contention that the disavowal of Stalin did not mean a true change of mind, and hence no change of direction, for the Communists. The blood bath, the terror regime, the deportations, the continuing show trials in Hungary revealed beyond a shadow of a doubt the true face of the Communist system, stripping all pretensions of "peaceful coexistence" of their inherent hypocrisy. I have always felt sure that the only aim of the strategy of the big smile and the diplomacy of reassurance was to sow confusion in the Western camp, to undermine the unity of the free world, and to gain control over the Federal Republic by means of a phony "neutralization" and a reunification in slavery. The Eastern European events amounted to a confirmation of this view, destroying a great many illusions of our political opponents in the process.

And, last but not least, the Near Eastern developments have shown that the Soviet Union persists in its attempts to subvert the free nations, not disdaining to inject the poison of nationalism into its philosophy of dialectic materialism, so as to further its imperialistic ends more effectively. On the other hand, the events in the Eastern Mediterranean, especially in Egypt, have led to some important repercussions in the Western world. They revealed certain cracks and flaws in the structure—to which we cannot possibly shut our eyes. But the West has learned from these events, and we may say already today that the bitter lesson of these days in October and November 1956 has led to a realistic self-scrutiny. The unity of the free world remains unshaken at the core; in fact, it is firmer today than it ever has been.

The year 1956 has strongly corroborated our efforts to strengthen the community and cooperation among all the free nations. In this, we agree with President Eisenhower who said at the height of the Suez crisis last October: "We believe that integrity of purpose and action is the fact that must most surely identify and fortify the free world in its struggle against Communism. We cannot proclaim this integrity when the issue is easy—and stifle it when the issue is hard. To do this would be to do something much worse than merely making our great struggle in the world more difficult. For if we were ever to lose that integrity, there would be no way to win true victory in that struggle. That would be a surrender that we shall not make."

To preserve this integrity of purpose and action is the chief concern of the Christian Democratic Union, which has not adopted the adjective "Christian" as a mere slogan, but is committed to a literal interpretation of the implicit ethical obligation, feeling deeply serious about the realization of Christian principles in the world of politics. We in Germany have had the bitter experience of the Nazi system; other nations have experienced different dictatorships, or are still subject to them today. We all know that the removal of the ethical element from the political life leads to the deification of the state, until human freedom and dignity sink into the materialistic morass. After those bitter lessons who would deny that there is no genuine freedom in a true democracy, unless it is tied to the eternally valid principles of Christian ethics? It is the only possible foundation for any legislation and any attempt to influence creatively the life of the nations in its multiple aspects—whether in the political, economic, cultural or social sphere. Only he who feels this permanent link with the living wellspring of divine strength can hope to last in the fight against communism and materialism.

I am happy that I may recall another statement by President Eisenhower to which I subscribe wholeheartedly, a statement which highlights the meeting of Western philosophy with the idea of the leadership of the West: "It is our faith in the deathless dignity of Man, governed by eternal morals and natural law. This faith defines our full view of life. It establishes, beyond debate, those gifts of the Creator that are Man's inalienable rights and that make all men equal in His sight."

I have said above that the Federal Republic represents today one of the most stable factors in the free world. The ultimate reason for this is in the profound commitment of my party, the Christian Democratic Union, to these basic tenets of Christian ethics. I myself, as well as all those who share with me the leadership of this party or who are going to succeed me, shall remain loyal to this commitment.